Cambridge Imperial and Post-Colonial Studies Series

General Editors: **Megan Vaughan**, King's College, Cambridge and **Richard Drayton**, King's College London

This informative series covers the broad span of modern imperial history while also exploring the recent developments in former colonial states where residues of empire can still be found. The books provide in-depth examinations of empires as competing and complementary power structures encouraging the reader to reconsider their understanding of international and world history during recent centuries.

Titles include:

Peter F. Bang and C. A. Bayly (*editors*)
TRIBUTARY EMPIRES IN GLOBAL HISTORY

James Beattie
EMPIRE AND ENVIRONMENTAL ANXIETY, 1800–1920
Health, Aesthetics and Conservation in South Asia and Australasia

Rachel Berger
AYURVEDA MADE MODERN
Political Histories of Indigenous Medicine in North India, 1900–1955

Robert J. Blyth
THE EMPIRE OF THE RAJ
Eastern Africa and the Middle East, 1858–1947

Larry Butler and Sarah Stockwell
THE WIND OF CHANGE
Harold Macmillan and British Decolonization

Kit Candlin
THE LAST CARIBBEAN FRONTIER, 1795–1815

Hilary M. Carey (*editor*)
EMPIRES OF RELIGION

Esme Cleall
MISSIONARY DISCOURSE
Negotiating Difference in the British Empire, c.1840–95

Michael S. Dodson
ORIENTALISM, EMPIRE AND NATIONAL CULTURE
India, 1770–1880

Bronwen Everill
ABOLITION AND EMPIRE IN SIERRA LEONE AND LIBERIA

Ulrike Hillemann
ASIAN EMPIRE AND BRITISH KNOWLEDGE
China and the Networks of British Imperial Expansion

B. D. Hopkins
THE MAKING OF MODERN AFGHANISTAN

Ronald Hyam
BRITAIN'S IMPERIAL CENTURY, 1815–1914
A Study of Empire and Expansion (*Third Edition*)

Iftekhar Iqbal
THE BENGAL DELTA
Ecology, State and Social Change, 1843–1943

Robin Jeffrey
POLITICS, WOMEN AND WELL-BEING
How Kerala Became a 'Model'

Javed Majeed
AUTOBIOGRAPHY, TRAVEL AND POST-NATIONAL IDENTITY

Francine McKenzie
REDEFINING THE BONDS OF COMMONWEALTH 1939–1948
The Politics of Preference

Gabriel Paquette
ENLIGHTENMENT, GOVERNANCE AND REFORM IN SPAIN AND ITS EMPIRE 1759–1808

Sandhya L. Polu
PERCEPTION OF RISK
Policy-Making on Infectious Disease in India 1892–1940

Jennifer Regan-Lefebvre
IRISH AND INDIAN
The Cosmopolitan Politics of Alfred Webb

Sophus A. Reinert and Pernille Røge
THE POLITICAL ECONOMY OF EMPIRE IN THE EARLY MODERN WORLD

Ricardo Roque
HEADHUNTING AND COLONIALISM
Anthropology and the Circulation of Human Skulls in the Portuguese Empire, 1870–1930

Michael Silvestri
IRELAND AND INDIA
Nationalism, Empire and Memory

Julia Tischler
LIGHT AND POWER FOR A MULTIRACIAL NATION
The Kariba Dam Scheme in the Central African Federation

Jon E. Wilson
THE DOMINATION OF STRANGERS
Modern Governance in Eastern India, 1780–1835

Cambridge Imperial and Post-Colonial Studies Series
Series Standing Order ISBN 978–0–333–91908–8 (Hardback)
978–0–333–91909–5 (Paperback)
(outside North America only)

You can receive future titles in this series as they are published by placing a standing order. Please contact your book-seller or, in case of difficulty, write to us at the address below with your name and address, the title of the series and one of the ISBN quoted above.

Customer Services Department, Macmillan Distribution Ltd, Houndmills, Basingstoke, Hampshire RG21 6XS, England

---

The Political Economy of Empire in the Early Modern World

Edited by

Sophus A. Reinert
Assistant Professor of Business Administration, Harvard Business School

and

Pernille Røge
Assistant Professor in French and French Imperial History, University of Pittsburgh

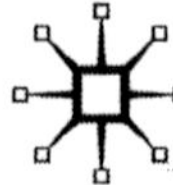

First published 2013 by
PALGRAVE MACMILLAN

Palgrave Macmillan in the UK is an imprint of Macmillan Publishers Limited, registered in England, company number 785998, of Houndmills, Basingstoke, Hampshire RG21 6XS.

Palgrave Macmillan in the US is a division of St Martin's Press LLC, 175 Fifth Avenue, New York, NY 10010.

Palgrave Macmillan is the global academic imprint of the above companies and has companies and representatives throughout the world.

Palgrave® and Macmillan® are registered trademarks in the United States, the United Kingdom, Europe and other countries

ISBN: 978–0–230–23064–4

This book is printed on paper suitable for recycling and made from fully managed and sustained forest sources. Logging, pulping and manufacturing processes are expected to conform to the environmental regulations of the country of origin.

A catalogue record for this book is available from the British Library.

A catalog record for this book is available from the Library of Congress.

Contents

Foreword: Of Empire and Political Economy

Richard Drayton

In the formative period for political economy, Europeans mainly understood 'empire' as government and the activity of the state.[1] It was only in the application of arguments about the reason of state to territorial expansion, colonies, and trade that 'empire' came to mean overseas possessions and the spaces beyond Europe.[2] 'Political economy' itself emerged in discussions of how government, and in particular monarchs, should intervene in economic and social life. Xenephon's *Oeconomicus*, an ancient dialogue about the management of the household ('oikos' in Greek), was applied, as in Sully's *Oeconomies Royales* (1572–1593), to a discussion of how the resources and activity of the kingdom should be regulated. By 1615, the phrase itself first surfaces in Antoine de Montchrétien's *Traicté de l'Oeconomie Politique* (1615), where an argument dedicated to the king and queen urging 'the growth of [their] empire in power and glory' explained that 'all society, to speak generally, is composed of government and commerce'.[3]

To this extent, 'political economy' was always about 'empire'. In 1615 both categories referred to ideas about what was prudent for particular European polities, even to 'techniques of secretive statecraft'.[4] A century later, however, a very different idea of 'political economy' began to emerge which its advocates understood to be 'philosophical' or scientific, which was public, and which was based on a theory of the world. The physiocrats, to whom we owe the modern idea of economics, chose to call themselves 'economistes' because they wished to identify themselves with the regalist reform programme of the *arbitristas* of the era of Sully and Richelieu. But they believed, if we address them as a group, that economic life might be governed through laws that could be discovered in nature itself, applied in every nation, and which encompassed production, exchange, and consumption across the world. In Adam Smith's *Wealth of Nations* (1776), we may see the culminating expression of this idea of a global vision of economic life ordered in the universal interest.

Political economy, which had begun as a discussion of policy particular to European kingdoms, by Smith's age had become a theory of international society for which the question of empire, in our sense of overseas possessions, was central. It is this shift, across the span of the early modern period, which is at the centre of *The Political Economy of Empire*. This collection of essays shows, first, how economic government became a trans-European 'science', both as ideas and texts which moved around Europe, and as doctrines and governmental practices indigenised in national contexts. Second, it explores how political economy became a global 'science', as it responded to problems thrown up by European overseas trade and conquest (by 'empire' in our modern sense of the word).

The success of this edited collection lies in how it weaves key strands of this transition of political economy from a kind of magic of monarchical statecraft to a rational and public ideology of cosmopolitan society. Hartman and Weststeijn (pp. 11–31) examine how Pieter de la Court (1618–1685), a figure closer to Montchrétien than Smith, received Italian and French ideas of economic *ragione di stato* and applied them to the Netherlands' commercial and imperial predicament. Røge's physiocrats (pp. 32–52), on the other hand, two generations later, saw France as a global nation to be remade after the humiliations of 1763 on the natural commercial conversation of temperate metropole and tropical colonies. Hopkins (pp. 53–75) shows how critical a theory of the colony within global exchange was for Adam Smith. Paquette (pp. 76–104) examines how Spanish and Portuguese intellectuals applied British political economy first to the reform of the Iberian overseas empires, and ultimately to programmes for sovereign states in Latin America. Reinert (pp. 105–28) offers a dazzling portrait of how economic ideas moved across Europe through translation, so constituting a common terrain of theory and practice. Parkinson (pp. 131–46) looks at the complex impact which the birth of a modern capital market in England had on making imperial Britain, at once providing the sinews of war and providing a means for European migrants to be integrated into the nation. Levenson (pp. 147–72) focuses on the problem of the surface of contact between emerging European ideas of market norms and the indigenous gift economy of colonial North America. Lees (pp. 173–91) provides a study of how the East India Company emerged as a classic 'military-fiscal' state. Finally, Mandelblatt (pp. 192–220), in an essay which echoes Røge's, maps how colonial economic realities, in the form of the constraints of the food provisioning networks of the French Atlantic, imposed themselves on political economic doctrine.

* * *

No other study before this has so explicitly and comparatively explored the interactions of the new political economy and

Europe's new overseas interests. It is startling to notice that historians of European economic ideas rarely address the impact of European expansion on them. For empire, in our modern sense, was clearly fundamental to the rise of the new science.

At the centre of these new doctrines, after all, lay the problem of how the European economy after 1492 was turned upside down by the dramatic increase in the supply of gold, silver, and trade. The new liquidity of exchange and its partner price inflation, the rise of new externally directed domestic economic interests, and the impact on European peace and security of overseas wealth and interests all propelled increasingly complex and interwoven debates about the regulation of the economy during the sixteenth and seventeenth centuries.[5]

These doctrines, furthermore, were needed by a European political order in which ultramarine wealth sustained the growth of the apparatus of the state and of its ambitions, whether 'absolutist' or republican, in Spain, France, Holland, and England. Economic life provided at once a critical resource for political power and a theatre in which an aggrandised royal, ecclesiastical, or republican power might seek to demonstrate its efficiency, even through the militant expression of theological commitment.

Connected to the new economies and politics of the sixteenth and seventeenth centuries arose permanent competition and war. It may be argued that three key waves of militarised European crises – one ca. 1580–1600s, another ca. 1618–1690s, and the third ca. 1740–1780s – propelled the three most important transitions in the rise of modern political economy. The conflicts of the 1580s and 1590s, which pitted the Counter-Reformation Habsburg 'monarchia catholica', that is to say the unified global state of Spain, Portugal and its dependencies in the Americas and Asia, against Holland, France, and England, engendered both a family of debates across Europe about 'commercial reason of state', the terrain of Sully's *Oeconomies Royales*, and theories of competitive colonial and commercial expansion. Out of the Thirty Years' War (1618–1648) came a new urgency for the raising of revenue and for state action in economic life represented in Cameralist projects for German princes to increase the wealth of their nation, and in a broader spectrum of doctrines about the government of trade, ranging from Colbertism on the one hand, and the mercantilist systems of England and France, to the flirtations with liberalising trade of Petty and Fourbonnais on the other. Lastly the combined impact of the connected War of the Austrian Succession, Seven Years' War, and War of the American Revolution, felt across Europe as a burden of public debt, gave prestige to a further wave of both dirigiste visions of Crown intervention in economic life, and to circulationist doctrines of liberalised trade.

Finally, this new global European economic and political order meant more exchange, and not just more competition, between states. Perhaps even under the pressure of competition, and attracted by the actual and potential riches of a wider world, the early modern period saw unprecedented intellectual mobility, collaboration, and convergence. This trans-European intellectual response to the world found expression in what historians, at different moments, refer to as the Scientific Revolution and the 'Republic of Letters'. Theories of government and the world were now open to international debate and reconsideration, with the soundness of a principle to be found, like a sound coin, in its accepted value when in circulation across national boundaries.[6] If we are increasingly learning how Newtonian science depended upon opportunities for observation and measurement opened up by European commerce and overseas empire, so reciprocally, economic thought, in the hands of Quesnay and Smith, modelled itself on natural philosophy, claiming laws founded upon nature, universally applicable and subject to universal criticism, free of mere custom and tradition. Political economy, in its mature form, was both a means and a product of cosmopolitan exchange, a new global kind of reason.

* * *

Why was such a collection not previously attempted? One explanation lies, of course, in that way of seeing which assumed that European political economy might be understood through studying intra-European phenomena. But it is also true that the national focus of European historiography, where both the domestic and colonial histories of Spain, Holland, or England were examined in separate compartments, also inhibited a comparative perspective. *The Political Economy of Empire* points suggestively toward how new trans-European research programmes might open up new lines of sight into the shared intellectual, institutional, and imperial history of Europe. It might even be the foundation for a future masterwork on how, from Suarez to Keynes, overseas empires shaped economic thought.

Notes

1. R. Koebner, *Empire* (Cambridge: Cambridge University Press, 1961); I. Hont, *Jealousy of Trade: International Competition and the Nation-State in Historical Perspective* (Cambridge, MA: Harvard University Press, 2005), 1–156.
2. D. Armitage, *The Ideological Origins of the British Empire* (Cambridge: Cambridge University Press, 2000); A. Pagden, *Lords of All the World: Ideologies of Empire in*

Spain, Britain, and France c. 1500–1800 (New Haven, CT: Yale University Press, 1995).

3. 'Pour l'acroissement de cet empire en puissance et en gloire' and 'Toute société...semble estre composée de gouvernement et de commerce', Antoine de Montchrétien, *Traicté de l'Oeconomie Politique* (Paris, 1615), f. 14 and f. 137, http://gallica.bnf.fr/ark:/12148/btv1b8610768t/f14.image (accessed 10 July 2012).
4. Hont, *Jealousy of Trade*, 12.
5. P. Vilar, *A History of Gold and Money, 1450–1920*, J. White (trans.) (New York: Verso, 1991); M. Grice Hutchinson, *The School of Salamanca and Early Economic Thought in Spain, 1177–1740* (London: Allen and Unwin, 1978).
6. S. A. Reinert, *Translating Empire* (Cambridge, MA: Harvard University Press, 2011).

Acknowledgements

The contributions in this volume are the result of a conference on 'The Political Economy of Empire in the Early Modern World' organised at King's College, University of Cambridge, on 4 November 2006. The editors would like to thank the History Faculty at the University of Cambridge and the Centre for History and Economics at Magdalene College and King's College, University of Cambridge, for making that conference possible. They are also grateful to Richard Drayton, Istvan Hont, and Emma Rothschild for intellectual and moral support, to the anonymous peer reviewer, to Inga Huld Markan for practical assistance, and to the participants of the conference for making it such a memorable event. This book is dedicated to the memory of Istvan Hont.

Notes on Contributors

Jan Hartman is writing a PhD thesis on the political thought of the seventeenth-century Hollanders Johan and Pieter de la Court. He was a researcher at the Erasmus University Rotterdam and the Erasmus Center for Early Modern Studies and is now a part-time independent scholar.

Thomas Hopkins is a postdoctoral researcher with the Research Project Europe 1815–1914 at the University of Helsinki since 2009. He holds a PhD in History from the University of Cambridge and is currently working on a monograph on political economy in post-Napoleonic Europe, with particular reference to the thought of Jean-Baptiste Say and J.-C.-L. Simonde de Sismondi.

James Lees holds a BA in English Literature and an MA and PhD in British Imperial-South Asian History, all from King's College London. His research examines power relations and bureaucratic culture among the European civil servants of the East India Company state in late eighteenth-century Bengal. He has taught history at KCL and London Metropolitan University, and at NTU in Singapore. He currently works as a research funding administrator at the University of London's Institute of Historical Research.

Claire S. Levenson is an executive communications officer in the Office of Communications and Public Affairs at Columbia University in New York City. Prior to that, she was a producer at *Charlie Rose*, the PBS television program in which politicians, business leaders, artists, and scholars from around the world come to be interviewed. She earned a PhD in history from the University of Cambridge and a BA degree from Columbia University.

Bertie Mandelblatt is an assistant professor in the Department of History and the Program for Caribbean Studies at the University of Toronto. Her teaching and research interests concern French overseas expansion, environmental history, commodity exchanges, and consumption in the Atlantic world of the seventeenth and eighteenth centuries, with a focus on the greater Caribbean. Her current book project measures global and local elements of colonial/slave food provisioning of the Franco-Caribbean during the period of French colonisation.

Gabriel Paquette is an assistant professor of History at Johns Hopkins University. He is the author of *Imperial Portugal in the Age of Atlantic Revolutions: The Luso-Brazilian World, c. 1770–1850* (2013) and the coeditor of *Connections after Colonialism: Europe and Latin America in the 1820s* (2013).

Giles Parkinson graduated in 2005 from Durham University with a degree in history. He then went on to graduate from St. John's College, Cambridge, with an MPhil in Historical Studies. In 2006 Giles joined Newton Investment Management as a research analyst. He joined Artemis Investment Management in September 2010 to work alongside William Littlewood on the Artemis Strategic Assets Fund.

Sophus A. Reinert is an assistant professor of Business Administration in the Business, Government, and the International Economy unit at Harvard Business School. He has written extensively on the history of political economy and is the author of *Translating Empire: Emulation and the Origins of Political Economy* (2011).

Pernille Røge is a historian of eighteenth-century France and its colonial empire. She completed her doctoral studies at the University of Cambridge in 2010, after which she took up a research/lectureship at Corpus Christi College, Cambridge. In 2012 she was appointed to an assistant professorship in History at the University of Pittsburgh. She has published widely on French political economy, slavery and imperial policy.

Arthur Weststeijn is Director of Historical Studies at the Royal Netherlands Institute in Rome. His recent publications include *Commercial Republicanism in the Dutch Golden Age* (2012) and 'Republican Empire. Colonialism, Commerce, and Corruption in the Dutch Golden Age', *Renaissance Studies* 26, no. 4 (2012).

Introduction: The Political Economy of Empire

Sophus A. Reinert and Pernille Røge

'Commerce', the archbishop of Aix, de Boisgelin, wrote in a 1785 commentary on Montesquieu, 'seems to have a propensity to create one single empire of all empires, one single people of all peoples, to found one single, immortal nation which has no other name but that of mankind'.[1] More than two centuries later, we like to think that commerce is indeed a uniting force between peoples, creating if not an 'immortal nation' called 'mankind', at least a 'global community'. Trade, we assume, is the antithesis of warfare; it creates prosperity for all parties involved, rendering conflict impossible, polities more stable, and governments largely redundant. On the one hand there is the discord of empires; on the other there is peaceful commerce – warfare is the tool of the former, political economy that of the latter.

In the early modern period, political economy was in effect seen by many as an antidote to the evils of imperialism, an alternative to empire and its bloody collaterals which had so grimly tinted the age. As one journal optimistically summarised this new discipline in the wake of the costly and destructive Seven Years' War, 'political economy' was a 'science' allowing one to '*increase the greatness, power, and wealth of the Nation, without at the same time aiming to enlarge the borders of what one possesses*'.[2] Ideally, political economy allowed for competition and greatness by more peaceful means.[3]

History, however, reminded others that the relationship between trade and empire often was less black and white, and more a subtle chiaroscuro. From the Italian city-states of the Renaissance, through the Dutch Golden Age to the rise of the British Empire, trade had worked wonders, but most often through conscious policies and seldom, if ever, without bloodshed. One of the continent's most experienced practical imperialists, the Dutch officer of the East India Company and twice governor-general of the East Indies Jan Pieterszoon Coen, had his finger on the pulse of a widespread economic culture when he explained to the governing body of the Netherlands that 'one cannot do commerce without war, nor war without commerce', for similar statements were legion across Europe in the seventeenth and eighteenth centuries.[4] Contrary to what is often assumed, the idea that trade could also be a means of coercion in international relations was in fact clearly articulated in the mainstream of early modern political economy by some of its most celebrated practitioners.[5] As one professor of political economy warned in 1781, aggressive export strategies had bestowed upon Britain 'dominion' even where it sent no troops, 'a different kind of Empire'.[6]

So though there was a tradition of thought emphasising the incompatibility of trade and war, there was also a parallel tradition that conceived of trade, and thus liberty and national security, as competitive rather than collaborative. In practice, the case is even clearer. England and later Britain rose to prominence in the eighteenth century through the vigilance of the Royal Navy, and its factories were protected by some of the most prohibitive tariffs in European history well into the nineteenth century. Military and economic power were not opposites as Britannia came to rule the waves; they were part and parcel of her imperial project, to which Adam Smith's memorable praise of the draconian Navigation Acts testifies.[7] There certainly existed a political economy of internal development, based on the idea that territorial policies, improving technologies of cultivation and production, and policing could bring about worldly melioration in a peaceful manner, but the limits and possibilities of the discipline could also be conceptualised very differently. The same insights into the benefits of administering possessions and dominions could validate imperial expansion and global competition for resources. Empire and political economy were not necessarily counteracting in the early modern world; they could also function in tremendous synergy.

'She who commands the Commerce, commands the Wealth', Thomas Brooke Clarke thus concluded in 1799, 'and she who commands the Wealth of the World, must command the World itself'.[8] As European powers sought to embrace the globe in the early modern period, the acquisition of their empires was inexorably intertwined with the acquisition of profits, and the two were seldom discussed in isolation. It is therefore not surprising that the political economy of empire is a growing theme in contemporary imperial and intellectual historiography.[9] Taking cues from neighbouring fields like Atlantic history and the history of globalisation, not to mention the history of economic thought, historians of early modern and modern Europe have become increasingly interested in tying together the categories 'empire' and 'political economy' in order to reflect upon Europe's confrontation with its mounting world dominance and the dynamic relationship between intellectual history and the unfolding cultural, military, and economic history of global trade and conquest. In this context, the seventeenth and eighteenth centuries have proven to be particularly fruitful periods for analysis. Not only did they witness the rise of political economy as a discipline and a concomitant acceleration of European imperial expansion overseas, but they also form an intriguing backdrop against which the simultaneously introvert and extrovert nature of early modern Europe can be considered and through which the origins and consequences of imperialism can be ascertained.

The Political Economy of Empire in the Early Modern World takes this important historical moment as its subject as well as its point of departure. Inspired by monographs and comparative studies already published on the political economy of empire, it aims to open the field to its larger European and extra-European context. Though many of the contributions to our volume focus on the political economy of Europe's Atlantic empires – both theoretically and practically – these are enriched and made more trenchant by being put in a comparative global context. This both clarifies the unique and salient characteristics of western expansion and makes it historically intelligible as part of a larger imperial imagination of political and economic possibilities, in the metropolitan centres as well as in their colonial peripheries. Originating in a conference organised under the auspices of the Faculty of History at the University of Cambridge and the Centre for History and Economics at King's College, Cambridge, this collection of essays treats the diverse range of theoretical and practical manifestations of the science of political economy in and among the five largest European imperial powers: Spain, Portugal, France, England and Holland. While the volume does not claim to encompass all the possible horizons and perspectives inherent in the subject matter, and indeed a comprehensive treatment is not conceivable in a single volume, the multifaceted representation of its topic and its embodied dialectic between theory and practice do weave together a coherent picture of the political economy of empire in the early modern world and identify certain recurring themes and problems.

The organisation of the book, divided in two parts, is thematic. Part I groups together five contributions that predominantly treat intellectual developments and debates over empire in Europe, but also demonstrate the multidirectional influences between imperial centres and peripheries.

The essays in this section, entitled 'Theorising the Early Modern Empire', are arranged chronologically, starting with Jan Hartman and Arthur Weststeijn's on Pieter de la Court's (1618–1685) critique of the Dutch East India Company and the possibilities of imperial expansion eastward and northward as a means of resisting the rise of England. Their study is followed by Pernille Røge's examination of the physiocratic vision of colonial France after the Seven Years' War and this school's attempt to reconceptualise 'colonies' in the West Indies as 'overseas provinces' of the French agricultural kingdom. Shifting from continental to Scottish political economy, Tom Hopkins reinterprets the role played by colonies and formal empires in Adam Smith's political economy. The fourth and fifth chapters change perspective from the prosopographic and monographic to the comparative. Gabriel Paquette surveys the impact of British political economy on Spanish and Portuguese's colonial reform (1740–1810), highlighting the theoretical tensions resulting from the transfer of economic knowledge from core to periphery as colonies became sovereign states. Sophus A. Reinert concludes the section with a quantitative analysis of economic translations in Europe (1500–1849) that gauges the way in which international economic competition triggered imperial emulation of politico-economic theory and practice. Together, the five chapters illustrate how European powers faced very similar concerns and anxieties regarding their empires and greeted political economy as a possible solution to the many financial and political disputes the management of empire entailed.

Part II shifts the focus from theoretical to practical aspects of empire and, with the exception of Giles Parkinson, from metropolitan centres to colonial peripheries. Entitled 'Imperial Experiences', part II opens with Giles Parkinson's study on the role of the stock market in financing Britain's imperial wars against France, and how successful imperial expansion overseas can be seen to have solidified national sentiments in the metropolis and provided an oriflamme around which immigrant interests could consolidate their adoptive identities. Claire S. Levenson's contribution relocates to the Americas with a study of the economic encounter between the Yamacraw Indians and the British in Georgia Low Country, problematising the relations between different cultures of exchange: indigenous gift-giving and the European market principle. James Lees turns eastward again in his survey on practices of military-fiscalism in the East India Company, and particularly so on the relationship between fiscal measures and the success and consequence of the colonial economy of violence. Bertie Mandelblatt ends part II with a study on food provisioning in the French Caribbean world. Drawing attention to the movement of material commodities among colonial and intercolonial networks of exchange rather than between colony and metropolis, the study offers an alternative mapping of mercantile networks in the French Atlantic.

Together, the two parts of this volume begin to address the ever-vexing and dynamic relationship between theory and practice in early modern political economy. Much as the real linkages between science and industry defy the transparency too often allotted them, so the relationship between early modern economic ideas, policies, and real-world consequences remains elusive and can perhaps never be resolved in a generalisable manner. The imperial encounter with political economy was in other words neither uniform across political, economic, cultural, and religious constellations nor static across time. Yet the essays here do justify the drawing of some larger conclusions, both historical and historiographical.

First of all, they all highlight the imperative importance of advancing the international and comparative dimensions of early modern history, not merely in terms of considering imperial cores and peripheries but also the dynamic relationships between polities, empires and the liminal lands between them. Whether statesmen, theorists, or practitioners, Native Americans, Indian peasants, or small-scale British investors, this volume's protagonists kept at least one eye perpetually across the horizon, whether their intentions were to understand, resist, reform, conquer, or emulate the proverbial 'other'. Many of the essays in the volume in effect place particular importance on the role played by emulation at the time, on the myriads of ways in which theories and practices were received, mediated, and implemented across time, borders, and languages in the early modern world – from the reception of Italian reason of state in Holland to the engagement with British imperial policies in the Luso-Hispanic dominions and the changing patterns of economic translations in the very long eighteenth century. Emulation, this book suggests, is a crucial cypher for making sense of the enormous changes taking place in the European world during its first period of globalisation.

Secondly, essays from the book's two parts highlight the importance of considering intellectual and material histories together, analysing the same problematic – in this case regarding the theories and practices of physiocratic imperialism in the wake of the Seven Years' War – from disparate but mutually illuminating angles. Similarly, gift-giving diplomacy in seventeenth-century Georgia, Adam Smith's theory of colonialism, and tax violence in eighteenth-century British India were facets of the same imperial prism, disparate yet related aspects of the same vast historical phenomenon. As such, the essays here collected demonstrate the historiographical value of considering the history of political economy, one of the currently fastest growing and most innovative subfields of the historical profession, in a holistic fashion. The contributions collected in this volume address, with undeniable pertinence for the struggles of later periods, the moral and military ambiguity of profits and power as well as the often jealous interactions between different solutions to the problem of empire, whether theoretical or practical. By synthesising economic, intellectual, and cultural historiographies, *The Political Economy of Empire in the Early Modern World* lays a mosaic of imperial theories and practices contributing to the creation of the modern world.

David Hume understood that a revolution took place in human affairs once 'trade' became an 'affair of state'.[10] Success in the international economy had become an existential concern, and to many eighteenth-century observers it seemed obvious that 'commerce' had come not only to influence but to 'decide' the 'superiority of one nation over another'.[11] We are still struggling with the aftershocks of this revolution and with the exigencies it continues to present for the global economy. Together, the essays in this volume present a prolonged meditation on the origins and nature of this moment in world history, on the ways in which trade curtailed and reinforced dominion, and ultimately on the dynamic relationship between empire and political economy in a globalising world.

Notes

1. In Simona Cerutti, 'Società Di "Eguali" E "Comune Umanità": La Critica Al Processo Tra Il Piemonte E La Francia Del Settecento', in Antonella Alimento (ed.), *Modelli D'Oltre Confine: Prospettive Economiche E Sociali Negli Antichi Stati Italiani* (Rome, 2009), 191–208, 205.
2. *Giornale d'Italia*, 21 July 1764 (Rome), 17.
3. The classic discussion of 'sweet commerce' is in Albert O. Hirschman, *The Passions and the Interests: Political Arguments for Capitalism before Its Triumph* (Princeton, 1977), but see also Pocock, *Barbarism and Religion*, 4 vols. (Cambridge, 1999–2005), I: 109, II: 79, 221, III: 309, 377–8; Stephen C. Neff, *Friends but No Allies: Economic Liberalism and the Law of Nations* (New York, 1990), 30; Katherine Barbieri, *The Liberal Illusion: Does Trade Promote Peace* (Ann Arbor, 2002); Michael P. Gerace, *Military Power, Conflict and Trade* (London, 2004).
4. In Maria Fusaro, *Reti commerciali e traffici globali in età moderna* (Bari, 2008), 71; emphasis added. See, for equivalent English statements at the time, Ronald

Findlay and Kevin H. O'Rourke, *Power and Plenty: Trade, War, and t Economy in the Second Millennium* (Princeton, 2007), 244.

5. See for example Simone Meysonnier (ed.), *Traites sur le commerce a Child suivis des Remarques de jacques Vincent de Gournay*, (Paris, 200), 242; Girolamo Belloni with annotations by Giovanni Battista Zanobetti, *Del commercio...* (Leghorn, 1751), 70n.
6. Michele de Jorio, *Storia del commercio e della navigazione: Dal principio del Mondo sino a' giorni nostri...*, 4 vols. (Naples, 1778–1783), I: 21.
7. Example, Patrick K. O'Brien, 'Inseparable Connexions: Trade, Economy, Fiscal State, and the Expansion of Empire, 1688–1815', in P. J. Marshall (ed.), *The Oxford History of the British Empire*, vol. 2, *The Eighteenth Century* (Oxford, 1998), 53–77; J. V. C. Nye, *War, Wine, and Taxes: The Political Economy of Anglo-French Trade, 1689–1900* (Princeton, 2007); Adam Smith, *An Inquiry into the Nature and Causes of the Wealth of Nations*, Edwin Cannan (ed.), 2 vols. (Chicago, 1976), I: 486.
8. In Istvan Hont, 'The "Rich Country-Poor Country" Debate Revisited: The Irish Origins and French Reception of the Hume Paradox', in Carl Wennerlind and Margaret Schabas (eds), *David Hume's Political Economy* (London, 2008), 243–323, 299
9. Example, Richard Drayton, *Nature's Government: Science, Imperial Britain, and the 'Improvement' of the World* (New Haven, 2000); Jose Luis Cardoso, *A Economia Política e Os Dilemas do Império Luso-Brasileiro (1790–1822)* (Lisbon, 2001); Emma Rothschild, 'Global Commerce and the Question of Sovereignty in the Eighteenth-Century Provinces', *Modern Intellectual History* 1, no. 1 (2004): 3–25; Gabriel Paquette, *Enlightenment, Governance, and Reform in Spain and Its Empire, 1759–1808* (Basingstoke, 2008); Paul Cheney, *Revolutionary Commerce: Globalization and the French Monarchy* (Cambridge, MA, 2010).
10. David Hume, *Political Essays*, Knud Haakonssen (ed.) (Cambridge, 1994), 52.
11. *Giornale d'Italia*, 12 April 1766, 327.

Part I

Theorising the Early Modern Empire

1
An Empire of Trade: Commercial Reason of State in Seventeenth-Century Holland

Jan Hartman and Arthur Weststeijn

In his reinterpretation of 1688 as the 'first modern revolution', Steve Pincus argues that England's revolutionary epoch of the 1690s involved a significant change in the way people thought about the relation between politics and economics.[1] The 'new political economy', which rose to prominence in public discourse and state policy, held that wealth and power were based on manufacture instead of agriculture, on labour instead of land. Its underlying principle was that property was man-made and t-hus infinite instead of flowing from (finite) natural resources. This changing vision of political economy culminated in the financial policies of king-stadholder William III, such as the establishment of the Bank of England in 1694. Pincus shows that opponents of William III in the 1690s were prone to dismiss these novel policies as coming from Holland.[2] Was this a cheap polemic trick of guilt by association with the alien interest of Britain's natural enemy? Or was the 'new political economy' really a Dutch import?

To answer these questions, we first need to establish what the dominant ideas on politics and economics were during the period in which young William III (1650–1702) grew up in Holland. Recent scholarship, in particular by Erik Reinert and Jacob Soll, has laid some of the groundwork for this task by highlighting the international significance of seventeenth-century Dutch economic theory and practice, explicitly couched by Soll as 'the rise of political economy'.[3] According to Soll, a crucial role in this process should be ascribed to Pieter de la Court's *Interest van Holland*, an influential political treatise, first published in 1662, that had a large impact on foreign perceptions of Dutch mercantile success.[4] De la Court's work is particularly important in the context of European commercial emulation, or 'jealousy of trade', a leitmotif of the age that has been adopted by Istvan Hont to describe the gradual development of a Machiavellian theory of international trade at the end of the seventeenth century.[5] Yet surprisingly Hont has paid very little attention to Dutch theorising about politics and commerce, even though the Netherlands were the principal object of much of the jealousy in question. To mention just one example, Josiah Child stressed in 1668 that the 'prodigious increase of the *Netherlands* in their domestick and foreign Trade, Riches, and multitude of Shipping, is the envy of the present, and may be the wonder of all future Generations'.[6] The Dutch themselves shared this assumption. A pamphleteer argued in 1661 that Dutch primacy in world trade, 'the Soul and the life of the Netherlands', had caused it to be that 'several Nations have become jealous, especially the English, who cannot bear the prosperity of the Dutch'.[7]

In this chapter we aim to uncover this Dutch theorising about commerce as the pivot of international competition, focusing on the work of de la Court in the context of the development of reason of state theory throughout Europe. De la Court's case, we argue, shows that the term 'political economy' does not adequately describe seventeenth-century Dutch thought about politics and economics, which involved a distinctive application of conventional 'reason of state' to a seaborne, mercantile polity. As an alternative to 'political economy', therefore, we propose the concept of 'commercial reason of state' as a more useful term to understand the context and development of Holland's 'jealousy of trade' in the early-modern period.[8]

The rise of commercial reason of state

When William III came of age in the Dutch Republic, Pieter de la Court ranked among the most important Dutch theorists on the relation between politics and economics. De la Court was born in 1618 as the eldest son of a Walloon immigrant family in Leiden. Educated at Leiden University during the 1640s, he and his younger brother Johan, born in 1622, became successful entrepreneurs in Leiden's textile industry, which was by then the largest in Europe and employed more than half of the town's population.[9] The combined scholarly and economic background of the brothers de la Court resulted in their large oeuvre of political treatises which critically commented upon the remarkable 'Golden Age' of Dutch primacy in world trade. The initiative for this intellectual enterprise had come from Johan de la Court, yet after his premature death in 1660, Pieter took over the project, adapted his brother's work and published a range of treatises until his own death in 1685.[10] All in all, the brothers' common oeuvre, which merged a radical critique of all forms of monarchy with a groundbreaking study of the origins of Dutch prosperity, was highly contested and debated throughout the Dutch Republic – and it remained influential far beyond the country's borders.

The very first treatise of the brothers de la Court comprised a comprehensive analysis of the economic and political situation in their hometown of Leiden. Dedicated to the local magistrate Johannes Eleman, Pieter de la Court's brother-in-law, the treatise offered a critical assessment of the policies of the municipal government, which according to the de la Courts fundamentally obstructed the economic, religious and political liberties of Leiden's citizens.[11] This treatise, which circulated in manuscript and would not be published during the brothers' lifetime, formed the foundation of a general theory of a commercial republic that was developed in their subsequent works and applied to the case of Holland at large in the 1662 *Interest van Holland*. Significantly, the de la Courts started their treatise on Leiden with the explicit statement that the politics of their hometown should be conceived 'sopra la raggion di Stato'(on the basis of reason of state).[12] From the outset, they thus positioned themselves in the tradition of reason of state: an intellectual current comprising a heterogeneous array of political treatises which, from the end of the sixteenth century onward, flooded the European markets with intricate accounts of how to preserve and enlarge a dominion according to the notorious adage 'necessity has no law'.[13] What exactly was the sort of reason of state that the de la Courts adhered to?

One of the first and foremost contributions to the reason of state tradition was Giovanni Botero's *Della ragion di stato*, first published in 1589. Writing in the large shadow of Machiavelli, Botero (ca. 1544–1617) chiefly argued that princes should promote the *grandezza* (greatness) of their 'state' (defined as 'a firm dominion over peoples') through the expansion of territory, population and, in particular, wealth. Reason of state, then, entailed a practical framework to achieve such greatness, offering princes 'the knowledge of the means of establishing, preserving and enlarging a Dominion'.[14] In its opening passages, Botero's work revealed to be deeply indebted to the Machiavellian obsession of how to establish and pursue such a durable empire that would not be consumed by external violence and envy or internal corruption.[15] Yet unlike Machiavelli, Botero did not propose republican Rome as a paragon of greatness, but rather middle-sized polities such as Sparta or Venice – examples repudiated by Machiavelli.[16] More importantly, Botero duly emphasised the mercantile over the military means of attaining greatness, substituting a predominantly economic approach to politics for Machiavelli's praise of militant *virtù*. He developed this economic approach further in the treatise *Delle cause della grandezza delle città*, which was regularly appended to *Della ragion di stato*. This work entailed a reason of state of cities, yet still with a focus on the central role of a prince and his urban residence. Significantly, Botero referred in this context in particular to the example of the 'Cities of Flanders' and their economic achievements. Some of these cities, and here Botero mentioned Antwerp and Amsterdam, were indeed 'almost the masters of merchandize and trade because of their convenient location for many nations, to which they serve as warehouse and entrepôt'.[17] Botero thus stressed the structural geographic causes behind the enviable mercantile success of the Netherlands, but he also favourably discussed the concrete policies that engendered Dutch prosperity, in particular 'the frankness of taxes'.[18] In short, Botero implicitly taught that the Dutch model of commercial greatness should not only be envied, but also imitated.

An important follower of Botero's economic approach to reason of state who clearly understood this lesson was Sir Walter Raleigh (ca. 1552–1618).[19] In his *Observations Touching Trade and Commerce with the Hollander and Other Nations*, written around 1618 but only published in 1653, Raleigh adopted Botero's envious praise of the Dutch mercantile model, which so patently outshone its competitor across the North Sea. How could it be, Raleigh wondered, that Holland had no natural resources but was still able to build more and cheaper ships than England or Spain? How could Holland be a supplier of grain to many European countries if the country mostly consisted of pastures? Raleigh postulated as the main reason for this commercial success the fact that in Holland 'the liberty of free Traffick for Strangers to buy and sell ... maketh great intercourse'. The low duties levied on existing trades and the free customs for new trades attracted many foreign merchants to Holland, thus enlarging the country's population and wealth. Moreover, Dutch fishing at the coasts of England guaranteed a continuous source of income, while the transportation and storage of other countries' commodities enabled the Dutch to sell corn in times of scarcity and thereby make tremendous profits.[20] Like Botero, Raleigh thus argued that the Dutch commercial success was primarily due to low taxation and staple market function, and again like Botero, he also stressed that these achievements could easily be imitated. Having 'undergone the pains to look into their Policies', Raleigh pointed out to James I that England was located conveniently enough to take the place of Holland as a storehouse and transporting country for other parts of Europe.[21] The Dutch might have had a head start, but Raleigh claimed that the English would sooner or later outdo them – a warning that de la Court was clearly aware of, given his explicit reference to Raleigh's *Observations* in the *Interest van Holland*.

While Botero and Raleigh primarily discussed the economic policies that underlay Dutch commercial primacy, another important representative of the reason of state tradition, the Italian satirist Traiano Boccalini (1556–1613), argued that the Dutch success was predominantly due to its republican constitution. In his *Ragguagli di Parnasso* (1612–1613), Boccalini tells of a fictional gathering of Europe's potentates. They are disturbed by the popping up of many republics among the Germanic peoples (the Swiss, Grisons and Bernese), and especially those of the Hollanders and Zeelanders in the Low Countries. The potentates pleaded that from the world's beginning to that day, monarchy was the most praised and preferred form of government, and monarchies had ever been victorious against republics, their natural enemies. History showed that aristocratic, democratic and mixed republics degenerated, after which these governments would soon be subjected to the rule of a single man. The demise of Rome was a certain fate for all republics, even mixed ones. Now, however, the potentates noticed that the Swiss – skilled watchmakers – had invented 'subtle and acute artifices' to safeguard eternal liberty. These successful institutions in turn threatened monarchies with extinction.[22] If the neighbouring monarchs did not extinguish the small seed of Swiss liberty, revolution might spread throughout Europe, because 'the least spark, if neglected, can easily cause great fires'.[23]

With this imaginative tale of international competition between princes and republics, Boccalini clearly followed in the footsteps of Machiavelli's famous analysis of the superiority of free states over monarchies.[24] However, Boccalini departed from Machiavelli's path when he claimed that the most important precept of the Germanic peoples was not to desire military conquest or offensive warfare, for this had been, pace Machiavelli, the cause of the demise of Rome. Boccalini explained that the Germanic peoples remained at peace with their neighbours and searched the conservation of their own liberty rather than the appropriation of the liberty of others. This also gave them military prowess, for 'each man who defends his liberty has twenty hands and as many hearts'.[25] The outstanding example of this was given by the military strength of the insuperable Hollanders and Zeelanders. They had miraculously defended themselves against the mighty open force of Spain and the clever intrigues of the French, the English and William I of Orange – who was not seen by Boccalini as a liberator of the Low Countries, but as someone who secretly aspired to become sovereign.

Boccalini's propagation of a peaceful commercial republic as a viable alternative to a territorial monarchy, together with Botero's and Raleigh's analysis of the economic policies that favour trade, figure prominently in the work of the brothers de la Court as authoritative international sources on the politics of the Dutch economy. Clearly, then, the 'reason of state' that the de la Courts referred to as the basis of their critical discussion of Leiden's welfare implied that favourable taxes, the attraction of foreign merchants, and a protective foreign policy would achieve the commercial *grandezza* of the state. Whilst 'state' meant in the work of Botero the personal dominion and status of a prince, for the de la Courts the state involved the collective body of both rulers and ruled, that is, the city or commonwealth at large – the traditional idiom of the Italian Renaissance republics as developed from Machiavelli to Boccalini.[26] The brothers' idea of 'reason of state' implied the precepts for governing such a republican state within the European balance of military and commercial power.

A somewhat different perspective is suggested by the term 'political economy'. The earliest known usage of this term is that by the French author Antoine de Montchrétien in his *Traicté de l'oeconomie politique* of 1615, a long advisory treatise to the French King Louis XIII. Montchrétien explains the term by claiming that the wealth of an empire does not simply depend on its extent or on the number of its inhabitants, but primarily on the cultivation of all lands and the proper allocation of offices.[27] In the state, just as in the family, people should be governed according to their inclination, for the science of acquiring goods is common to governments as well as families. Therefore, 'against the opinion of Aristotle and Xenophon', who distinguished the *oikos* from the *polis*, Montchrétien maintains that 'one would not be able to separate economy (*l'oeconomie*) from politics (*la police*) without thereby amputating the main part from the whole'.[28] The main task of the prince is therefore to balance the household book as a national *pater familias*: the ruler has to spend less than he earns.[29] As we explain in the next section of this chapter, such an emphasis on the individual prince as a public householder who ensures the cultivation of lands, the allocation of offices and the bookkeeping of the state is entirely absent from the thought of the brothers de la Court.

Free trade as the highest law

The foundation of the de la Courts' account of Holland's reason of state was formed by their critical analysis of the economic policies of Leiden, the city where the brothers were born, where they had studied and where they made their fortune. According to the conventional reason of state logic, Leiden posed a difficult case. Botero had argued that the *grandezza* of cities follows from the quantity of the people and their belongings, for which, apart from the splendour of a princely court, a favourable geographical position and fecund surroundings are essential.[30] Yet Leiden, as the brothers de la Court insisted, lacked all these assets. Therefore, the city should resort to two highly unpredictable means of attaining civic *grandezza*: the world of learning, embodied by Leiden's famous university, and the world of industry and trade.[31] With this double claim as a starting point, the de la Courts embarked upon a fervent criticism of the corporate politics of Leiden's society, which resulted in a passionate and remarkable plea for an 'open' city where entrepreneurial liberty fosters prosperity.[32]

The de la Courts primarily insisted that Leiden's trade and industry were based on the consumption of its goods outside the city walls. Hence, the general welfare was dependent on the large mercantile entrepreneurs who exported textiles across the borders and, thanks to their ability to make large investments, employed small producers and petty artisans. Yet these international merchants could only make high revenues if they would be left unhindered in their decisions and actions, for 'he who has to eat the porridge cooks and cools it best'. As the de la Courts stressed,

> Everyone ought to be totally free and unrestrained in producing and dealing with his own commodity.... Where everyone takes care of himself, everyone is fine, and no one gets lost. This is the natural liberty that the Rulers should never take away from their subjects.[33]

The core assertion of the de la Courts is that Leiden's corporate regulation through the establishment of textile halls and guilds fundamentally obstructed such natural liberty – and as a result, Leiden's reason of state.

In view of the vicissitudes of international trade, the exclusivist policies and unifying regulations of these corporate associations were, for the de la Courts, fundamentally counterproductive.[34] 'None of our industries is fixed to the ground', they argued, 'and therefore they do not resemble the trees, from which one may cut some branches that bear little fruit'.[35] In the realm of commercial Lady Fortune, characterised by cross-border competition and the capriciousness of fashion, a pragmatist mercantile *virtù* was necessary to maintain Leiden's industry and to improve its competitiveness. The de la Courts therefore claimed that all production should be deregulated, wages should be set free, levies and cartels should be abolished and everyone should be able to choose with whom to trade.[36] Such economic freedom would increase manufacturing, attract foreigners, and thus enhance Leiden's overall *grandezza*, whereas corporate regulation would result in the direct opposite.

This critical analysis of Leiden's economic prospects forms the inductive foundation of a general theory of commercial reason of state that Pieter de la Court subsequently applied to the case of Holland at large. The core of this theory lies in the Ciceronian maxim *salus populi suprema lex* (the welfare of the people shall be the highest law), a powerful and widespread early-modern commonplace that could be mobilised for various political purposes – for the de la Courts as a reason to comment that the phrase was like 'a nice doll praised by all outwardly, but by only a few valued and cared for inwardly'.[37] The case of Leiden revealed that the maxim truly implies that the health of the people in a mercantile republic consists of two intrinsically connected elements: commercial greatness and the advancement of liberty. Commerce must be the means to achieve the preservation and increase of the polity, and commerce thrives in liberty. Hence, freedom of trade ranked for the de la Courts as the supreme law that leads to commercial greatness.[38]

This fundamental claim that free trade forms the essence of commercial reason of state starts from the assertion that human natural liberty should be maintained as much as possible within the boundaries of the law in order to promote general prosperity and the growth of society. A commonwealth where all inhabitants enjoy such liberty will improve its competitiveness with the surrounding polities and therefore fulfil its chief goal, the increase of its population. Indeed, a city like Leiden 'will only be able to subsist by giving its inhabitants much more freedom than they can find in any nearby or better situated Cities or places'.[39] The de la Courts therefore stressed the need to grant all immigrants citizenship rights and the same opportunities to make a living as the indigenous population, for 'absolute uniform freedom for all inhabitants, bearing uniform burdens', is apart from a natural right a 'powerful means to attract foreigners'.[40] Such freedom of immigration and occupation is all the more important since immigrants will also bring 'knowledge and goods', and are therefore essential for the survival of a commonwealth of learning and industry. Newcomers do not own any fixed property, and therefore they will have to invest their foreign experience and capital 'to invent and create new fisheries, manufactures, trade, and navigations'. Hence, a constant influx of immigrants will guarantee the constant renewal and improvement of trade and industry.[41] Commercial increase and liberty are thus mutually dependent:

> *Trade* is a very powerful means to employ and feed many people. ... Yet Trade is not fixed to one place only. Where Merchants are burdened least and where they are given more freedom to make and keep profits, there they will remain. But where, on the contrary, the freedom to make profits is restricted, or where the rich Merchants are harshly charged, there they are chased away or extinguished.[42]

In short, in an emerging era of international commercial competition, Leiden and Holland more generally could only endure by conceding all inhabitants a range of liberties – 'freedom in Religion, Study, trade, manufactures, arts, citizenship and Government'.[43]

Pieter de la Court's reworking of the manuscript on Leiden's welfare to the 1662 *Interest van Holland* and eventually the 1669 *Aanwysing* amounted to an extensive discussion of the concrete policy measures that would promote free trade and thus enhance Holland's commercial greatness. Like Leiden, he argued, Holland was plagued by numerous natural burdens, especially the small size and scarcity of the country's soil. As a result, Holland's population 'should by all means search its food abroad and continuously attract new Inhabitants from foreign Countries'.[44] Commerce and immigration are necessary for survival, and here Holland had an obvious advantage because of its favourable geographical position, which had led to the growth of Dutch fishery, soon followed by trade, industry and seafaring, all essential sources of welfare. Indeed, de la Court claimed self-assuredly that '*in Europe no Country is more capable for* Trade *than Holland*', and in spite of war, international competition and jealousy of trade, 'the Hollanders have navigated almost all Nations out of the great Ocean, the Mediterranean, the Indian Ocean, and the Baltic'.[45]

De la Court's vision of Holland's interest pivoted on the claim that the continuation of this commercial success depended on a range of liberties which would lure foreigners to settle in Holland and promote the growth of trade: freedom of immigration, comprehensive religious freedom, and freedom of enterprise. Following the plea for entrepreneurial liberty in Leiden, de la Court claimed that commercial enterprise in Holland at large should not be obstructed by the imposition of too heavy a tax burden. De la Court thus adopted Botero's and Raleigh's favourable discussion of the earlier taxation policies in Holland, yet he continued to argue that the current reality in Holland had deviated from this admirable past. Although the 'Freedom of *Fishery* and *Trade* is still greater than elsewhere', the tax burden was far too heavy, and de la Court claimed that taxes 'have risen now that high, that the like has never been seen or heard of in any Republic in the World, much less in a Country only subsisting of commerce'.[46] This assertion involved only a little hyperbole, for per capita taxation in seventeenth-century Holland was indeed considerably higher than in other countries.[47] Facing this reality, de la Court insisted that such '*heavy and numerous* imposts' threatened to divert Holland's commerce and thus 'eventually chase away the Country's welfare'.[48]

De la Court concluded that Holland's commercial reason of state required a protectionist policy of taxation that 'burdens *least* the means of *subsistence* which matters us *most*, which we lose the *soonest* and which, once lost, we *cannot easily* recover'.[49] It were therefore the pillars of Holland's economy, the fishermen, artisans, and especially the international merchants, that should be exempted from taxation, since they, 'bringing profit from *abroad into* the Country, are very necessary for the State, yet they can, because of their commerce and correspondence, divert themselves, their goods, and their arts very easily into other Countries'.[50] Facing international competition, a commercial commonwealth such as Holland should favour those who make profits abroad: the entire community depends on their wealth, and if they would be taxed excessively they would leave the country. Accordingly, the manufacturing of goods should not be taxed, nor should any tariffs be raised on the export of these goods or on the import of raw materials needed for the industry. In contrast, de la Court insisted that taxation of consumption and landed property offered an easy and necessary means to secure the state's revenue, while foreign goods that competed with Holland's trade and industry were to be levied as much as possible.[51]

This combined argument for free enterprise within the commonwealth and a protectionist policy vis-à-vis foreign competitors amounted to de la Court's further claim that chartered monopolies in international trade, such as the Dutch East India Company (VOC), go against true commercial reason of state. This claim takes centre stage in the *Interest van Holland* and subsequently the *Aanwysing*, reflecting a significant development in the brothers' economic thought, from unrestricted entrepreneurial freedom in the domestic sphere of Leiden's economy, toward a more regulative approach in order to promote Holland's trade in the expanding arena of international competition overseas. Given his growing involvement in international commerce and state policy during the 1660s, de la Court increasingly realised that Holland's commercial success led to the envy of other polities, for even though 'all Republics that are founded on peace and commerce share the same *Interest* with Holland', they would still try to obstruct 'our main *design*, namely the increase of commerce'.[52] Therefore, all competitors, and in particular England, should be outplayed by a mercantile policy that imposes high tariffs on foreign merchandise while promoting free trade for Holland's own merchants.

Such free trade, so de la Court claimed, should also entail free competition on the colonial market, and hence the abolition of the monopoly of trading companies like the VOC. The roots of this claim lie in the strong condemnation of the economic monopolisation by Leiden's guilds. Like guilds, de la Court insisted, the Dutch trading companies curtailed the '*free trade* of the common inhabitants' and 'their natural liberty of seeking a livelihood in their fatherland'.[53] Moreover, facing a globalising economy and growing international rivalry, it was deemed necessary that all of Holland's merchants were able to trade with the vast territories outside of Europe so that commerce and foreign consumption could continue to increase. Yet as de la Court argued, these opportunities for worldwide commerce were discarded because the private interests of the trading companies necessarily conflicted with the public interest of society at large. Besides, their monopolistic position meant that trading companies were not encouraged to open up new markets. 'Certain profits make them stupid and slow', de la Court asserted repeatedly, 'for necessity makes an old wife trot, hunger makes raw beans sweet, and poverty begets ingenuity'.[54]

Significantly, this criticism of the Dutch trading companies was not confined to pure theory. In the summer of 1664, de la Court and a number of fellow entrepreneurs asked the states-general for permission to search for a northern passage toward China along the shores of Siberia, thus circumventing the monopoly on Asian trade enjoyed by the VOC.[55] A first request was turned down by the States-General after it heard the objections of the directors of the VOC, yet de la Court *cum suis* did not give in and they sent a subsequent request to the States of Holland. Their petition insisted that the general interest of Holland would be greatly enhanced if all of its merchants were allowed to trade in Asia, while 'the particular interest of the Chartered East Indian Company is, on the contrary...to alienate and exclude for eternity the common inhabitants from all knowledge, navigation and commerce of those Asian countries'.[56] Yet this second request was also rejected and the VOC maintained its monopoly – for the petitioners a clear sign of 'the perniciousness of the company, which prefers that other nations come into the possession of such a considerable passage (if it could be found) instead of our own nation'.[57] This remark clearly referred to the growing international competition confronting Dutch overseas trade in the course of the 1650s and 1660s. Since the establishment of the Council of Trade in England in 1650 and the French *Conseil du Commerce* in 1664, Navigation Acts, naval confiscations and tariff wars increasingly obstructed Holland's merchants.[58] At the absolute apex of Dutch primacy in world trade, de la Court perceptively prophesied its immanent decline in respect to its European rivals. Surely, this criticism of the Dutch economic situation reflected de la Court's personal commercial interests, defending entrepreneurial independence against the regulative and exclusivist policies of the corporate establishment.[59] Yet his argumentation also testified to a principled political stance, which went beyond mere self-serving rhetoric and amounted to a comprehensive theory of republican liberty.

This theory postulated that the only remedy for the Dutch consisted of a truly republican government that would safeguard free trade as the highest law of Holland's reason of state. While the de la Courts followed Botero and Raleigh in their analysis of commercial and taxation policies, here they adopted the republican precepts of Machiavelli and Boccalini with the unequivocal claim that '*a* Republic *is better than a* Monarchy', even that '*the* best Monarchical *Government is not as good to the Subjects as the* worst Republican *Government*'.[60] For the de la Courts, the liberties needed to foster Dutch trade could only be maintained under a broad governing assembly without any single ruler such as the Dutch stadholder – in their logic merely a monarch in disguise. Monarchical rule, so they claimed time and again, fundamentally thwarts the preservation and increase of the polity, the prime principle of reason of state. Kings always enforce large taxes to weaken their subjects and to finance their decadent court, frustrating all trading activity. Moreover, they forsake the necessary defence of the country, and instead of promoting the growth of trade, they wage offensive wars to conquer new territories. Thus a commercial commonwealth will necessarily disintegrate when it is enslaved to princely domination, for merchants 'shun and should flee from such a government like from *a deadly Plague*'.[61] Wherever a people lives under domination by the arbitrary will of one man, commerce will collapse: because 'in general, commerce always disappears from those countries and cities where one single man can rob a Merchant at his pleasure of his goods; that is, in short, from all monarchical government'.[62]

This ranting accusation of the principle of monarchy as the arch-enemy of commerce forms the pivot of the de la Courts' entire oeuvre. Appropriating the various commercial and republican lessons of the reason of state tradition from Machiavelli to Raleigh, the brothers constructed a comprehensive account of Holland's interest as an empire of trade where freedom is the highest law. Tellingly, there is nothing in this account that reminisces on the idea of the prince as national *pater familias* who governs the economy of his state as a public bookkeeper, the idea that is central to Montchrétien's notion of 'political economy'. The brothers de la Court were not primarily concerned with issues such as the value of money or the establishment of price levels, but rather with the economic dominance of manufactured products that can be traded, and the resulting need to attract and promote individual mercantile activity. Their model of a commonwealth is not a polity governed as if it were an *oikos*, but rather a republic where no single head can thwart the principles of commercial reason of state. These principles include the promotion of free trade for domestic merchants and the imposition of protectionist measures against foreign competitors: the crucial means to advance the conservation and expansion of the homeland's trade. Unlike economic theorists in a later age, the brothers de la Court did not think about free trade in terms of universal consensus but rather in terms of international strife. Their concept of free trade meant primarily the freedom of Dutch merchants to outdo their rivals abroad, and thus to safeguard Holland's – and none but Holland's – welfare.

Conclusion

By way of conclusion, it is important to highlight two significant features of the Dutch context and the international impact of the work of the brothers de la Court. First of all, the *Interest van Holland* not only entailed the most significant insider's account of the intricacies of Dutch commerce in the later seventeenth century; it was also directly linked to the very nucleus of Dutch republican power, the regent oligarchy around the grand pensionary Johan de Witt. De Witt and a number of his allies were closely involved in the publication of the treatise in 1662, which they intended to use as propaganda for the policies of the States of Holland vis-à-vis the other provinces of the Dutch Republic and the House of Orange. Two chapters of the work were even based on a draft written by de Witt himself, clearly meant to vindicate his rule.[63] This interference in the text should not lead to the conclusion that the de la Courts can be characterised as mere propagandists of the de Witt regime, for such a conclusion does not pay justice to the brothers' strong criticism of the regent oligarchy in power. Nonetheless, the fact that the *Interest van Holland* was published in close cooperation with de Witt shows that the thought of the de la Courts was far from marginal. Indeed, other authors duly adopted their development of a Dutch commercial reason of state, such as the 1665 treatise *Vrije politieke stellingen* (Free Political Tenets), which directly followed in the de la Courts' footsteps by merging a Machiavellian critique of monarchy with a strong plea for liberty of trade.[64] The author of this treatise was Franciscus van den Enden, Spinoza's teacher of Latin. In his radical political treatises of the following decade, Spinoza proved to be equally indebted to the thought of the de la Courts.[65]

While the brothers de la Court thus played a foundational role in the earliest stages of the Radical Enlightenment in the Dutch Republic, their work also had an important impact on political and economic thinking on the other side of the North Sea. This is the second concluding point that should be emphasised. In the course of the 1670s and the 1680s, a number of English authors adopted, either directly or indirectly, the de la Courts' precepts of commercial reason of state. The most significant of these authors was Slingsby Bethel, who had been exiled in the Dutch Republic during the 1660s and who directly reproduced the argumentation of *Interest van Holland* in his own writings, especially in the 1680 *Interest of Princes and States*.[66] True interest, so Bethel insisted, is commercial interest, and commerce thrives through a policy of comprehensive liberty. This de la Courtian claim was also put forward by other Whig theorists such as Roger Coke and Carew Reynell, whose treatises on commerce equally praised the Dutch trading model.[67] With these Whig theorists, we turn back to the very start of this chapter, for they are the protagonists in Steve Pincus's account of the rise of the 'new political economy' in England around 1688. Much more research can and should be done on the de la Courts' influence on this Whig economic and political thought, but it seems justifiable to adopt the claim of contemporary Tory opponents that England's 'new political economy' was clearly indebted to the Dutch.[68]

So how 'new' was this political economy, and does it make sense to speak of 'political economy' at all? This chapter suggests that Whig theorising about politics and economics was not radically innovative but stood in a long international tradition of thinking about the relation between statecraft, freedom and commerce – a tradition rooted in sixteenth-century Italy and developed further on both sides of the North Sea during the seventeenth century. The term 'political economy' does not fully cover the various dimensions of this tradition. To authors like the brothers de la Court, 'political economy' was as much an oxymoron as it was to ancient Greeks. The mere analogy of family and state – in terms of origins or function – and the resulting focus on the prince as a national householder is far removed from the brothers' commercial republican principles.[69] These principles centred on comprehensive freedom of trade, not as an abstract economic formula or a lofty ideal to spread in the world, but as a necessary element of national prosperity, as the pivot of Holland's reason of state in the burgeoning arena of international competition. Using the term 'political economy', with all its connotations of a developing economic science 'before Adam Smith', only obscures the specific historical context in which these principles were developed.

Notes

1. Steve Pincus, *1688. The First Modern Revolution* (New Haven, CT: Yale University Press, 2009), 366–99.
2. Ibid., 395.
3. Jacob Soll, 'Accounting for Government: Holland and the Rise of Political Economy in Seventeenth-Century Europe', *Journal of Interdisciplinary History* 40, no. 2 (2009): 215–38; Erik S. Reinert, 'Emulating Success: Contemporary Views of the Dutch Economy before 1800', in Oscar Gelderblom (ed.), *The Political Economy of the Dutch Republic* (Farnham: Ashgate, 2009), 19–39. See also P. W. Klein, 'A New Look at an Old Subject: Dutch Trade Policies in the Age of Mercantilism', in S. Groenveld and M. Wintle (eds), *State and Trade: Government and the Economy in Britain and the Netherlands since the Middle Ages* (Zutphen: Walburg Pers, 1992), 39–49; Theo van Tijn, 'Dutch Economic Thought in the Seventeenth Century', in Jan Daal and Arnold Heertje (eds), *Economic Thought in the Netherlands 1650–1950* (Aldershot: Ashgate, 1992), 7–28; and Gijs Rommelse, 'The Role of Mercantilism in Anglo-Dutch Political Relations, 1650–74', *Economic History Review* 63, no. 3 (2010): 591–611.

4. *Interest van Holland, ofte gronden van Hollands-welvaren* (Amsterdam: Joan. Cyprianus vander Gracht, 1662), republished in a significantly expanded version as *Aanwysing der heilsame politike Gronden en Maximen van de Republike van Holland en West-Vriesland* (Leiden and Rotterdam: Hakkens, 1669). This latter edition was first translated into English as *The True Interest and Political Maxims of the Republick of Holland and West-Friesland*. Written by John de Witt, and Other Great Men in Holland (London: s.n., 1702). For its international impact, cf. Kenneth E. Carpenter, 'The Economic Bestsellers before 1850', *Bulletin of the Kress Library*, entry no. 3, May 1975, available online at http://www.othercanon.org/uploads/AJALUGU%20THE%20ECONOMIC%20BESTSELLERS%20BEFORE1850.pdf (accessed on 23 October 2011).
5. Istvan Hont, *Jealousy of Trade: International Competition and the Nation-State in Historical Perspective* (Cambridge, MA: Harvard University Press, 2005), esp. 5–17.
6. Josiah Child, *Brief Observations Concerning Trade, and Interest of Money* (London: Henry Mortlock, 1668), 3, reprinted in Child, *A New Discourse of Trade* (London: John Everingham, 1693).
7. *Verthooninge, ghedaen aen die van de Vereenichde Nederlanden* (s.1., s.n., 1661), sig. A2: '...de Ziel ende het leven van de Nederlanden...dat verscheyde Natien daer over jaloers sijn geworden en boven alle de Engelse, dewelcke niet kan verdragen de prosperiteyt van de Nederlanders'.
8. We are not the first to use this term, yet thus far it has not been applied to the Dutch case. See Hont, *Jealousy of Trade*, 61, and David Armitage, *The Ideological Origins of the British Empire* (Cambridge: Cambridge University Press, 2000), 145, 168.
9. For a biographical introduction, see Theo van Tijn, 'Pieter de la Court, zijn leven en zijn economische denkbeelden', *Tijdschrift voor geschiedenis* 69 (1956): 304–70. For the background of Leiden's textile industry and Flemish immigration, see Leo Lucassen and Boudien de Vries, 'Leiden als middelpunt van een Westeuropees textiel-migratie-systeem, 1586–1650', *Tijdschrift voor Sociale Geschiedenis* 22 (1996): 138–67.
10. A complete bibliography can be found in Ivo W. Wildenberg, *Johan & Pieter de la Court (1622–1660 & 1618–1685). Bibliografie en receptiegeschiedenis* (Amsterdam: APA-Holland University Press, 1986).
11. Johan and Pieter de la Court, *Het welvaren van Leiden. Handschrift uit het jaar 1659*, F. Driessen (ed.) (The Hague: Martinus Nijhoff, 1911). For a useful analysis of the development of this treatise, see Jan Lucassen, 'Het Welvaren van Leiden (1659–1662): de wording van een economische theorie over gilden en ondernemerschap', in Boudien de Vries, Erik Nijhof and Lex Heerma van Voss (eds), *De kracht der zwakken. Studies over arbeid en arbeidersbeweging in het verleden* (Amsterdam: IISG, 1992), 13–48.
12. De la Court, *Welvaren* 1, 3: 'Sullende mine gedaghten laten gaen, sopra la raggion di Stato, over 't Welvaren der Stad Leiden, soo moet in 't begin werden geseid, dat ick daer mede verstae de Conservatie ende vermeerderingh der Leidsche Republieke, en menschelicke societeit bestaande uijt Regeerders ende Onderdanen'.
13. For useful surveys of the reason of state literature, see esp. Peter Burke, 'Tacitism, Scepticism, and Reason of State', in J. H. Burns and Mark Goldie (eds), *The Cambridge History of Political Thought, 1450–1700* (Cambridge: Cambridge University Press, 1991), 479–98; Michael Stolleis, *Staat und*

Staatsräson in der frühen Neuzeit. Studien zur Geschichte des öffentlichen Rechts (Frankfurt: Suhrkamp, 1990); and Maurizio Viroli, *From Politics to Reason of State: The Acquisition and Transformation of the Language of Politics, 1250–1600* (Cambridge: Cambridge University Press, 1992), 238–80.

14. Giovanni Botero, *Della ragion di stato e delle cause della grandezza delle città* (Venice: Gioliti, 1598), I, 1: 'Stato è un dominio fermo sopra popoli ... Ragione di Stato è notitia di mezi atti a fondare, conservare, e ampliare un Dominio cosí fatto'.
15. The classic account of this obsession is J. G. A. Pocock, *The Machiavellian Moment: Florentine Political Thought and the Atlantic Republican Tradition*, 2nd ed. (Princeton, NJ: Princeton University Press, 2003).
16. See Botero, *Della ragion di stato*, esp. 9–10: 'I mediocri sono i più durabili; concio sia, che né per molta debolezza sono cosi esposti alla violenza, né per grandezza all' invidia altrui: e perche le ricchezze, e la potenza è moderata, le passioni sono anco meno veementi; e l'ambitione non ha tanto appoggio, né la libidine tanto fomento, quanto ne' grandi'. Cf. Niccolò Machiavelli, *Discorsi sopra la prima deca di Tito Livio*, Corrado Vivanti (ed.) (Turin: Einaudi, 2000), esp. I.6.
17. Botero, *Della ragion di stato*, 346: 'sono quasi signore delle mercatantie, e de' traffichi per lo sito comodo à molte nationi, alle quali esse servono di fondaco, e di magazzino'.
18. Ibid., 343–44: 'Le Città di Fiandra sono state le più mercantili, e le più frequentate Città d'Europa: Se tu ne ricercherai la cagione, troverai essere stata tra l'altra, la franchezza dalle gabelle'.
19. For Botero's influence in early seventeenth-century England, see Andrew Fitzmaurice, 'The Commercial Ideology of Colonization in Jacobean England: Robert Johnson, Giovanni Botero, and the Pursuit of Greatness', *William and Mary Quarterly*, 3rd series, 64 (2007): 791–820.
20. Sir Walter Raleigh, 'Observations Touching Trade and Commerce with the Hollander and Other Nations as It Was Presented to King James', in *Remains of Sir Walter Raleigh* (London: Henry Mortlock, 1702), 121–59, 130.
21. Ibid., 131, 156.
22. Traiano Boccalini, *Ragguagli di Parnasso e scritti minori*, Luigi Firpo (ed.) (Bari: Laterza, 1948), II.6: 'gli Alemanni, sottilissimi e acutissimi artefici non meno di orologi che di prestantissime republiche, quelle eterne libertadi hanno finalmente saputo inventare'.
23. Ibid.: 'che qualsivoglia piccola scintilla disprezzata è atta a cagionar incendi grandi'.
24. See Machiavelli, *Discorsi*, II.2.
25. Boccalini, *Ragguagli*, II.6: 'perché l'uomo che difende la libertà ha venti mani e altrettanti cuori'.
26. See, e.g., de la Court, *Aanwysing* I.24, 118: 'de *politike Regeerders*, over alle Onderdaanen *gesaamentlik* een Politik lighaam uitmaakende, welke wy den *Staat* noemen'. On the shifting vocabulary of the state in early-modern Europe, see Quentin Skinner, 'From the State of Princes to the Person of the State', in *Visions of Politics*, 3 vols. (Cambridge: Cambridge University Press, 2002), II, 368–413.
27. Antoine de Montchrétien, *Traicté de l'oeconomie politique: dédié en 1615 au Roy et à la Reyne Mère du Roy*, Théophile Funck-Brentano (ed.) (Paris: Plon, 1889), 31: 'La richesse d'un Estat ne dépend pas simplement de sa large estenduë,

ni de l'abondance de ses peuples, mais de n'y laisser nulle terre vague et de disposer avecques jugement un chacun à son office'. Cf. the analysis in Henry C. Clark, *Compass of Society: Commerce and Absolutism in Old-Regime France* (Lanham, MD: Lexington, 2007), 10–14.

28. Montchrétien, *Traicté de l'oeconomie politique*, 31: 'contre l'opinion d'Aristote et de Xenophon, que l'on ne sçauroit diviser l'oeconomie de la police sans demembrer la partie principale de son Tout, et que la science d'acquerir des biens, qu'ils nomment ainsi, est commune aux républiques aussi bien qu'aux familles'.
29. Cf. Gerard de Malynes, *A Treatise of the Canker of Englands Common Wealth* (London: William Iohnes printer, 1601), 2.
30. Botero, *Della ragion di stato*, 309, 318–30.
31. De la Court, *Welvaren* 1, 3–5.
32. See Jan de Vries and Ad van der Woude, *The First Modern Economy: Success, Failure, and Perseverance of the Dutch Economy, 1500–1815* (Cambridge: Cambridge University Press, 1997), 175–76.
33. De la Court, *Welvaren* 16, 44: 'En die de pap selvs eeten moet, kookt en koelt se best ... een ijder in 't maken van sijn eigen goed, ende besteden desselvs gansch vrij en onbedwongen behoorde te weesen ... daer een ijder sich selven soekt, vind men sich best, en gaet niemand verlooren. Dit is de naturelijcke vrijheid, die de Regeerders noit hunne onderdanen behoorden te beneemen'.
34. On the prominence of guilds in early-modern Dutch corporate politics, see Maarten Prak, Catharina Lis, Jan Lucassen and Hugo Soly (eds), *Craft Guilds in the Early Modern Low Countries: Work, Power, and Representation* (Aldershot: Ashgate, 2006).
35. De la Court, *Welvaren* 26, 61: 'dat geen onser neeringen aen onse grond vast sijn, en dat sij dienvolgende de boomen niet gelijcken, daer men eenige weinigh vrughtdragende tacken mach afsnijden'.
36. De la Court, *Welvaren*, 46–52; de la Court, *Politike Discoursen, handelende in Ses onderscheide Boeken van Steeden, Landen, Oorlogen, Kerken, Regeeringen en Zeeden*, 2nd ed. (Amsterdam, 1662), I.I.1, I.I.6.
37. De la Court, *Welvaren* 61, 141: 'Salus populi Suprema Lex ... waerelijck het is een schoone pop bij allen uijterlijck gepreesen, bij weinigen innerlijck besorght ofte geaght'. Cf. Peter N. Miller, *Defining the Common Good. Empire, Religion and Philosophy in Eighteenth-Century Britain* (Cambridge: Cambridge University Press, 1994), 39–40.
38. See for a lucid analysis of the position of the brothers de la Court in the context of seventeenth-century Dutch views on free trade, Hans-Jürgen Wagener, 'Free Seas, Free Trade, Free People: Early Dutch Institutionalism', *History of Political Economy* 26, no. 3 (1994): 395–422. For the period following the de la Courts, see Ida Nijenhuis, 'De ontwikkeling van het politiek-economische vrijheidsbegrip in de Republiek', in E. O. G. Haitsma Mulier and W. R. E. Velema (eds), *Vrijheid: een geschiedenis van de vijftiende tot de twintigste eeuw* (Amsterdam: Amsterdam University Press, 1999), 233–52; and Karel Davids, 'From De la Court to Vreede: Regulation and Self-Regulation in Dutch Economic Discourse from c. 1660 to the Napoleonic Era', *Journal of European Economic History* 30, no. 2 (2001): 245–9.

39. De la Court, *Welvaren* 80, 171: 'gansch niet subsisteeren kan, dan met den inwoonderen veel meer vrijheid te geeven, als sij in eenige nabij, of beeter geleegene Steden, ofte plaetsen konnen beleeven'.
40. Ibid. 2, 8: 'hoe kraghtigen middel om vremde inwoonders aentelokken ... de absolute eenparige vrijheid voor alle inwoonders, eenparige lasten dragende, intevoeren'.
41. De la Court, *Aanwysing* I.15, 69: 'alle haare kennise en goederen te besteeden, om nieuwe visserien, handwerken, koopmanschap, ende navigatien te bedenken, en te formeeren'.
42. De la Court, *Politike Discoursen* I.I.1, 4: 'dat de *koopmanschap* een zeer kragtig middel is, om zeer veele menschen besig te houden ende te voeden ... Maar de Koopmanschap is aan geen plaats vast, daarmen den Koopluiden minst beswaard, en meer vryheids geeft om haare profiten te mogen doen, ende te conserveeren, daar heeftmense: ende daarmen ter contrarie de vryheid om winsten te doen besnoeit, ofte de rijke Koopluiden hard taxeert, daar verjaagd of blustmense uit'.
43. De la Court, *Welvaren* 80, 171: 'door vrijheid in Religien, Studien, koopmanschappen, manufacturen, konsten, borgerschap en Regeeringh'.
44. De la Court, *Aanwysing* I.3–5, 21, 27: 'voor den menschen ongesond weeder'; 'dat het in allen manieren sijn voedsel buiten 's Lands moet soeken, ende geduurig niewe Ingesetenen uit vreemde Landen tot zig trekken moet'.
45. Ibid. I.7, 31: '*In Europa is geen Land tot de* Negotie *bequaamer als Holland*'; ibid. I.13, 58: 'dat de Hollanders by naast alle Natien, soo uit den grooten Oceaan, Middelandse, Indise, als Belt-Zee, gevaaren hebbende'.
46. Ibid. I.19–21, 84, 91: 'De Vryheid van *Visseryen* en *Negotie* aangaande is nog grooter als ergens'; 'soo hoog gereesen, dat nooit diergelijke in eenige Republijke ter Weereld, veel min in eenen Lande op koopmanschap, en nergens anders op bestaande, is gehoord of gesien geweest'.
47. See the comparison in Jan Luiten van Zanden and Maarten Prak, 'Towards an Economic Interpretation of Citizenship: The Dutch Republic between Medieval Communes and Modern Nation-States', *European Review of Economic History* 10 (2006): 111–45, 130.
48. De la Court, *Aanwysing* I.21, 90: 'Dat de swaare ende eenigvuldige imposten, 's Lands welvaaren endelik sullen verjaagen'.
49. Ibid. I.24, 115: 'dat men nogtans *minst* beswaren mag dat middel van *subsistentie* waar an ons *meest* gelegen is, en welk wy *allerligst* verliesen, en verloren zijnde *niet ligtelik* wederom bekomen'.
50. De la Court, *Politike Discoursen* I.I.1, 19: 'want alle deesen van *buiten* winst *in* 't Land brengende, zeer noodsaakelik voor den Staat zijnde, nogtans zeer gemakkelik door haare correspondentie ende koopmanschap, haare personen, goederen en konsten in andere Landen konnen brengen'.
51. See ibid. I.II, 29–30, and the more regulative elaboration in *Aanwysing* I.21–24.
52. De la Court, *Aanwysing* II.6, 275–76: 'dat alle Republiken, op vreede en koopmanschap gefondeerd zijnde, het selve *Interest* met Holland hebben ... ons in ons voornaemste *dessein*, namentlik het vermeerderen der koopmanschap, altijds naar haar vermoogen sullen dwersdrijven'.

53. Ibid. I.7, 32: '*vrijen handel* der gemeene Ingeseetenen'; Ibid. I.16, 71: 'haare naturelike vryheid van 's leevens middelen in haar vaderland soekende, te besnoejen met *geoctroyeerde* ofte *geslootene Compagnien* en *Gildens*'.
54. Ibid. I.16, p. 72: 'soo maaken haar de seekere profijten dom en traag. Daar aan de andere zijde waarhaftig is, *dat de nood een oud wijf doed draaven*; ende de *honger raawe boonen soet maakt*; alsmede *dat de armoede list soekt*'.
55. All the documents concerning the project are published in J. C. Overvoorde (ed.), 'De Noord-Oostelijke doorvaart naar China', *Bijdragen en mededelingen van het historisch genootschap* 47 (1926): 249–331.
56. Ibid., 285: 'het particulier interest der Geoctroyeerde Oostindische Compagnie ter contrarie is... Gemeene ingeseetenen van alle kennisse, navigatie en negotie der opgemelde Asiatische landen te vervremden en te secluderen in der eewigheid'.
57. Ibid., 299: 'blijckt hieruijt de quaedaerdigheijt van de compagnie, die liever heft dat andere natien de possessie van soo consideraebelen passage (bijaldien het te vinden waere) soude becomen dan onse eijgene natie'.
58. Rommelse, 'The Role of Mercantilism'.
59. A detailed discussion of the connection between de la Court's thought and his social background can be found in Van Tijn, 'Pieter de la Court, zijn leven en zijn economische denkbeelden'. According to the Marxist historian Van Tijn, the treatise *Het Welvaren van Leiden* is an 'oratio pro domo' (p. 337), a piece of self-serving rhetoric.
60. De la Court, *Politike Discoursen* II.V.4, 105: '*Dat een* Republijk *beeter is als een* Monarchie'; Ibid. II.V.9, 131: '*De* beste Monarchale *Regeering, is den Onderdaanen soo goed niet, als de* geringste Republikse *Regeering*'. For a lucid analysis of the de la Courts' republican claims, see Wyger Velema, '"That a Republic Is Better Than a Monarchy": Anti-monarchism in Early Modern Dutch Political Thought', in Martin van Gelderen and Quentin Skinner (eds), *Republicanism: A Shared European Heritage*, 2 vols. (Cambridge: Cambridge University Press, 2002), I, 9–25.
61. Johan and Pieter de la Court, *Consideratien van Staat, ofte Politike Weeg-schaal*, quoted from the 4th ed. (Amsterdam, 1662), I.I.13, 72: '*de Koopluiden*, van zoodanige regeeringe niet min schuw zijn, en vlieden moeten, als van *een doodelike Pest*'.
62. De la Court, *Welvaren* 37, 82: 'in 't generael verloopt de negotie altijds uijt ende van die landen en steden, daer een eenigh mens een Negotiant na sijn gelieven, van sijn goederen kan berooven, dat is met eenen woorde geseght van alle monarchale regeringe'.
63. See the printer's copy of the work in The Hague Royal Library, Ms 73 B17, which has been analysed in detail in an unpublished MA thesis by Leo van Rossum, 'Het aandeel van Johan de Witt aan het *Interest van Holland*' (Utrecht University, 1964). For the contacts between de la Court and de Witt, see also Herbert H. Rowen, *John de Witt, Grand Pensionary of Holland, 1625–1672* (Princeton, NJ: Princeton University Press, 1978), 391–8.
64. Franciscus van den Enden, *Vrije politieke stellingen*, Wim Klever (ed.) (Amsterdam: Wereldbibliotheek, 1992), esp. 211–13.
65. On the de la Courts' influence on Spinoza, see the analysis in E. O. G. Haitsma Mulier, *The Myth of Venice and Dutch Republican Thought in the Seventeenth Century* (Assen: Van Gorcum, 1980), 170–208. Cf. also Jonathan Israel, 'The

Intellectual Origins of Modern Democratic Republicanism (1660–1720)', *European Journal of Political Theory* 3 (2004): 7–36.

66. Slingsby Bethel, *The Interest of Princes and States* (London: John Wickins, 1680), 111–13.
67. See esp. Roger Coke, *A Discourse of Trade* (London: H. Brome and R. Horne, 1670) and Carew Reynell, *The True English Interest* (London: Giles Widdowes, 1674), and cf. the analysis in Pincus, *1688*, 369–72.
68. Throughout the late seventeenth and eighteenth centuries, de la Court's writings were widely read in Germany, France, and Britain. See Wildenberg, *Bibliografie en Receptiegeschiedenis*, 40–73, and Clark, *Compass of Society*, esp. 62–3, 129–43, 221–8.
69. Cf. the critique of Robert Filmer's *Patriarcha* in Jean-Jacques Rousseau, 'Discourse on Political Economy', in Victor Gourevitch (ed.), *The Social Contract and Other Political Writings* (Cambridge: Cambridge University Press, 1997), 5–6. Rousseau refers to the first book of Aristotle's *Politics*, which refutes the confusion of the public economy (of the state) with private economy (of the household).

2
A Natural Order of Empire: The Physiocratic Vision of Colonial France after the Seven Years' War

Pernille Røge

> Rome understood how to defeat and subjugate many nations, but it did not understand how to *govern*. It ruined the affluent agriculture of the countries subjected to its domination, and from that moment on its military strength disappeared, the valuable conquests were lost, and it found itself defenceless against the pillage and violence of its enemies.
>
> Quesnay, *Analyse du Tableau Économique* (1763)[1]

In the aftermath of the Seven Years' War, France stood defeated at the hands of its enemy. The 1763 Treaty of Paris stripped France of most of its Canadian and North American possessions, reduced its colonial empire to one-tenth the size of its prewar territorial grandeur, and plunged the Crown into decades of financial instability.[2] To the emerging group of French political economists, known as the physiocrats, the war and its consequences was the result of a long-standing misconception of what type of state France was and by which laws it should be governed. They therefore began promoting a programme for French regeneration based on their 'new science' of political economy. The physiocratic view was that prosperity and peace between France and its imperial rivals would resume if France placed agricultural production at the heart of its economy, replaced its obscure fiscal system with one based on a single land tax, and opened up to free trade. In 1763, the physiocrats presented this view in *La philosophie rurale*, which had as its second title *Économie générale et politique de l'agriculture, réduite à l'ordre immutable des loix physiquse & morales, qui assurent la prospérité des empires.* Despite the emphasis on the prosperity of empires in the second title, the majority of scholarly work on the physiocrats focuses only on the domestic side of their ideas.[3] Colonies are treated only in passing, and often with the view that physiocratic political economy embodied an anticolonial slant.[4] Yet while the physiocrats certainly launched a scathing critique of the existing French colonial system (known as the *Exclusif*), they were not against colonial empire. Their main goal was to bring France and its colonies back into line with what they called the *natural order*. In arguing their case, they not only pushed for a liberalisation of trade but also offered a potent reconceptualisation of what was understood by the French 'metropole' and its 'colonies'. In doing so, they suggested changing both the meaning of, and the reasons for, a French colonial empire, a suggestion which would prove influential at the time and even down to the present day. To elucidate this further, and to exhibit the imperial side of physiocratic political economy, this chapter examines first how the founders of physiocracy came to develop a new colonial vision for France, and second, how they attempted to influence French imperial policy after the Seven Years' War.

Quesnay's French agricultural kingdom and Mirabeau's art of colonisation

The physiocratic school originated in 1756–1757 when François Quesnay published the articles 'Fermiers' and 'Grains' in the *Encyclopédie*. Soon after the publication of his encyclopaedic entrees, he started collaborating with Victor de Riquetti, Marquis de Mirabeau, the author of *L'ami des hommes* (1757). The two spent most of the war developing the core tenets of what would become physiocracy. In late 1763 they presented their doctrine to the wider public in the three-volume *La philosophie rurale*, published in Mirabeau's name.[5] At this point, they had acquired such followers as Pierre Samuel Dupont de Nemours and Pierre-Paul Mercier de la Rivière.

Quesnay's 'Fermiers' and 'Grains' were propositions for how to alleviate the French monarchy of its current political and economic ills. Inspired by the successes of Sully's agrarian policies during the reign of Henri IV, Quesnay projected that prosperity would re-emerge if France gave preference to the cultivation of land and if the government facilitated agricultural growth by implementing a system of free trade. This emphasis on agriculture was grounded in Quesnay's insistence that France was predominantly an agricultural kingdom rather than a commercial one.

As he explained in 'Grains', it was Colbert's efforts to favour commerce and industry above agriculture, and monopoly trade over free trade, that had proven so counterproductive to the French economy and caused the current predicament.[6]

In these texts Quesnay also developed several components of the conceptual arsenal for which the physiocrats would later become famous. It hinged on his view that agriculture was the source of all riches and that a 'natural order' governed society. As Simone Meysonnier has argued, this approach had a rich genealogy leading back to Boisguilbert's *Le Détail de la France* from 1695, where Boisguilbert introduced the idea of a natural economic order.[7] As Hopkins demonstrates elsewhere in this volume, there were different interpretations of what this natural order was. To Quesnay, the natural order was the order that would arrive when the governance of human society followed those laws intended for it and which could be derived from the physical laws (it was on the basis of this understanding, moreover, that the physiocrats later claimed that their political economy was a veritable science).[8] In these writings, Quesnay also stressed that if property rights were respected, and underpinned by a system of free trade, France would become the champion of the grain trade on the international market. If the Crown, in turn, could agree to abolish its obscure tax policies impeding production and replace them with a single land tax drawn from the net product [*produit net*] of agricultural produce, France would divest itself of a ruinous fiscal system and the monarchy would find a reliable and lavish source of revenue.[9] To illustrate in a scientific model how this worked, Quesnay began circulating his famous *Tableau Économique* in 1758.[10]

While Quesnay fathered such tenets of physiocracy, the global orientation of the doctrine was not to be found in his early economic writings. Colonies, for instance, entered only as a subclause to his elaborations on the benefits of free trade and free trade's function as a regulator of price. 'Fermier' twice mentioned the British colony of Pennsylvania with reference to its high export of corn and its subsequent role in regulating corn prices in England.[11] 'Grains' made a mention of colonies only to quell the anxieties of free trade sceptics. In this entry, Quesnay claimed that at no given time would a society regulated by free trade jeopardise national interests. Competition between an agricultural colony and its mother country (i.e., France) would tilt in France's favour, 'the quality of French grain being superior to grain from [the colonies] and all other places.'[12]

The Marquis de Mirabeau, on the other hand, was deeply interested in the colonial question. His *L'ami des hommes* was influenced by Richard Cantillon's doctrine of *populationisme*, which took population size to be the indicator of national wealth and colonisation the means by which the world was populated.[13] Moreover, his brother, the Chevalier de Mirabeau, had moved to Guadeloupe in December 1753 to fill the post of governor. During his stay, the two had kept an ongoing correspondence in which they debated the deficiencies of the French colonial system. As their correspondence reveals, several of the colonial ideas Mirabeau promoted in *L'ami des hommes* had in fact already been discussed with his brother. In 1754 the governor had written a letter to Mirabeau complaining about the metropole's attitude toward the colonies, noting that colonies were considered 'the farms of French commerce'.[14] Hearing that it was the British rather than the French who provisioned the colonies by means of contraband trade, the political economist wrote in response that 'if I was a public figure, I would encourage the development of agriculture and "laissez aller le commerce"'.[15]

In *L'ami des hommes*, Mirabeau repeated and developed this message. Presenting the colonising activity as an art form which developed through historical stages, he classified 'l'art des colonies' to be only in its third age, or – as he also said – in its most 'imbecile infancy'.[16] At the heart of Mirabeau's disapproval lay a strong aversion to the established perception that colonies existed purely to serve the commerce of the metropole. To Mirabeau, such a paradigm would never accomplish the task of founding strong colonies. As he said, '[T]he spirit of commerce is in itself completely incapable of forming, populating and fortifying colonies'.[17] He prophetically commented that without a real effort to settle Canada, the colony would soon be lost to the British – just like Acadia already was.[18]

In general, Mirabeau constantly stressed that France's colonial problem was the inevitable outcome of having prioritised metropolitan commerce before colonies had developed into sustainable entities. As he saw it, proper settlement and cultivation had to be in place before commerce between them could begin. He pointed out that to pave the way for proper cultivation, provisioning of the colonies should be open to other nations. He suggested letting the grain-producing colonies in the Americas supply the Antilles with foodstuffs and letting French agriculture find a natural outlet closer to home. Exports to the colonies could consist of 'metal goods, fine clothing, a range of merchandise, useful and agreeable, which the Creoles consume and that our commerce purchase from Paris and the provinces'.[19] An early abolitionist, Mirabeau also stressed that by 'settlement', he did not mean transplanting enslaved Africans to the Americas, slave labour being an inefficient form of labour. Later on, he and Quesnay would join forces in rejecting slavery, describing it as a perversion of the natural order. Such antislavery views were of course entirely unconventional in the mid-eighteenth century.[20]

Genesis of the physiocratic colonial vision

Once Mirabeau and Quesnay began collaborating in 1757, the two would have to reconcile the catalogue of ideas propagated in *L'ami des hommes* with the basic tenets of Quesnay's doctrine before agreeing on the core of physiocracy. Mirabeau shared Quesnay's preference for agricultural production and rejected a political system rooted in Colbertian mercantilism, yet his *populationisme* clashed with Quesnay's outlook, a disagreement reducible to the 'chicken and egg' dilemma of what came first, people to produce food or food to produce people. Mirabeau once explained that this discrepancy disappeared after his first meeting with Quesnay, during which Quesnay would 'break the skull of Goliath' who wrongly had 'put the plough in front of the oxen.'[21] Despite Mirabeau's modesty, 'David', however, had not left the battle unaffected. In his efforts to convert Mirabeau to his own doctrine, Quesnay had been forced to address the colonial question more directly. When Mirabeau published the fourth edition of *L'ami des hommes* in 1758, we find inserted Quesnay's *Questions intéressantes sur la population, l'agriculture et le commerce*, within which article XXIV of the subchapter 'Commerce des Denrée du Cru' questioned a series of issues regarding the colonies.[22]

The adjustment of disparate theories was only one issue which the two had to consider while writing their ideas. Another was the geographical damage wrought by the war. By 1763, France only possessed a few fisheries in Canada, its sugar islands in the West Indies, and trade stations in Africa and India. Once *La philosophie rurale* appeared, and in contrast to Mirabeau's *L'ami des hommes*, the discussion on colonies was thus confined to the sugar islands in the West Indies. These islands were unmistakably subjected to the crudest version of the *Exclusif*. Solidified with the *Lettres patentes* of 1717 and 1727, the *Exclusif* had carved into the metropolitan colonial conscience that the sugar colonies existed exclusively to provide France with exotic goods and as protected markets for French commodities.[23] The sugar trade, of course, was the most lucrative of French colonial commerce. From 1716 to 1757, the value of Antillean produce had risen from 4.4 million *livres* to 77 million and constituted one of France's largest export markets.[24] But as the governor of Guadeloupe had explained to the Marquis de Mirabeau in his letters, the Antilles suffered greatly under the sclerotic pace at which the metropole met their basic needs. The colonial administration had permitted some free trade in the colonies during the war, a policy in keeping with the recommendations of the political economist François Véron de Forbonnais, who in 1756 had suggested that merchants from neutral nations such as Denmark, Sweden, Holland, Spain, Italy and Hamburgh should be granted permission to provision the French colonies with foodstuffs in time of war. In 1763, however, the *Exclusif* resumed due to pressure from the French ports.[25]

All these issues were tackled in the eleventh chapter of Quesnay and Mirabeau's *La philosophie rurale*. They appropriately began their presentation by branding colonial commerce 'today's apple of discord'.[26] As they saw it, the *Exclusif* caused an ever-present air of hostilities between nations and inevitably degraded most colonies to a state of ruin and desertion. Shifting to a more targeted assault, they set upon monopolies and protectionism: 'Nothing is as singularly contradictory to the *natural order* as the current condition whereby European powers appear to accord their colonies right to protection and sovereignty.' The gloss of paternal protectionism and benevolence concealed an abusive exploitation of the colonies and an obfuscation of the nation's general interests: 'All these beautiful measures, it is true, appear to support authority and force, but under false appearances that hide a monopoly as disadvantageous to the metropole as to the colony and the Sovereign'.[27] The deception stemmed from the fact that France had developed a colonial system modelled on the Dutch system. To Quesnay and Mirabeau, however, this was a fundamental mistake since France was not a republic of merchants but an agricultural empire:

> The example of the small nations who are in a strong state by means of their mercantilist commerce, and amongst which some associations of merchants have created trade stations [*établissemens*] successfully at the edges of the world to be able to bring back certain commodities, most notably rare goods which excite our curiosity; this example, I say, has led the larger Nations, in an age of infatuation with commerce, to enter into competition with these. But they have not wished to see that for those who set the example, the profit of the merchants was the profit of the State, since the State was only an association of merchants, who drew their profit from other States who were rich in production.[28]

In a country like France, however, the Crown should take into account the interest of all involved, not just merchants. Landowners, for instance, who were the real producers of wealth, did not benefit from monopoly trade, and by extension, therefore, neither did France.

This notion that colonial and national interests were betrayed had formed the crux of Quesnay's critique in the *Questions intéressantes*. His very first question in section XXIV read, 'The commerce of a metropole with its colonies, which procure the merchant with enormous gains thanks to commercial restrictions, is it not more seductive than it is concrete and advantageous to the nation?'[29] To illustrate the flaws of the *Exclusif*, and to promote a set of rules beneficial to both nation *and* colonies, Quesnay and Mirabeau availed themselves of this and several other of Quesnay's questions. In an almost complete reproduction of these, they asked, is it beneficial to the *colons* that their colonial produce is resold to foreigners at overpriced rates by merchants with monopoly? Would the *Colons* not profit more from a structure where merchants from all nations compete for the colonial markets within a system regulated by free trade? Is this not the greatest way of making the colonies and all other territories in the world prosper?[30] While these questions were left unanswered in the fourth edition of *L'ami des hommes*, they received a detailed reply in *La philosophie rurale*.

Aside from free trade, Quesnay and Mirabeau's reply was based on a fascinating reconceptualisation of a 'colony' and on the development of the idea of the sovereign as *copropriétaire* of the net product of all French land.[31] The latter was explained in the following way:

> The progress of colonies depends on the progress of the cultivation of their land. From this progress results the successive development of the colony and its contribution, that is, its population, consumption and reproduction, and of the net product of which the Sovereign is *Copropriétaire* together with the owners of the cultivated land.[32]

The strategy of tying the sovereign to French land – whether located at home or abroad – would guarantee the best possible system for agricultural development since, according to the physiocratic system, the sovereign's revenues should derive solely from the net product of the land.

But the concept of the *copropriétaire* was only a first step toward reconciliation between colonial and metropolitan interests. The second entailed a reconceptualisation of what was understood by the term 'colony', a category Mirabeau and Quesnay chose to frame within their domestic vocabulary: 'What is a colony, they inquired, if not a province, like other provinces of the state which should enjoy the same prerogatives in order to prosper.' (Provinces' prerogatives had been discussed earlier on in the chapter 'Rapports des dépenses avec l'Agriculture,' where Quesnay and Mirabeau had stressed the need for the free circulation of grain between provinces and foreigners.)[33] Looking at a draft of *La philosophie rurale* stored among Mirabeau's private papers, it becomes clear that it was Quesnay who had insisted on this reconceptualisation. He had scribbled the following in the margin next to the answer to the second question: 'Are colonies then only defeated foreign nations treated as enemies? But if we conceive of them as provinces of one and the same empire...'.[34] The draft leaves the remark pending. Yet the insistence upon a colony as a province in the finished draft shows how important it was to Quesnay to ensure that if colonies were to have a place in the physiocratic economic system they would have to be cast in a domestic vocabulary.

A third move which Quesnay and Mirabeau needed in developing their attack on the current colonial system was to call attention to the danger of confusing merchant interests with national interests. As if speaking directly to the Crown and the Ministry of the Navy, they stated, 'What are you doing instead with your exclusive and barbaric system? You, protectors of cumbersome, inept and fearful merchants, you allow them to increase expenses at their will. It is to assure them their fortune that you tyrannise your colonies, harm your commerce, and treat your neighbours as enemies.'[35] The critique of squaring merchant interests with national interests concluded a line of criticisms against the existing colonial system. It also gave additional weight to Quesnay's view that merchant interests in France had, since Colbert, been given priority above everything else.

Thus, the physiocratic colonial model in *La philosophie rurale* had maintained several of the principles advocated by Quesnay in 'Grains', while it also accommodated the global orientation to be found in Mirabeau's *L'ami des hommes*. The colonial views sketched by Mirabeau, however, were far from merely grafted onto Quesnay's axioms. Gone were Mirabeau's *populationisme* and the social dimension it entailed. The attack on the *Exclusif* was maintained, yet Mirabeau's suggestion to focus on the export of luxuries to the colonies had disappeared. Quesnay, in turn, was now no longer indifferent to colonialism. The question is whether he had become a supporter of colonisation or was an 'anti-colonialist' as Merle and others have argued.[36] A return to the draft of *La philosophie rurale* stored among Mirabeau's private papers initially suggests the former. In the margins, Quesnay had jotted down that newly created colonies should be exempt from taxation until they had developed a sustainable cultivation; he had mentioned that companies with monopoly rights were 'enemies of the state'; and he had continuously pointed to the importance of free trade. Quesnay, however, had one substantial amendment to the draft, which sows doubt about his full adhesion to the French colonial project. After his stress on exempting new colonies from tax burdens, Quesnay noted that the same should be said for newly cultivated domestic land. Upon this remark he further added that a country that still possessed much fallow land 'should not think about forming colonies in far-away regions...'. This argument remained in the published version of *La philosophie rurale*. It drew a direct line back to the articles 'Fermiers' and 'Grains' in which Quesnay had bemoaned that one-quarter of French land was still left uncultivated (he estimated that France had 50 million *arpents* of cultivatable land in total and that 36 million *arpents* were cultivated). Leaving the comment in the published version of *La philosophie rurale* does not indicate, however, that Quesnay was against colonial expansion. It merely shows that he believed that French expansion should not begin until France had brought all its domestic territory into production.

Le Mercier de la Rivière and the dissemination of the physiocratic colonial model

While Quesnay and Mirabeau prepared the publication of *La philosophie rurale*, one of their future followers, Le Mercier de la Rivière, was employed as *intendant* of the Isles-du-Vent (from 1757 to 1762 and of Martinique from 1763 to 1764). Le Mercier de la Rivière had been in touch with Mirabeau before going to Martinique, but it is unclear to what degree he had adopted Quesnay and Mirabeau's views wholesale.[37] In his study of Le Mercier de la Rivière, L. P. May convincingly showed that the *intendant*'s activities in the colonies were underpinned by physiocratic thinking.[38] May also pointed out that Le Mercier de la Rivière, at this point, had a more realistic view of which aspects of physiocracy were applicable in practice and which ones were not. Nevertheless, several memoranda within the colonial archives bear proof of his wish to disseminate at least some of Quesnay and Mirabeau's ideas in France and the colonies. Two of these memoranda shall be considered here: his address to the *colons* in June 1760 and his 1762 memorandum to the minister of the marine, the Duc de Choiseul.

Le Mercier de la Rivière's address to the *colons* came with the opening of the Chambre mi-partie d'agriculture et de commerce.[39] The chamber at

Martinique was one of three chambers of agriculture and commerce that the colonial administration had authorised in the Antilles the previous year. Represented by a deputy in the Bureau of Commerce in Paris, the role of the chambers was to debate and communicate the interests of the colonies to the metropole.[40] They had, however, no real power.[41] As a representative of the Crown, Le Mercier de la Rivière had to provide the opening speech. To begin with, his speech reflected the official concern regarding the contested loyalty between metropole and colony. Using the metaphor of the body to explain the nature of a state, Le Mercier de la Rivière proclaimed that the provinces, including the colonies, were its essential body parts. In a reference to the 'natural order' of things, he then noted that the particular interests of each limb were subordinate to the general interests of the entire body: 'Thus, Gentlemen, when we consider here the propositions for the good of the colony, our considerations should include the other provinces; we should take the general interests of the state to be the same as those of the colony and each of the provinces.'[42] Without calling colonies 'overseas provinces', he thus placed colonies and the French provinces on a par, just as Quesnay and Mirabeau would do.

Underscoring the state as one *corps politique*, Le Mercier de la Rivière then shifted to address the *Exclusif*. He explained that although trade with foreign merchants might benefit the colony in the short term, the loss such commerce would represent to provinces back in France would reduce the metropole's willingness to supply and protect its colonies. What first appeared as advantageous to the colony would thereby end up as a drawback.[43] Nevertheless, Le Mercier de la Rivière was not conceding to the Colbertian system. Going farther than his position as the king's representative in the colonies permitted, he granted the *colons* some leeway vis-à-vis the *Exclusif*: 'Gentlemen, do not conclude from this that all commerce of the colony should uniquely be with France. If you are able to make a great profit with a foreign merchant, I'll say: if it does not damage French commerce, if it is not unfavourable to it, such transaction will necessarily become an advantage to French commerce as much as to you.'[44] Le Mercier de la Rivière hastened to emphasise that this leeway should not be abused. Nevertheless, it was clear that he saw a huge gain in liberalising the *Exclusif* and did not find that the metropole should be the only source of provisions, nor a colony's only customer. This view was obviously well received by the *colons*. However, the Chamber of Commerce in Bordeaux, which was opposed to foreign commerce in the colonies, took a less positive interest in Le Mercier de la Rivière's speech. It had his opening discourse read to the assembled merchants on 21 August 1760 after receiving it in a letter sent from Martinique.[45] After the war, the same port would nervously write to Choiseul requesting that a full restoration of the *Exclusif* would be assured.[46]

To the distress of French merchants, Le Mercier de la Rivière's speech to the Chambre mi-partie d'agriculture et de commerce helped spread the view that colonies should be equal to domestic provinces and that free trade would be advantageous to the colonial system. Two years after this, he obtained an opportunity to advocate his outlook to the colonial administration. During preparations for peace, Choiseul commissioned Le Mercier de la Rivière to present the value of Martinique and Guadeloupe to help the administration decide whether to fight for Canada or these islands in the peace negotiations with Britain. In making a case for Martinique, however, Le Mercier de la Rivière also seized the opportunity to lecture Choiseul on political economy.[47] He promoted subordinating particular interests to general interests and explained how a liberalisation of trade within sectors pertaining to colonial commerce would make colonies prosper. Additionally, he repeated the arguments stated by Quesnay in 'Grains', stressing that agriculture was the source of riches. It was therefore in the interests of the Crown to see its colonial lands cultivated in the best possible way – something Le Mercier de la Rivière thought unattainable without liberalising the system.[48] However, Le Mercier de la Rivière did not promote Quesnay and Mirabeau's doctrine wholesale. They differed strongly on the crucial question of slave labour. In *La philosophie rurale*, Mirabeau and Quesnay would stress that slavery was a perversion of the natural order and that slave labour was inefficient.[49] In sharp contrast to this, Le Mercier de la Rivière believed that slave labour was crucial to a well-functioning plantation system. Although stressing that agriculture was the source of riches, he also implied that slaves produced wealth, thus developing the notion of a *produit net des nègres*.[50] To the *intendant* of Martinique, wealth creation, in other words, could also come from labour.[51]

Le Mercier de la Rivière also proved more practical minded than the founders of physiocracy when it came to free trade. He was acutely aware of the difficulties of implementing a liberal system immediately. As he told Choiseul, 'The political system of all commercial nations prevents us from allowing foreigners to trade freely in our colonies. It is therefore in the reform of our own economic system that we have to find a way to indemnify our colonies of the losses they suffer due to the freedom we cannot grant them.'[52] Such a reform, to Le Mercier de la Rivière, relied on France accepting its incapacity to fully meet the material needs of its colonies. Instead, it should allow foreigners to supply colonies with those essential goods which France could not. Recommending that international merchants, and particularly the British, should contribute to the provisioning of the French colonies, he suggested that this especially should be applied to the slave trade.

Le Mercier de la Rivière, however, again echoed Quesnay and Mirabeau when explaining the advantages of giving up certain trades. He stressed that this would help France concentrate on developing its agriculture. Returning to the benefits of free trade, particularly with Britain, Le Mercier de la Rivière made it clear what France and its empire would have looked like had it not adhered to Colbertian mercantilism: 'If our general plan had been based on…the abundance of the production of our islands and our domestic land and on free trade with England, we would have seen our colonies rich in population and production, our commerce a hundred times wealthier and widespread. Commerce would have been healthy because it would have been based on what is best for our land and cemented by interests common to our rivals as well as us'.[53] Had such policy been followed, Le Mercier de la Rivière concluded, France would not have lost its North American, Canadian and Indian possessions.

It is well known that Le Mercier de la Rivière fell victim to his own ideas. Having made every possible effort to save Martinique from occupation, he eventually had to give in to the defiant planter aristocracy who subsequently turned the island over to the British on 13 February 1762. Upon the end of the war, Choiseul ordered Le Mercier de la Rivière back to Martinique to reinstate order and rebuild the colony. To replenish food stocks, Le Mercier de la Rivière opened trade to foreigners, a measure in line with Choiseul's temporary admittance of a very restricted selection of foreign goods to Martinique.[54] Yet Le Mercier de la Rivière's extension of the permit to include slaves provoked an outcry in the French ports, leading to his discharge.[55] Back in France Le Mercier de la Rivière gave up his role as a colonial official temporarily and embarked on his famous contribution to physiocracy and the French Enlightenment, *L'ordre naturel et essentiel des sociétés politiques* (1767). Yet as May has stressed, Le Mercier de la Rivière's masterpiece was more a tribute to Quesnay's doctrine than a freestanding contribution to it.[56] If we judge *L'ordre naturel* against Le Mercier de la Rivière's colonial reports, he had in fact entirely left his practical-mindedness in the colonies. It is paradoxical that the very words 'colony' and 'metropole' feature nowhere in the text, while empire and international commerce appear only in the abstract, the latter as a *pis-aller*.[57] Why this flight from specificity?

One guess is that if physiocratic thinking were to be carried to its logical conclusion and illustrate a system in harmony with the 'natural order', the very notion of a colony would be unfitting. As Le Mercier de la Rivière specified in *L'ordre naturel*, 'Every nation is therefore merely a province of nature's great kingdom'.[58] In nature's great kingdom, there were only provinces, and the category of a colony was thus superfluous. Another theme missing was the question of slavery. It would, of course, also be entirely anti-physiocratic to introduce the notion of a *produit net des nègres*, since physiocracy was built on the idea that only agricultural production could produce a net product and that slavery was a perversion of the natural order.

The debate on the *Exclusif* in the *Journal de l'agriculture, du commerce et des finances*

Le Mercier de la Rivière's personal intervention was not the only opportunity that the physiocrats would have to advocate a new vision of empire. Another arose in the mid-1760s. Choiseul had long been keen to liberalise the *Exclusif*. To help him with this, he had appointed Jean Dubuc, who was part of the rich Dubuc family in Martinique, as *premier commis* of the Bureau des colonies after the war.[59] Dubuc had been the representative chosen by the Chambre mi-partie d'agriculture et de commerce in Martinique as their representative to Paris.[60] He had thus been present when Le Mercier de la Rivière gave his opening speech. To pave the way for this liberalisation, Dubuc wrote a memorandum on the need to relax the *Exclusif* which was presented to the Conseil royal de commerce on 9 April 1765. In it, Dubuc affirmed the soundness of the *Exclusif* at first but then stressed the need to allow foreigners to provision the colonies with certain goods, slaves in particular. Unsurprisingly, the proposal was rejected on 9 September 1765 because it upset the interests of the French ports.[61] Nevertheless, the matter was far from settled. Immediately after the rejection of Dubuc's memorandum, the physiocratic organ, the *Journal d'agriculture, commerce et finances* (edited by Dupont de Nemours), published it in extenso in December 1765 under the title 'Mémoire sur l'étendue & les bornes des loix prohibitives du commerce étranger dans nos colonies.'[62] How exactly the physiocrats got hold of it is unknown, but it is plausible that Choiseul and Dubuc had passed it to them – particularly given Quesnay's close links to Versailles (he was the physician of Madame de Pompadour). As Chaussinand-Nogaret has noted, Choiseul often availed himself of the enlightened sector in his administration to prepare public opinion for a new policy. This had been the case in 1763 when Choiseul commissioned Abbé Morellet to publish a piece arguing for the liberalisation of the press. Likewise, in 1764, he used Turgot, Dupont de Nemours and Trudaine to prepare the ground for the edict authorising the free exportation of grain.[63]

After the publication of Dubuc's memorandum, each issue of the journal carried articles on colonial regulations until June 1766. To present both sides of the argument, the first article was a defence of the *Exclusif*, to which the journal had added counterarguments in the footnotes (the footnotes were written by Le Mercier de la Rivière, who had started writing for the journal in November 1765, under the name of M.G.[64]). After yet another defence of the *Exclusif* in the March issue, Quesnay published his response to the debate in April. Entitling his article 'Remarques sur l'opinion de l'auteur de *L'esprit des lois* concernant les Colonies', Quesnay used Montesquieu's justification of the Colbertian system in *L'esprit des lois* as a means to combat supporters of the *Exclusif*. Montesquieu had maintained that the goal of establishing colonies was the extension of commerce. As he had said, 'It has been established that only the metropole can trade with the colonies: and that with good reason because the aim of the colonies (établissement) has been the extension of commerce, not the foundation of a town or a new empire'.[65] Quesnay would agree to this in part, but he noted that the ultimate goal of this extension was 'the greater good of the *patrie*'. The greater good of the *patrie*, however, was not best served by the *Exclusif*.[66] To prove this, Quesnay pointed to what he saw as a vagueness in Montesquieu's argument. He stressed that Montesquieu had been unclear when speaking about 'the metropole', 'colonies', and their reciprocal commerce.[67] As he said, 'It does not seem that he [Montesquieu] has noticed the difference in applying the word *metropole* to a republic of merchants or an agricultural empire where one has to distinguish between the sovereign, the state, the nation and the merchants who trade overseas and from which emerges different interests which needs to be regulated by a government conforming to the constitution of society.'[68] Quesnay then listed different types of colonies, some of which could be subjected to monopoly trade. However, when he spoke of the French Antilles, he noted, 'The colonies are no more dependent on the metropole than the provinces of the metropole are dependent on each other. And yet the commerce of these provinces happens freely between each other and outside'. Quesnay then stressed that the contribution of the colonies derived from their agricultural production. They, like the domestic provinces, should therefore be subjected to a system of free trade as well, given that free trade allowed for the highest level of agricultural production.[69]

It is important to understand why Quesnay found it necessary to repeat what he and Mirabeau had already explained in *La philosophie rurale*. The rejection of Dubuc's memorandum showed how rooted the view of the metropole's exclusive right to trade in the colonies was in France. Even in the opus of the Enlightenment, the *Encyclopédie*, the conventional vision prevailed. In the *Encyclopédie*, Forbonnais had authored the article 'Colonies'. Here he had divided colonies into six classes, with the first four pertaining to the premodern period. The fifth type was defined as trade stations on the coast of Africa and in the East Indies; the sixth type was that of the Americas. With respect to these colonies, Forbonnais stated, 'These colonies were established only for the usages of the metropole, it therefore follows: 1° That they should be immediately dependent on and protected by the metropole. 2° That commerce should be exclusive to the founders.' Later on, Forbonnais explained that free trade in the colonies was 'to steal from the metropole'.[70] Thus, other political economists writing for the *Encyclopédie* did not necessarily deviate on this matter from the view of the port cities or the view of Colbert.[71]

Within a year after the debate in the *Journal d'agriculture, commerce et finances*, the Crown authorised the opening of two free ports in the Caribbean, one at Môle Saint-Nicolas and one on Saint-Lucie. At these ports, the colonies could purchase wood, animals and hides from foreigners in exchange for syrups and *taffias*. Free ports were nothing new in the Caribbean. The Dutch and the Danish had used such ports to gain access to foreign markets for decades. They had, however, never appeared in the French colonial context. As Bertie Mandelblatt shows in this volume, the establishment of free ports in the French Caribbean was partly due to the failure to turn French Guyana into a source of provision for the Antilles. Yet it was also a result of the acceptance that the needs of the colonies should be accommodated. Speaking of the instalment of the free ports, Chaussinand-Nogaret states that 'the colonial ethos had transformed, from then on the rights of the colonies to prosperity had been recognised and the royal administration sought to ameliorate the well-being of the inhabitants'.[72] With reference to this transition, rooted in a shift from the *Exclusif* to the *Exclusif mitigé*, Jean Tarrade stressed that the efforts of the physiocrats had no role to play.[73] This claim seems peculiar, since it was only after Dubuc's initially rejected memorandum was taken up in the physiocratic journal that France moved to a more liberalised version of the *Exclusif*. As a platform from which a liberalisation of the mercantile rapport between Franc colonies was forcefully promoted, the physiocrats, as the only intellectuals who persistently argued for such a transformation : late 1750s, could only have helped prepare the way for Choi... ... Dubuc when they finally managed to have their decree passed in the Conseil royal de commerce.

The colonial vision which the physiocrats promoted after the Seven Years' War turned out to be an inescapable critique of the French colonial system. To the physiocrats, France would have to undergo a total makeover in order to prosper as an agricultural empire. The means to achieve this would be to treat colonies as if they were provinces of the metropole and allow them to cultivate their land and develop their riches within a system of free trade, with only a single land tax to pay as their contribution to the general good of the empire. It would be up to France to decide whether to follow these ideas or stick to the old structure. Daubigny observed long ago that after the Seven Years' War the colonial administration was faced with the choice between Quesnay and Montesquieu.[74] It could easily be argued that the manifest transition from the *Exclusif* to the *Exclusif mitigé* in 1767, embodied in the establishment of the free ports, Carénage in St. Lucie and Môle Saint-Nicolas at Saint-Domingue, signalled that the choice had fallen in Quesnay's favour. These measures, however, cannot be claimed a physiocratic victory since trade with the colonies remained heavily regulated. In fact, only for a brief period during the French Revolution, when the commercial restrictions on the colonies were entirely ignored, did the colonies enjoy free trade. The view that colonies were 'overseas provinces' briefly triumphed during the French Revolution. The Constitution of the year III, article 6, stated that the French colonies were part and parcel of the Republic and subject to the same constitutional laws. Yet both the *Exclusif* and the subservience of the colonies to the metropole remained an integral feature of nineteenth-century French colonial policy, with slight modifications and the new misleading name of the Pacte Coloniale. In the mid-twentieth century, French colonies and provinces would again acquire a similar status with the creation of the DOM-TOM (Départements et Territoires D'outre-Mer).[75] These latter changes are often seen as pertaining to France's 'second' empire, or even pertaining to the period of decolonisation. However, the conceptual foundations of these changes go back at least to the French colonial crisis of the Seven Years' War when a handful of political economists were trying to promote a new vision for the French colonial empire, one in which the empire would be in line with the natural order.

Notes

1. François Quesnay, in Auguste Oncken (ed.), *Œuvres Économiques Et Philosophiques De F. Quesnay* (Paris, 1888), 319. All translations in this essay are my own.
2. For a study on the way in which public debt was discussed and feared in eighteenth-century France, see Michael Sonenscher, *Before the Deluge: Public Debt, Inequality, and the Intellectual Origins of the French Revolution* (Princeton, 2007).
3. On physiocracy, see George Weulersse's publications: *Le Mouvement Physiocratique En France (de 1756 À 1770)*, 2 vols. (Paris, 1910); *La Physiocratie Sous Les Ministères de Turgot Et de Necker (1774–1781)* (Paris, 1950); *La Physiocratie À La Fin Du Règne de Louis XV (1770–1774)* (Paris, 1959); *Physiocratie À L'aube de La Révolution 1781–1792* (Paris, 1985). On the origins of the physiocratic school, see Elizabeth Fox-Genovese, *The Origins of Physiocracy: Economic Revolution and Social Order in Eighteenth-Century France* (London, 1976). More recent studies include Yves Charbit and Arundhati Virmani, 'The Political Failure of an Economic Theory: Physiocracy', *Population* (English edition) 57, (November–December 2002): 855–83; T. J. Hochstrasser, 'Physiocracy and the Politics of Lissez-Faire', in Mark Goldie and Robert Wokler (eds), *The Cambridge History of Eighteenth-Century Political Thought* (Cambridge University Press, 2006), 419–42; Henry C. Clark, *Compass of Society: Commerce and Absolutism in Old-Regime France* (Lanham, 2007); Christine Théré and Loïc Charles, 'The Writing Workshop of François Quesnay and the Making of Physiocracy', *History of Political Economy* 40 (2008): 1–42; Liana Vardi, *The Physiocrats and the World of the Enlightenment* (Cambridge, 2012).
4. On the physiocrats and anticolonialism, see Marcel Merle, 'L'Anticolonialisme', in Marc Ferro (ed.), *Le Livre Noir Du Colonialisme xvie–xxiie Siècle: De L'Extermination À La Repentance* (Paris, 2003), 815–62, 835. See also Alain Clément '"Du bon et du mauvais usage des colonies": politique coloniale et pensée économique française au XVIIIe siècle', *Cahiers D'Économie Politique* 56 (2009): 101–27, 115–7. In his recent study on economic thought and globalisation in eighteenth-century France, Paul Cheney offers a discussion of the colonial ideas of the physiocrats. He argues that there was a physiocratic 'desire to call the French back to the land'. See Cheney, *Revolutionary Commerce Globalization and the French Monarchy* (Cambridge, MA, 2010), 160–2. The only studies specifically focusing on the colonial ideas of the physiocrats are André Labrouquère's, 'Doctoral Dissertation', *Les Idées Coloniales Des Physiocrates* (Paris, 1927) and Henri Sée, 'Les Économistes Et La Question Coloniale Au XVIIIe Siècle', *Revue De L'Histoire Des Colonies Françaises* 4 (1929): 381–92. For a study on the impact of physiocratic thought on imperial Britain, see Richard Drayton, *Nature's Government Science, Imperial Britain, and the 'Improvement' of the World* (Yale, 2000).
5. Marquis de Mirabeau, *La Philosophie Rurale Ou Économie Générale Et Politique De L'agriculture, Réduite À L'ordre Immuable Des Loix Physique And Morales, Qui Assurent La Prospérité Des Empires*, 3 vols. (Amsterdam, 1764).
6. Quesnay, 'Grains', in Auguste Oncken (ed.), *Œuvres Économiques Et Philosophiques De F. quesnay* (Paris, 1888), 208.

7. Simone Meysonnier, *La Balance Et L'horloge. La Genèse De La Pensée Libérale En France Au XVIIIe Siècle* (Paris, 1989), 36.
8. Quesnay, 'Le Droit Naturel', in Auguste Oncken (ed.), *Œuvres Économiques Et Philosophiques De F. Quesnay* (Paris, 1888), 374.
9. On Quesnay's basic ideas, see Philippe Steiner, *La 'Science Nouvelle' De L'économie Politique* (Paris, 1998).
10. On Quesnay's Tableau Economique see Loic Charles, 'The Tableau Economique as Rational Recreation', *History of Political Economy* 36 (2004): 445–74.
11. Quesnay, *Œuvres Économiques*, 173 and 183.
12. Quesnay, *Œuvres Économiques*, 232.
13. Mirabeau stressed his adoption of Cantillon's doctrine in Marquis de Mirabeau, *L'ami Des Hommes*, 3 vols. (Avion, 1756), 238–9.
14. Chevalier de Mirabeau to Marquis de Mirabeau Guadeloupe le 10 January 1754. Musée Arbaud, Aix-en-Provence, Fonds Mirabeau, volume 23.
15. Marquis de Mirabeau to Chevalier de Mirabeau Paris le 5 juin 1754. On the impact of the governor's views on the Marquis de Mirabeau's and the physiocrats' later writings, see my '"Legal Despotism" and Enlightened Reform in the Îles du Vent: The Colonial Governments of Chevalier de Mirabeau and Mercier de la Rivière, 1754–1764', in Gabriel Paquette (ed.), *Enlightened Reform in Southern Europe and Its Atlantic Colonies, c. 1750–1830* (Basingstoke, 2009), 167–82.
16. Mirabeau, *L'ami des hommes*, iii, 293.
17. Ibid., 388.
18. Ibid., 377.
19. Ibid., 380–1.
20. On Mirabeau's antislavery views, see Pernille Røge, 'The Question of Slavery in Physiocratic Political Economy', in Manuela Albertone (ed.), *Governare Il Mondo. l'Economia Come Linguaggio Delle Politica Nell'europa Del settecento* (Feltrinelli, 2009), 149–69, 155. See also Marcel Dorigny, 'The Question of Slavery in the Physiocratic Texts: A Rereading of an Old Debate', in Manuela Albertone and Antonino De Francesco (eds), *Rethinking the Atlantic World: Europe and America in the Age of Democratic Revolutions* (London: Palgrave Macmillan, 2009), 147–62.
21. Louis de Loménie, *Les Mirabeau, Nouvelles Études Sur La Société Française Au XVIIIe Siècle*, 5 vols. (Paris, 1879–1891), 172, 156. On Mirabeau's conversion from Populationism to Physiocracy, see Paul Chanier, 'Le Dilemme de Mirabeau: Cantillon ou Quesnay?' In Michel Vovelle (ed.), *Les Mirabeau Et Leur Temps: Actes Du Colloque d'Aix-en-Provence, 17 et 18 Décembre 1766* (Paris, 1968), 23–35.
22. Marquis de Mirabeau, *L'ami des hommes ou Traité de la population*, 6 vols. (Haye, 1758), iv.
23. Jean Tarrade, *Le Commerce Colonial De La France à la Fin de l'Ancien Régime: l'évolution de 'l'Exclusif' de 1763 à 1789*, 2 vols. (Paris, 1972), i, 88.
24. Paul Butel, *L'Économie Française Au XVIIIe Siècle* (Paris, 1993), 116–7.
25. François Véron Duverger de Forbonnais, *Essai sur l'admission des navires neutres dans nos colonies* (1756).
26. Mirabeau, *La philosophie rurale*, iii, 195.
27. Ibid., 195–7.

28. Ibid., 214–5.
29. Quesnay, *Œuvres Économiques*, 292–3.
30. These questions are largely a reproduction of those posed by Quesnay in his 'Questions Intéressantes sur la Population, l'Agriculture et le Commerce' inserted in the 1958 version of Mirabeau's *L'ami des hommes*. See Quesnay, *Œuvres Économiques*, 293–4.
31. This use of the term '*copropriétaire*' appears as part of the physiocratic terminology from *La philosophie rurale* onward. It is applied in several articles in the *Éphémérides du citoyen* from 1767 on and by Mercier de la Rivière in *l'Ordre naturelle* from 1767.
32. Mirabeau, *La philosophie rurale*, 204.
33. Ibid., 203–4.
34. Draft of *La philosophie rurale*, chapter 11. Paris, Archives Nationales, Mirabeau Papers, M799, bobine 3.
35. Mirabeau, *La philosophie rurale*, iii, 213.
36. Marcel Merle, 'L'Anticolonialisme', in Marc Ferro (ed.), *Le Livre Noir Du Colonialisme: XVIe–XXIe Siècle: De L'Extermination à La Repentance* (Paris, 2003), 626.
37. In 1768, Dupont de Nemours claimed that Le Mercier de la Rivière was indeed a disciple of Quesnay during his intendancy. Pierre Samuel Dupont de Nemours, in A. Dubois (ed.), *De l'Origine Et Des Progrès d'Une Science Nouvelle (1768)* (Paris, 1910), 9.
38. L. P. May, *Le Mercier De La Rivière (1719–1801) Aux Origines De La Science Économique* (Paris, 1975), 42. See also Florence Gauthier, 'À l'Origine De La Théorie Physiocratique Du Capitalisme, La Plantation Esclavagiste. L'Expérience De Le Mercier De La Rivière, Intendant De La Martinique', *Actuel Marx* 32 (2002): 51–72.
39. Le Mercier de la Rivière, 'Discours d'Ouverture De La Chambre Mi-Partie d'Agriculture Et De Commerce', in L. P. May (ed.), *Le Mercier De La Rivière (1719–1801): Mémoires Et Textes Inédits Sur Le Gouvernement Économique Des Antilles* (Paris, 1978).
40. Some argue that such agricultural chambers were part of a scientific colonial machinery. See François Regourd, 'La Société Royale D'Agriculture De Paris Face à l'Espace Colonial (1761–1793)', *Bulletin Du Centre D'Histoire Des Espaces Atlantiques* 8 (1997/1998): 155–94; James E. McClellan and Francois Regourd, 'The Colonial Machine: French Science and Colonisation in the Ancient Regime', *Osiris* 15 (2000): 31–50. In contrast, Tarrade sees the chamber as part of the transformation toward the accommodation of the colonies' perspective within the colonial administration. See Jean Tarrade, 'L'Administration Coloniale En France à La Fin De l'Ancien Régime: Projets De Réforme', *Revue Historique* 229 (1963): 103–22.
41. Henri Joucla, *Le Conseil Supérieur Des Colonies Et Ses Antécédents* (Paris, 1928).
42. Le Mercier de la Rivière, 'Discours D'Ouverture De La Chambre Mi-Partie D'Agriculture Et De Commerce', 93.
43. Ibid., 94–5.
44. Ibid., 96.
45. Deliberations of the chamber, 21 August 1760, Bordeaux, Archives départementales de la Gironde (ADG), Chambre du Commerce de Guienne (C) 4256.
46. Letter to Choiseul from Bordeaux, 7 December 1762, ADG, C4264.

47. Le Mercier de la Rivière, 'Mémoire', in *Le Mercier De La Rivière (1719–1801): Mémoires Et Textes Inédits*, 102.
48. Ibid., 126, 128, 131, 141.
49. Pernille Røge, 'The Question of Slavery in Physiocratic Political Economy', in Manuela Albertone (ed.), *Governare il mondo. L'economia come linguaggio delle politica nell'Europa del Settecento* (Feltrinelli, 2009).
50. See Philippe Steiner, 'L'Ésclavage Chez Les Économistes Français (1750–1830)', in Marcel Dorigny (ed.), *Les Abolitions De l'Esclavage De L. F. Sonthonaz à V. Schœlcher 1793 1794 1848* (Paris, 1995), 165–75, 168–9.
51. Le Mercier de la Rivière, 'Mémoire', 132–3, 124.
52. Ibid., 146.
53. Ibid., 148. This strategy was almost identical to the one Dupont de Nemours would propose to Vergennes more than twenty years later, which resulted in the 1786 Anglo-French commercial treaty. On Dupont de Nemours and the 1786 Anglo-French Commercial Treaty, see Orville T. Murphy, 'Dupont De Nemours and The Anglo-French Commercial Treaty of 1786', *Economic History Review* 19 (1966): 569–80.
54. With permission granted on 18 April 1764, 175 foreign ships obtained access to the island between July 1763 and April 1764. Dorothy Burne Goebel, 'The "New England Trade" and the French West Indies, 1763–1774: A Study in Trade Policies', *William and Mary Quarterly* 20 (1763): 331–72, 335–6, 345.
55. May, *Le Mercier De La Rivière*, 55 and Le Mercier de la Rivière, *Le Mercier De La Rivière (1719–1801): Mémoires Et Textes Inédits*, 73.
56. May, *Le Mercier de la Rivière*, 65, 67 and Mercier de la Rivière, *Le Mercier de la Rivière (1719–1801): Mémoires Et Textes Inédits*, 61.
57. Mercier de la Rivière, *Le Mercier De La Rivière (1719–1801): Mémoires Et Textes Inédits*, 265–6.
58. Paul Pierre Mercier de la Rivière, in Edgard Depitre (ed.), *L'ordre naturel et essentiel des sociétés politiques* (Paris, 1910), 243.
59. Tarrade, *Le Commerce Colonial*, i, 183, 201.
60. De la Rivière and de la Touche to Choiseul, 23 February 1761, Aix-en-Provence, Centre des Archives d'Outre-Mer, Col C8A 63 F1.
61. Tarrade, *Lee Commerce Colonial*, i, 241–80
62. Ibid., i, 275–80. See also Gustave Schelle, *Dupont de Nemours et L'École physiocratique* (Paris, 1888), 32–7.
63. Guy Chaussinand-Nogaret, *Choiseul – naissance de la gauche* (Paris, 1998), 181–3, 206.
64. May, *Le Mercier De La Rivière*, 60. See also Dupont de Nemours, *De l'origine et des progrès d'une science nouvelle*, 10.
65. Charles-Louis de Secondat Montesquieu, in Destutt de Tracy (ed.), *Œuvres de Montesquieu*, 3 vols. (Paris, 1822), iii, 447.
66. Quesnay, 'Remarques sur l'opinion de l'auteur de *L*'esprit des lois concernant les colonies', in *Œuvres Économiques Et Philosophiques*, 425–6. Originally printed 10 February 1766 in *Journal d'Agriculture, commerce et finances*. Montesquieu's ideas on colonisation and empire have recently been the topic in a special issue of the *Revue Montesquieu*. See Céline Spector (ed.), 'Montesquieu et L'empire', *Revue Montesquieu* 8 (2005–2006).

67. Philippe Steiner notes that this procedure was typical of Quesnay. Steiner, *La 'science nouvelle'*, 22. Fox-Genovese criticises Quesnay for committing the same mistake when defining 'the State'. See *The Origins of Physiocracy*, 115.
68. Quesnay, 'Remarques sur l'opinion de l'auteur de L'esprit des lois concernant les colonies', 428.
69. Ibid., 432.
70. Forbonnais, 'Colonies', in Denis Diderot and Jean le Rond D'Alembert (ed.), *Encyclopédie, ou dictionnaire raisonné des sciences, des arts et des métiers* (University of Chicago, ARTFL Encyclopédie Project), Winter 2008 edition, Robert Morrissey (ed.), http://encycopedie.uchicago.edu.
71. On 'Colbertisme' in this period, see Philippe Minard, *La fortune du Colbertisme. État et industrie dans la france des Lumières* (Paris, 1998).
72. Chaussinand-Nogaret, *Choiseul*, 212–3.
73. Tarrade, *Le commerce colonial*, i, 283.
74. E. Daubigny, *Choiseul et la France d'outre-mer après le traité de Paris: Étude sur la politique coloniale au XVIIIe siècle* (Paris, 1892), 242–4.
75. Clément also makes this point in 'Du Bon Et Du Mauvais Usage Des Colonies', 122.

3

Adam Smith on American Economic Development and the Future of the European Atlantic Empires

Thomas Hopkins

'The discovery of America, and that of a passage to the East Indies by the Cape of Good Hope,' Adam Smith told readers of *An Inquiry into the Nature and Causes of the Wealth of Nations*, 'are the two greatest and most important events recorded in the history of mankind.' They had served, in certain respects at least, to unite 'the most distant parts of the world', and in so doing had opened the way to an era of global commerce. And yet, Smith continued, noting the relatively recent date of those discoveries, 'it is impossible that the whole extent of their consequences can have been seen'.[1] In view of the great crisis shaking the British Atlantic Empire in the 1770s, few of Smith's contemporaries would have staked a claim to any certainty regarding the future relations between European nations, their colonies and the wider world. Certainly one way of structuring those relations, the idea of empire, appeared in Britain's case to be gravely threatened by the unprecedented strain placed upon metropolitan-colonial ties by the cost of victory in the Seven Years' War. Smith we know to have been 'very zealous in American affairs', and numerous studies have attempted to situate him within the contemporary debate over these 'present disturbances'.[2] The general thrust of Smith's critique of the colonial trading regime is, perhaps, sufficiently well known to need little exposition; as Donald Winch has argued, it forms 'part and parcel of Smith's attack on the "monopolising spirit" of the mercantile system, and his general case for free trade between nations'.[3] More problematic, however, has been the question of how this economic analysis relates to Smith's assessment of the politics of empire. Winch saw Smith's concern with America as primarily prompted by a fear of factionalism, whether driven by the American colonists themselves or by the mercantile class in Britain, which he identified with a civic republican tradition running through Montesquieu, Hume and Madison.[4] Peter Miller's more recent account of the idea of the 'common good' in eighteenth-century Britain, however, places Smith beyond the 'limits of the civic tradition' in his writings on America. The idea of a commonality of interests between Britain and America, such as could be construed within the republican idiom of the common good at least, had begun to break down by the 1760s. To Miller, Smith's political economy represents an attempt to put 'natural liberty' in the place of the 'common good' as the guiding light of modern politics, and by extension of metropolitan-colonial relations.[5]

However, the analysis of European colonisation offered in the *Wealth of Nations* appears to point beyond this immediate context to a vision of colonial development that would set a term to European imperial pretensions, regardless of the outcome of the Anglo-American revolt. Smith saw before Europe a future prospect of relative economic decline in the face of the rising agrarian-based economies of the New World, a decline prompted not so much by the ill effects of the mercantile system as by the very nature of the colonial societies themselves, when conceived as possessed of unique capacities for rapid demographic and economic growth. This went beyond the problem of how sovereignty could be exercised over the most distant provinces of an empire. The long-term question was whether the radically divergent economic paths the two continents appeared to be on would admit of European imperial rule at all. In Smith's hands the political economy of the modern settler colony was elevated to the status of a major problem of eighteenth-century political science. This essay traces the development of his analysis of the particularity of the American economic experience as an account of divergence from a putative 'natural order'. Unlike Europe, however, dependent on commerce as a stimulus to growth, there was to be nothing 'retrograde' about America's developmental trajectory. Land, and the knowledge of how best to cultivate it, would propel the colonies to economic greatness. The political implications of the coming reversal of power were, as will be seen, harder for Smith to gauge.

There were two kinds of advantages, according to Smith, that could in general be expected by metropolitan powers from their colonial empires. The first kind consisted of the general benefits to be had from the governance of empire: firstly, the contribution made by the provinces subject to its dominion to the general defence of the empire, and secondly, the contribution of revenue for the support of civil government. Neither of these benefits, however, had been generally enjoyed by the modern European empires, for which the defence and governance of American colonies had proved more a charge upon the mother country than a boon.[6] One could of course hope to reform this imperial system. In Britain's case, the union that Smith proposed between Britain, Ireland, and the American colonies, the integration, as it were, of the empire into the British constitution, might provide a means of extending the taxation system to all of its provinces and spreading the burden more equitably.[7] However, by 1776, as Smith acknowledged, in practical terms this proposal could appear as little more than a new Utopia, even if 'not more useless and chimerical than the old one'.[8] The onus thus appeared to fall on the second kind of advantage, namely those advantages that were supposed to derive from the 'peculiar' nature of the American colonies, that is, their subjection to an exclusive trading regime, the economic advantage of which to the mother country, Smith was keen to urge, was purely illusory.[9]

To be sure, as Smith noted in discussing the English Navigation Acts of the mid-seventeenth century, economic advantage is not the only criterion that may determine policy. The pressing needs of maritime defence dictated measures intended to secure not the expansion of foreign commerce, but a national monopoly of shipping that served as a bulwark of military rather than commercial superiority. 'As defence, however, is of much more importance than opulence,' Smith argued, 'the act of navigation is, perhaps, the wisest of all the commercial regulations of England'.[10] Pace the more doctrinaire interpretations of Smith's defence of free trade, he was far from insensible to the various demands that politics might (necessarily) make on the economy. Smith nevertheless had little difficulty in distinguishing the monopoly on entry into Britain's ports, a monopoly that could be justified in the light of national defence, from the monopoly on colonial trade. In the latter case, the cost of defending the monopoly itself outweighed whatever benefits might derive from its maintenance.[11]

Notwithstanding the sceptical light under which he cast them, the distinction Smith drew between the 'common advantages' of empire and the 'peculiar advantages' of the American colonies was a significant one, suggestive of the conceptual ties that had served to make colonies so central a preoccupation for writers on political economy in the previous half century. As Montesquieu had noted in book XXI of *De l'Esprit des Lois*, the modern colonies in the New World presented certain novelties when compared with the practice of the ancients, or indeed that of the backward Spanish who had first arrived in the Americas. Modern colonies,

Montesquieu argued, had been established not to found a new city, or even a new empire, but purely to further the extension of commerce. As a corollary of this, they were held in dependence by their mother countries, a dependence of which there were but few examples in the ancient world, in order to best secure the advantages of this trade to the metropolis, and to deny them to other nations.[12] This neatly captured the prevailing logic of over a century of debate on the utility of colonies: their integration into what Smith termed 'the system of commerce', and Hume, rather more pithily, 'jealousy of trade'. Commerce had become one of the foundations of modern empire; empire in its turn had been asked to reciprocate. This was not a new observation; the importance of Montesquieu's account lay rather in his historicisation of this fact of modern political life. The link between commerce and colonies was a product of the rise of modern trading republics and monarchies in the course of the seventeenth century and the ensuing bid to marshal trade in the service of national power. Coupled with the discovery of America, this had opened up the way not merely to the foundation of new colonies, but also to the emergence of a new kind of colony, its very existence bound up with the fate of the exclusive European trade regimes.

This form of commercial imperialism had certainly marked the rise of the Dutch Republic and England in the seventeenth century and, as the continued restrictions on colonial trade in place in each of the European empires bore witness, remained of great importance in setting the terms of public policy. However, as Istvan Hont has shown, the Colbertian experiment in France, notwithstanding its failings, had worked a very significant shift in political economic thought, reorientating debate toward the preconditions for the advancement of *domestic* economic growth.[13] In the writings of early to mid-eighteenth-century neo-Colbertian theorists, we can see the new emphasis on the importance of encouraging population growth and agricultural expansion start to alter the terms of the colony debate, with greater attention given to the agricultural and human resources of the colonies.

This is evident in the work of François Véron Duverger de Forbonnais, an influential member of the 'Gournay school' of political economists, so-called after the prominent financier around whom its members clustered. Charged with writing the article 'Colonie' for the third volume of D'Alembert and Diderot's *Encyclopédie*, Forbonnais produced a text that was still being cited as a guide to colonial policy in France as late as the 1940s.[14] In it he identified no fewer than six distinct forms that a colony might take. In general, he explained, we should understand by the word *colonie* simply 'the movement of a people, or of a part of a people from one country to another'.[15] This meant that one could justly call colonies the migrations of peoples after the biblical flood, the flight of Greek colonists from overcrowded or politically disturbed cities to more sparsely populated regions, the conquests of Rome or Alexander, the mass migrations of barbarian peoples, the peopling of trading entrepôts by commercial peoples, and the modern settlement of the Americas by European migrants.[16] It was these last two that he identified as the forms of colonisation undertaken by the moderns; although, given that the colony as entrepôt was a familiar enough concept from the ancient Mediterranean, it was only the colonies of settlement that could be regarded as unique in their modernity. In singling these forms out, he would appear to have been following the example of J.-F. Melon, whose *Essai politique sur le commerce* had been published to widespread acclaim in 1736. Melon had taken a commercial objective in the foundation of colonies to be axiomatic, but he had nevertheless sought to distinguish between colonies established as entrepôts and colonies where a conquering nation undertook to 'repeople' the land it had conquered. It was the latter that Melon took to be the common model in the Americas, particularly in the case of the Spanish colonies. There was little room here for Montesquieu's distinction between a Spanish empire of conquest and the commercial colonies of other nations. The only difference to Melon had been the foolishness of the Spanish in depopulating their own country in a bid to people America. The French and English had proceeded more gradually, and more wisely. In essence, Forbonnais adopted Melon's distinction when it came to discussing the colonies of the moderns and developed it further in his own *Elemens du commerce* of 1754. There were colonies for commerce alone, he argued, and colonies for commerce and agriculture. The former were known to the ancients; the latter were a product of the discovery, and conquest, of America.

Forbonnais remained a staunch defender of the subordination of colonies to the metropolis, going so far as to urge their abandonment if they entered into competition with metropolitan industry or agriculture.[17] In this respect, whatever emphasis he placed on agricultural settlement as the defining characteristic of Europe's American colonies, he remained committed to the principles of commerce and dependency that Montesquieu had outlined. However, in emphasising the agricultural nature of the modern American colonies, he added a third component to their 'peculiarity', and one moreover that in other hands was beginning to lead to a reconsideration of just how essential either commerce or dependence were to the colonies. As Røge argues elsewhere in this volume, the emergence of physiocracy in France from the late 1750s led to an attack on the *Exclusif*, an attempt to reconceive colonies as provinces within the body politic proper, and a demand that agriculture be given primacy over commerce in the development of the colonial economy – the restoration of what Mirabeau, in *L'Ami des hommes*, written prior to his encounter with the works of Quesnay, had referred to as the 'system of population'.[18]

At the same time, the agricultural potential of the vast expanses of land as yet uncultivated in the Americas, and the projected size of the population such a territory could sustain, were likewise becoming matters of increasing public debate in Britain and its empire, a debate that only intensified as it became clear that victory in the Seven Years' War bid fair to give Britain unchallenged supremacy in continental North America. In 1760, Benjamin Franklin published his *Observations Concerning the Increase of Mankind, Peopling of Countries, &c.*, although the text had been circulating in manuscript since 1751.[19] It was, like so many of the publicist's works, a short piece, and was somewhat overshadowed by the celebrated dispute on ancient and modern demographics between Robert Wallace and David Hume.[20] Franklin's argument lacked the subtlety of Wallace and Hume's explorations of the myriad of factors whose interplay could determine population growth, but at its core lay a concern that the two Scots barely addressed: how demographic models might work in the very different environment of America. The key, Franklin stressed, was land. Land was the necessary basis for sustaining a population; its relative scarcity determined the size of a population. In Europe most land was already under the plough, and the scope for further expansion of the population was limited. In America, however, land was freely available to all who would work it; hence it was easy to support a family, marriages were earlier, and population growth was more rapid.

At the time of its writing, Franklin's *Observations* appears to have been directed principally against the perceived threat of the rising number of German-speaking immigrants into Pennsylvania and other colonies. Since America was destined to support an immense population, it was incumbent upon Britain to ensure that that population was English speaking and preferably English by origin (since they constituted 'the principal Body of White People on the Face of the Earth').[21] However, as the slow-moving crisis over taxation of the colonies gathered pace in the 1760s, the future populousness of America took on a new importance. Already by 1767, in a letter to the Scottish jurist and historian Lord Kames, Franklin was darkly hinting at the reversal in power relations such an increase in population must bring: America 'will in a less time than is generally conceiv'd be able to shake off any Shackles that may be impos'd on her, and perhaps place them on the Imposers'.[22] Proposals for a parliamentary union between Britain and the colonies did not lessen the potential for upheaval that such a reversal could bring, for, to some at least, it appeared to hold the prospect that the seat of empire would one day follow the logic of population, wealth, and power and transfer itself to an American city.[23] An 'idle Dream', wrote the English political economist Josiah Tucker sourly in 1774. But nevertheless, his dismissiveness did not derive from any scepticism regarding America's future prosperity, but from his belief that 'it is much more probable, were Things to come to such a dreadful Crisis, that the *English* would rather submit to a *French* Yoke, than to an *American*; as being the less Indignity of the two.' A Newtonian analogy sprung to mind: Britain was more likely to gravitate toward the continent of Europe than toward that of America.[24]

Smith was markedly less sceptical about the possibility of such a translation of power than Tucker. In the event of a union, he suggested, the colonists could indeed 'flatter' themselves with such a prospect.

> Such has hitherto been the rapid progress of that country in wealth, population and improvement, that in the course of little more than a century, perhaps, the produce of American might exceed that of British taxation. The seat of the empire would then naturally remove itself to that part of the empire which contributed most to the general defence and support of the whole.[25]

Taxation was the key. The principal source of revenue to the state must be the principal source and seat of power. This made the relative economic prospects of Britain and America of signal importance to the future of the colonies' political relationship with the mother country. This was not something that could be determined solely through reference to the trading regime operative between the two. As Franklin's essay suggested, American economic development had a dynamic of its own that derived, in essence, not from being either commercial or dependent, but from Forbonnais' additional characteristic – that is, from being agricultural. Smith, however, went much further than Franklin in an attempt to explain American prosperity and follow through its implications. In the chapter 'On Colonies' in book IV of the *Wealth of Nations*, he attempted to integrate colonial America into the broader models of economic development presented in his work, and in so doing he forthrightly set out his own understanding of American 'peculiarity'. Smith's strategy, we might say, was twofold: firstly to tie the colonies into a conceptual 'natural order', using this model to explain the trajectory of American development; and secondly, by tying this model to the 'Greek' ideal that had emerged from earlier writers, he appears to have been trying to advance what may be termed an anti-imperial conception of colonies.

It has long been recognised that central to the development of political economy in the later eighteenth century was the elaboration of ideal-type models of socioeconomic development, and exploration of the ways in which European historical development diverged from such a conjectured 'natural order'. These models have been fruitfully studied for the light they shed on the conceptual apparatus available to contemporaries in explaining the origins of complex human societies, and, significantly for historians of empire, in accounting for the way of life of the 'rude nations' encountered in the Americas and elsewhere.[26] The importance of such models in Smith's works, and the importance of Smith in the development of the study of this 'history of civil society', was quite apparent to his contemporaries. In his encomium on the lately deceased Smith, Dugald Stewart attempted to explain the nature and purpose of what he termed Smith's '*Theoretical* or *Conjectural History*': 'In examining the history of mankind,' he wrote, 'as well as in examining the phenomena of the material world, when we cannot trace the process by which an event *has been* produced, it is often of importance to be able to show *how it may have been* produced by natural causes'. How so? By extrapolation from 'the known principles of human nature'.[27]

The most significant of such models for Smith's work was what we have come to know as the four-stages theory – baldly speaking, the idea that human societies, as they grow and increase the pressure upon resources, pass successively through four modes of subsistence: hunting, pasturage, agriculture, and a little more ambiguously, commerce. Yet if such a progression could be extrapolated from 'the known principles of human nature', that extrapolation long predated Smith. Thanks to the work of Istvan Hont, Knud Haakonssen, Nicholas Phillipson, and other scholars, we now have quite a detailed picture of what Hont has called 'the intimate continuity between earlier natural law theories of property and Smith's four-stage theory of history'.[28] It is therefore unsurprising that Smith's stadial theory is most fully developed in the unpublished *Lectures on Jurisprudence* rather than in either *The Theory of Moral Sentiments* or the *Wealth of Nations* itself. It can be argued that the model provides the framework within which Smith operates in the latter work, yet aside from the discussion of the origin and development of government and police in book V, one would be hard-pressed to identify a detailed exposition. Smith's concern in the *Wealth of Nations* was primarily with the final two stages of the model, agriculture and commerce, and the relationship between the two was, for Smith, as for so many writers on political economy in the eighteenth century, a concern of the utmost importance.

This becomes clear in the account he gave of 'The different Progress of Opulence in the different Nations', the subject that forms book III of the work. The first question he turned to concerned 'the natural progress of Opulence', and his account here, not surprisingly, followed the logic of the natural order suggested by the four-stages theory. Agriculture naturally develops first, manufacturing and commerce follow in its wake for reasons that are quite simple: 'As subsistence is, in the nature of things, prior to convenience and luxury, so the industry which procures the former, must necessarily be prior to that which ministers to the latter.' In order for towns, the centres of commerce to arise, there had to be an agricultural surplus capable of supporting them: this was the 'order of things which necessity imposes in general'.[29] It was also something of a commonplace and could provide the foundation for systems of political economy as different from Smith's own as those of Sir James Steuart or the physiocrats. Smith's account, however, continued in a direction that, as Hont has argued, aligned him in important ways not with these latter but with the proponents of neo-Colbertism in France. The natural progress of opulence may be from agriculture to commerce, but that was not to say that the natural order could not be subverted. In Europe this was exactly what had happened. The introduction of feudalism into the post-Roman world, that barbarism that so fascinated the historians of civil society in the eighteenth century, had significantly impeded the development of agriculture, as the feudal nobility engrossed land to themselves. Yet the impasse, which the growth of the European economy might seem to have reached in such a situation, was broken, not by any encouragement to agriculture, but by the stimulus provided to the growth of commerce and the towns by long-distance trade with the East. Europe's economic development had been commercially driven, not dependent upon the expansion of the agricultural sector. This is not the place to follow Smith's account on this score in detail, or to follow the policy implications that issued from it.[30] For our purposes what is important to stress is Smith's insistence on the 'unnatural and retrograde' order of these developments (which is not to say that he sought their reversal). In bucking the natural, because logically necessary, model of development, he argued, Europe had committed itself to a less than optimal rate of growth.

Tellingly, in this account of the emergence of the 'unnatural and retrograde order' in Europe, the greatest problems were seen to emerge from the success of the feudal nobility in engrossing land to themselves. Smith was not intrinsically hostile to the landlord class, but he was insistent that for agriculture to flourish one needed an active market in land. Where little land was available, rent, even on unimproved and uncultivated land, would inevitably be high, a situation that would tend not only to discourage the improvement of land in itself but would place considerable pressure on the wages of labour, hardly an encouragement to the increase of population. When Smith turned to the question of colonies in book IV, his prescription for a flourishing colony reads in some ways as a simple negation of the pressures operating in medieval Europe: 'Plenty of good land, and liberty to manage their own affairs their own way, seem to be the two great causes of the prosperity of all new colonies'.[31] This would seem to be simply a restatement of the preconditions of the 'system of natural liberty' that is the underlying assumption of the 'natural progress of opulence'. Nicholas Phillipson has described this as 'Smith's masterstroke' – employing the American colonial experience 'as the classic, and indeed the only possible example of a society whose progress had been rapid and natural by comparison with that of Europe'.[32] However, a closer look swiftly reveals that Smith was ready to make a somewhat more pointed claim than this would suggest. 'The colony of a civilized nation', he laid it down, 'which takes possession, either of a waste country, or of one so thinly inhabited, that the natives easily give place to the new settlers, advances more rapidly to wealth and greatness than any other human society'.[33] Smith's move here was significant. He was setting up a contrast between the idea of the colony as the offshoot of a 'civilized nation', implying, as the phrase does in this context, a modern, commercial society, and a 'waste country'; but he went further in bringing these two terms together, suggesting that their interaction gives colonial society a claim to the status of a unique form of human society, distinguished principally by its potential for rapid growth.

The explanation for this potential continued to be structured around the initial contrast, and, in elaborating, Smith in effect was concerned with drawing out two sets of comparative advantage (to use the term in a somewhat looser sense than that associated with Ricardo) born of this interaction. The first such advantage must be seen as relative to ordinary human societies in the first stages of their development, at the hunting or pastoral stage, where agriculture has yet to be established, or, in what was something of a term of art, relative to 'savage and barbarous nations':

> The colonists carry out with them a knowledge of agriculture and of other useful arts, superior to what can grow up in the course of many centuries among savage and barbarous nations. They carry out with them too the habit of subordination, some notion of the regular government which takes place in their own country, of the system of laws which support it, and of a regular administration of justice; and they naturally establish something of the same kind in the new settlement. But among savage and barbarous nations, the natural progress of law and government is still slower than the natural progress of arts, after law and government have been so far established as is necessary for their protection.[34]

The status of the colony as an offshoot of a 'civilized nation' gives the colonists, at least potentially, access to a body of knowledge that would, in the natural course of things, take a new society many ages to acquire. Significantly, Smith divided this knowledge into two categories: firstly, 'a knowledge of agriculture and of other useful arts', which, one may well suppose, constitute the principal advantage the colonists would enjoy over a preagricultural society when faced with wasteland to be cultivated. Yet in fact it is to the second category of knowledge that Smith assigned priority: 'the habit of subordination', and knowledge of their country's law and government. One must be careful here; Smith was not suggesting that law and government are found uniquely in an agricultural or commercial society, and in the *Lectures on Jurisprudence* and in book V of the *Wealth of Nations* he devoted considerable attention to the progress of law and government in 'savage and barbarous nations'. The point at issue is the extent to which law and government have been 'so far established for [the] protection of agriculture and the other arts'. A bare knowledge of agriculture is not enough: institutional support, and, one is tempted to add, the support of *mores*, must be in place if this knowledge is to be productively used. In the natural progress of society, such developments arise slowly, but in tandem. It is the peculiar blessing of a colonial society to be confronted with a preagricultural environment when it is already well placed to exploit its full potential.[35]

A corollary should be added to this. In the text known as the *Early Draft of the Wealth of Nations*, believed to date from 1762, Smith made the point that 'a nation is not always in a condition to imitate and copy the inventions and improvements of its more wealthy neighbours; the application of these frequently requiring a stock with which it is not furnished'.[36] This was, Smith acknowledged, a problem facing new colonies. 'New colonies', he noted in the published *Wealth of Nations*, 'are always understocked. Their capital is much less than what they could employ with great profit and advantage to the improvement and cultivation of their land'. However, once again, their status as offshoots of a larger society in some measure works to alleviate this problem, through the opportunity it presents for borrowing the capital they need from the mother country.[37] Smith was sceptical, to say the least, that the success of the colonists in this regard would be to the advantage of their creditors, or to the metropolis more generally, yet it represented a further important respect in which colonists, presented with a waste country, enjoyed advantages unknown in the natural order of progress.

There is a certain superficial resemblance in the stress laid on the 'waste' status of the land to be colonised by the apologetics for European conquest offered by writers such as John Locke. Smith's characterisation of the colonists taking possession of a 'waste country, or of one so thinly inhabited, that the natives easily give place to the new settlers' is apt to raise such suspicions. The analogy, however, is misleading. For Locke the issue was a question of right. The failure (as he characterised it) by the indigenous peoples of America to cultivate the land on which they dwelt signalled a neglect of the divinely derived obligation to improve the earth, the foundation of property rights in land. Uncultivated land properly speaking had no possessor by right, and the claims of European settlers against Native Americans were thus perfectly just.[38] Smith, however, had little time for such apologetics; he was quite clear that the European conquest of America represented a grave injustice to the indigenous inhabitants and was purely the result of an accidental military preponderance, which may in future be overturned.[39] The stress he placed upon 'waste country', whilst undoubtedly intended to chime with the common characterisation of pre-Columbian America, was not intended to establish a precedence of right to whomsoever should first put the land to the plough. Rather, it served to establish the basis of the extraordinary potential for growth he attributed to colonial societies. That something of a polemical purpose underlay this equation is not in doubt, and this is an issue that we shall have cause to return to. However, it remains to explore the second set of comparative advantages that resulted from this concatenation of 'waste country' and 'civilized nations', advantages in this case relative to the societies from which the colonists first issued.

From this perspective, it is not from the colonists' origins that the advantage derives, but from their new environment. We return to the importance of land:

> Every colonist gets more land than he can possibly cultivate. He has no rent, and scarce any taxes to pay. No landlord shares with him in its produce, and the share of the sovereign is commonly but a trifle. He has every motive to render as great as possible a produce, which is thus to be almost entirely his own. But his land is commonly so extensive, that with all his own industry, and with all the industry of other people whom he can employ, he can seldom make it produce the tenth part of what it is capable of producing. He is eager, therefore, to collect labourers from all quarters, and to reward them with the most liberal wages. But those liberal wages, joined to the plenty and cheapness of land, soon make those labourers leave him in order to become landlords themselves, and to reward, with equal liberality, other labourers, who soon leave them for the same reason that they left their first master. The liberal reward of labour encourages marriage. The children, during the tender years of infancy, are well fed and properly taken care of, and when they are grown up, the value of their labour greatly overpays their maintenance. When arrived at maturity, the high price of labour and the low price of land, enable them to establish themselves in the same manner as their fathers did before them.[40]

This is, as was previously suggested, a complete reversal of the situation that produced the 'unnatural and retrograde order' of Europe. In a colony there is an abundance of cheap land, which as Smith noted has the crucial knock-on effect of drastically raising the price of labour. The upshot, as Smith argued, is that whereas in developed countries 'rent and profits eat up wages, and the two superior orders of people oppress the inferior one', in new colonies, at least where the inferior order is not in a state of slavery, 'the interest of the two superior orders obliges them to treat the inferior one with more generosity and humanity', a great encouragement to the increase of population.[41]

That proviso, however, excluding those in the state of slavery from this model, is crucial. In the immediate context of his discussion of colonies, Smith was curiously reserved on this subject. He explained at some length his conviction that slaves are treated better under an arbitrary government, such as that of France, which has the power to intervene in the affairs of their masters, than under a government such as Britain's, where the masters enjoy greater liberty.[42] However, he did not enter into detail on the subject of the profitability, or otherwise, of colonial slavery. David Hume's essay, 'On the Populousness of Ancient Nations', had begun a considerable debate on the question of whether slavery retarded the growth of a society, a debate to which other writers on political economy, such as Sir James Steuart, devoted considerable attention.[43] Smith's comments in the *Wealth of Nations*, however, were sparing. He agreed with Hume in supposing slavery to limit economic growth, noting in the case of Rome how slavery deprived free labourers of employment.[44] It seems clear that he regarded slavery as an expense, rather than an asset, noting in book III that it was only the great profits of the sugar and tobacco plantations in the Caribbean and in North America that allowed them the luxury of slave labour. Slavery was an indulgence of the 'pride of man' and his desire to domineer over others, and in this sense it stood outside the logic of the costs of labour. Smith's evasiveness regarding American slavery in the context of economic and demographic growth would thus seem to suggest a desire to minimise the importance of an institution whose negative consequences in these regards he explicitly accepted. Slavery, an increasingly important feature of American reality, appeared to have little place in the ideal-type of colony that Smith was keen to present.

What, then, were the characteristics of the 'American order'? In the first place, the motor of economic development, following the logic of the hypothetical 'natural order', was agriculture, as opposed to the commerce-driven European economy with its suboptimal growth rates. Secondly, American society is more egalitarian thanks to the opportunities for land ownership available, and this, following a logic familiar enough from Wallace and Hume, was itself a great incentive to population growth. This would certainly suggest a strong endorsement of America's potential for economic growth, whatever the consequences of that may prove to be. However, what of the pernicious effects of the colonial monopolies, Smith's critique of which has attracted so much scholarly attention, such as the exclusive trading companies, the restrictions on shipping or the imposition of tariff barriers? Surely these must represent a considerable check on the American economy, as they did on that of the mother country. Smith, however, was careful to minimise the impact of the monopolies on the colonies, at least for the present time, partly by downplaying the real efficacy of imperial control over the colonies, and partly by pointing to their lack of dependence, in their current situation, on trade to fuel expansion.

The first of these strategies was based not only on a careful assimilation of the American case to a 'natural' model of colonial development, but also in an insistence on the possibility of colonies existing outside of an imperial framework. Smith captured this distinction rather neatly in appealing to the classical precedents available. In Latin, *colonia*, to be sure, signified simply a 'plantation', a settlement of citizens or subjects amongst a conquered population that would remain subordinate to the mother city of Rome.[45] Yet there was another example one could draw upon for a very different sense of the nature of a colony. In the Greek world colonies had owed no obedience to their mother cities, and if they were to be considered as the children of the metropolis, they were, he noted, 'emancipated' children. Greek colonies were not founded amidst a conquered population, but in 'remote and distant' Italy and Asia Minor, at the time inhabited by 'barbarous and uncivilized [i.e., easily displaced] nations'. The very term used in Greek (αποιχια), 'signifies a separation of dwelling, a departure from home, a going out of the house'.[46]

There was, of course, nothing new in appealing to antiquity when attempting to understand the empires of the modern world. The ancient world, Anthony Pagden has written, exercised an 'imaginative dependency' over the minds of the theorists of colonial empire of modern Europe; Rome in particular provided them with 'the language and political models they required'.[47] By the mid-eighteenth century, however, the ancient world as it appeared in discussions of the question of colonies had become a good deal more heterogeneous. Montesquieu had seen a qualitative difference between the empire of Rome and the colonies of the Greeks that had, in an earlier age, spread across the Mediterranean. The latter, he suggested, had promoted the growth of commerce, although this may not have been the object of their foundation.[48] Rome, however, was an empire of conquest: the Romans had little taste for commerce. This distinction between Greece and Rome when discussing the colonies of the ancient world had begun to emerge in the seventeenth century in the writings of the natural jurists. Grotius had noted that the colonies of the Greeks had only the loosest of obligations toward their metropolis; Pufendorf had subsequently amplified his arguments.[49] By 1745, when the French Académie royale des inscriptions et belles lettres awarded their prize to Jean-Pierre Bougainville for his subsequently influential *Dissertation sur cette question, Quels étaient les droits des Métropoles grecques sur leurs colonies, et les devoirs des colonies envers les métropoles*, a well-defined trope had been established: Greek colonies had enjoyed autonomy from their mother cities, but the ties of a common origin had tended to make them faithful allies in war.[50] Here was a model of colonial government that appeared to offer an alternative to the subordinate status imposed on colonies under the present system. Unsurprisingly, it found favour amongst some of the advocates of the Anglo-American colonists as their dispute with Britain escalated over the course of the 1760s, to the extent that a defender of metropolitan primacy like James Abercromby felt compelled to expend considerable effort refuting the juridical basis for any comparison between Ancient Greece and modern New England.[51] Smith's evocation of the colonies of Greece was thus a loaded one.

With the Greek/Roman dichotomy in mind, Smith's natural order of colonial development takes on a new light. Let us recall his starting point: 'The colony of a civilized nation which takes possession, either of a waste country, or of one so thinly inhabited, that the natives easily give place to the new settlers, advances more rapidly to wealth and greatness than any other human society.'[52] Smith's move here is significant. In setting out his explanation of the prosperity of new colonies, he has subtly steered the reader away from the Roman model of colonisation, as occurring amongst a conquered population, toward what he has previously outlined as the Greek ideal. The link is underlined as Smith segues smoothly from the explanation of the causes of this prosperity into the statement that 'the progress of many of the antient Greek colonies towards wealth and greatness, seems accordingly [and note here the implicit link to the model implied in "accordingly"] to have been very rapid', whilst the progress of the Roman colonies was 'by no means so brilliant'.[53] However, his strategy becomes even clearer when we discover his ultimate goal: the tying in of the colonies of modern Europe, not to the Roman model, the archetypal imperial model, but to those of Greece:

> In the plenty of good land, the European colonies established in America and the West Indies resemble, and even greatly surpass, those of antient Greece. In their dependency upon the mother state they resemble those of Rome; but their great distance from Europe has in all of them alleviated more or less the effects of this dependency.[54]

Distance, it would seem, is the solvent of imperial authority, and Smith is able to state that the 'progress of all the European colonies in wealth, population, and improvement, has accordingly been very great'.[55]

Yet there was a complication involved in assimilating the model of natural colonial development to the Greek example. The most significant feature of Smith's account of Greek colonisation had been the freedom Greek colonies enjoyed from metropolitan authority. We have already seen how he attempted to sidestep this issue with regard to the European colonies in America, asserting that distance had mitigated its impact. However, the logic of his arguments against mercantilism and monopolies does indeed intervene at this point, pushing him to draw explicitly a further condition of colonial prosperity. Not only 'plenty of good land' but also 'liberty to manage their own affairs their own way' were the conditions for colonial prosperity. This may not come as any great surprise in a work dedicated to expounding the 'system of natural liberty'. However, it has interesting implications for consideration of Smith's views on the relations between colonies and empire. Each and every one of the European colonial regimes, designed as they were to keep the colonies in some measure dependent upon the metropolis, could reasonably be described as illiberal trading regimes. Britain's colonies may have suffered least in this general pattern, but the regime to which they were subject is only the 'least illiberal' amongst the European empires; it is not positively endorsed. It is at this point that Smith's examination of the colonial issue really begins to engage with the 'mercantilist' policies of the European states. In attempting to direct the economic development of their colonies, particularly in so far as it concerns their ability to trade freely in whatever and with whomsoever they wish, European governments have not only damaged their own interests, an issue which has received particular attention from scholars with regard to Smith's treatment of the British case, but have committed a grave wrong against their colonies. They are a 'badge of slavery', Smith claims, and contrary to the rights of nature: 'To prohibit a great people... from making all that they can of every part of their own produce, or from employing their stock and industry in the way that they judge most advantageous to themselves, is a manifest violation of the most sacred rights of mankind.'[56] There is an implicit tension here between the needs of colonies, as a society that is already semi-detached from its parent metropolis, and the demands of empire, and it may be suggested that it is in this context that the Greek model began to appear so attractive to Smith. In matching his model of the natural development of a colony so closely to the example of Greece, he had implicitly assimilated into it the crucial factor of Greek independence from the metropolis. If, as he was careful to insist, the only real contribution Europe had made to the development of her colonies had been to form the character of their founders, what advantage lay, to the colonies at least, in continued subjugation to European empires? The 'separation' that characterised the Greek concept of a colony began to look extremely attractive.

This would seem to take us back to the limiting effect of the mercantile system on colonial development, making dissolution of the political ties between colony and metropolis the precondition for future growth. A note of caution must be sounded here, however. The effects of the monopoly thus far had not, Smith noted, been terribly hurtful, given the continuing abundance of land, and hence the limited need for the colonies to engage themselves in manufacture and trade. True, this abundance may not continue forever and metropolitan regulations might appear under a worse light: 'In a more advanced state they might be really oppressive and insupportable.'[57] In the meantime, however, agriculture was a sufficient basis for growth, and growth, moreover, would ensure a decisive shift in the balance of political power between colony and metropolis. It was this shift in power that promised at some stage to upset the structures of imperial rule in each of the different European Atlantic empires; the mercantile system might retard this growth, but the potential of the Americas was such that it did not put a stop to it.

It would be wrong to read into Smith's insistence that Britain should give up its colonies a simple endorsement of the objections of the American colonists to the relationship of dependence in which they were held. As Andrew Skinner has observed, it was the dynamic of growth in both economies that necessitated *some* form of change in the imperial relationship, and both economies had suffered from the prerevolutionary arrangements.[58] At one level, the abandonment of empire by Britain, and by implication the other European states with trans-Atlantic empires as well, represented a simple matter of self-interest. The *Wealth of Nations* offered a comprehensive argument as to how a nation such as Britain could maintain its economic strength within a free trade economy: namely, through furthering the advantages to be gained from an extensive division of labour, a strategy only open to an economy already heavily capitalised. Colonial empires had little to offer in this light, whilst the expenses they entailed appeared rather clearer. However, Smith was well aware of the changes that the recent centuries of colonisation had brought and would continue to bring to the balance of global power. The destruction wrought upon the peoples of the Americas and the East Indies was evident enough, as in the latter case was the crippling economic burden that imperial exploitation had placed upon the Indian subcontinent. In the

American case, however, the destruction of the native peoples, whilst denounced, was somewhat sidelined by the adoption of the image of America as a waste country, allowing Smith to adopt, and apparently vindicate, the Greek model of colonisation, redescribing it as the operation of a natural order of colonial development. What this pointed to was an alternative route to economic power, one built not on the slow accumulation of capital since the middle ages, but on the exploitation of a vast and supposedly untapped supply of land. Uncertain as the future may have appeared in 1776, the potential of the American economy could not be ignored.

Notes

I am greatly indebted to Pernille Røge and Sophus A. Reinert for their comments on successive drafts of this essay. For comments on earlier drafts, I thank Istvan Hont, Gareth Stedman Jones, Iain McDaniel, Suzanne Marcuzzi, Graham Clure and Justin duRivage.

1. Adam Smith, *An Inquiry into the Nature and Causes of the Wealth of Nations*, R. H. Campbell, A. S. Skinner and W. B. Todd (eds), 2 vols. (Indianapolis: Liberty Fund, 1981), II, 626. Hereafter referred to as *WN*.
2. David Hume, on the authority of the Duke of Bucleugh, notes Smith's zeal on the subject of America. Letter to Smith, 8 February 1776, in A. Smith, *Correspondence*, E. C. Mossner and I. S. Ross (eds), (Indianapolis: Liberty Fund, 1987), 186. Emma Rothschild has written recently of the 'Sense of the Overseas Connections of Empire as Almost within Sight, in Eighteenth-Century Scotland', *The Inner Life of Empires: An Eighteenth-Century History* (Princeton, NJ: Princeton University Press, 2011), 220. The secondary literature on Smith's contribution to the debate on America is large, if sometimes antiquated. Helpful studies include I. S. Ross, *The Life of Adam Smith* (Oxford: Clarendon, 1995), 248–69; P. N. Miller, *Defining the Common Good: Empire, Religion and Philosophy in Eighteenth-Century Britain* (Cambridge: Cambridge University Press, 1994); D. Winch, *Adam Smith's Politics: An Essay in Historiographic Revision* (Cambridge: Cambridge University Press, 1978), 146–63 and the same author's *Classical Political Economy and Colonies* (London: G. Bell, 1965), 6–24; A. S. Skinner, 'Adam Smith and the American Economic Community: An Essay in Applied Economics', *Journal of the History of Ideas* 37 (1976): 59–78; D. Stevens, 'Adam Smith and the Colonial Disturbances', in A. S. Skinner and T. Wilson (eds), *Essays on Adam Smith* (Oxford: Clarendon, 1975), 202–17. J. Pitts, *A Turn to Empire: The Rise of Imperial Liberalism in Britain and France* (Princeton, NJ: Princeton University Press, 2005), 25–58, contains some useful insights.
3. Winch, *Adam Smith's Politics*, 148.
4. Winch, *Adam Smith's Politics*, 146–63.
5. Miller, *Defining the Common Good*, 399–412.
6. Smith, *WN*, II, 593. Spain and Portugal were a partial exception to the general rule – they had, Smith admitted, derived some revenue from their conquests in the New World.

7. Smith, *WN*, II, 619–26, 933–47. Smith's exploration of this possibility gave rise in the early twentieth century to the suggestion that he should be seen as a distant precursor of the late nineteenth-century advocates of imperial federation. See, for example, E. A. Benians, 'Adam Smith's Project of an Empire', *Cambridge Historical Journal* 1 (1925): 249–83. Duncan Bell accords Smith's legacy a more ambivalent role in nineteenth-century debate on empire: D. Bell, *The Idea of Greater Britain: Empire and the Future of World Order, 1860–1900* (Princeton, NJ: Princeton University Press, 2007), 198–9, and *Passim*.
8. Smith, *WN*, II, 934. Michael Sonenscher has recently suggested that this 'Utopia' be seen as a response to Sir James Steuart's 'rhapsody of public debt' that imagined the functioning of taxation in a world-state. Smith's union of the colonies and Great Britain appears on Sonenscher's account as a similar thought experiment, if with more limited ambitions. Michael Sonenscher, *Before the Deluge: Public Debt, Inequality and the Intellectual Origins of the French Revolution* (Princeton, NJ: Princeton University Press, 2007), 64–5.
9. Smith, *WN*, II, 594.
10. Smith, *WN*, I, 464–5.
11. Smith, *WN*, II, 613–5.
12. Charles-Louis de Secondat, Baron de La Brède et de Montesquieu, '*De l'Esprit des Lois, ou du rapport que les lois doivent avoir avec la constitution de chaque gouvernement, les mœurs, le climat, la religion, le commerce, etc. A quoi l'auteur a ajouté des recherches nouvelles sur les lois romaines touchant les successions, sur les lois françoises et sur les lois féodales*', in R. Callois (ed.), *Œuvres complètes de Montesquieu*, 2 vols. (Paris: Gallimard, 1951), II, 643.
13. Istvan Hont, 'Jealousy of Trade: An Introduction', *Jealousy of Trade: International Competition and the Nation-State in Historical Perspective* (Cambridge, MA: Harvard University Press, 2005), 1–37 and *Passim*.
14. For discussion, see Yves Benôt, 'L'Encyclopédie Et Le Droit de Coloniser', by Benôt, in R. Desné and M. Dorigny (ed.), *Les Lumières, L'esclavage, La Colonisation* (Paris: La Découverte, 2005), 164–72.
15. François Véron Duverger de Forbonnais, 'Colonie', in Denis Diderot and Jean Le Rond D'Alembert (eds), *Encyclopédie: Ou Dictionnaire Raisonné Des Sciences, Des Arts Et Des Métiers*, 17 vols. (Paris: Briasson et al., 1751–1765), III, 648. On Forbonnais and the Gournay group, see Sonenscher, *Before the Deluge*, 179–89, and I. Hont, 'The "Rich Country–Poor Country" Debate Revisited: The Irish Origins and French Reception of the Hume Paradox', in C. Wennerlind and M. Schabas (eds), *David Hume's Political Economy* (London: Routledge, 2008), 243–323.
16. Forbonnais, 'Colonie', *Encyclopédie*, III, 648–51.
17. François Véron Duverger de Forbonnais, *Elemens du Commerce*, 2 vols. (Paris: Briasson, 1754), II, 22.
18. Victor Riqueti and Marquis de Mirabeau, *L'Ami des hommes, ou Traité de la population* (Avignon, 1756–1760).
19. Benjamin Franklin, 'Observations Concerning the Increase of Mankind, Peopling of Countries, & c. (1751)', in A. Houston (ed.), *The Autobiography and Other Writings on Politics, Economics, and Virtue* (Cambridge: Cambridge University Press, 2004), 215–21.
20. David Hume, 'Of the Populousness of Ancient Nations', in E. F. Miller (ed.), *Essays Moral, Political and Literary* (Indianapolis: Liberty Fund, 1987), 377–464. Robert Wallace, *A Dissertation on the Numbers of Mankind in Ancient*

and Modern Times: In Which the Superior Populousness of Antiquity Is Maintained. With an Appendix, Containing Additional Observations on the Same Subject, and Some Remarks on Mr. Hume's Political Discourse, of the Populousness of Antient Nations (Edinburgh: G. Hamilton and J. Balfour, 1753).

21. Franklin, 'Observations Concerning the Increase of Mankind', 221. The trenchantly racist conclusion to the essay of 1751 was omitted in subsequent published versions, as Franklin scrabbled to win votes for a seat in the Pennsylvania assembly from the very 'Palatine Boors', now become electors, that he had so aggrieved.
22. Franklin, 'To Lord Kames' (25 February 1767), in *The Autobiography and Other Writings on Politics, Economics, and Virtue*, 284.
23. Some took this prospect in a very literal sense. Arthur Young, for example, in his *Political Essays Concerning the Present State of the British Empire; particularly respecting I. Natural advantages and disadvantages. II. Constitution. III. Agriculture. IV. Manufactures. V. The colonies. And VI. Commerce* (London: W. Strahan; T. Cadell, 1772) suggested that the monarch would do well to decamp for America in person: 'Let him man his royal navy, and at the head of a gallant army, and those who will follow royalty, transfer the seat of empire to that country, which seems almost peculiarly formed for universal domination.' Young, *Political Essays*, 430. See also N. Guyatt, *Providence and the Invention of the United States, 1607–1876* (Cambridge: Cambridge University Press, 2007), 76–82, for discussion of the prospect of *Translatio Imperii* in the 1760s and 1770s.
24. Josiah Tucker, *Four tracts, Together with Two Sermons, on Political and Commercial Subjects*, (Glocester [sic]: R. Raikes; J. Rivington, [1774]), 194. On Tucker, see J. G. A. Pocock, 'Josiah Tucker on Burke, Locke, and Price: A Study in the Varieties of Eighteenth-Century Conservativism', *Virtue, Commerce and History: Essays on Political Thought and History, Chiefly in the Eighteenth Century* (Cambridge: Cambridge University Press, 1985), 157–91 and Miller, *Defining the Common Good*, 399–412.
25. Smith, *WN*, II, 625–6.
26. Ronald L. Meek's, 'Pioneering Study', *Social Science and the Ignoble Savage* (Cambridge: Cambridge University Press, 1976), left something of a question mark hanging over eighteenth-century stadial theory, laying it open to the charge of legitimating European conquest of native American peoples and others deemed to fit the category of savage. This is not an issue that will be examined in any detail here. Jennifer Pitts' recent work, *A Turn to Empire*, has tried to refute the charges in the case of Smith, at least.
27. Dugald Stewart, 'Account of the Life and Writings of Adam Smith, LL.D' (1793), reprinted in Adam Smith, *Essays on Philosophical Subjects*, W. P. D. Wightman, J. C. Bryce and I. S. Ross (eds), (Indianapolis: Liberty Fund, 1982), 293.
28. Istvan Hont, 'The Language of Sociability and Commerce: Samuel Pufendorf and the Theoretical Foundations of the "Four-Stages" Theory', in A. Pagden (ed.), *Languages of Political Theory in Early Modern Europe* (Cambridge: Cambridge University Press, 1986), 253, reprinted in Hont, *Jealousy of Trade*, 160; and, most recently, Adam Smith's, 'History of Law and Government as Political Theory', in R. Bourke and R. Geuss (eds), *Political Judgement: Essays for John Dunn* (Cambridge: Cambridge University Press, 2009), 131–71. See also Knud Haakonssen, *Natural Law and Moral Philosophy: From Grotius to the Scottish Enlightenment* (Cambridge: Cambridge University Press, 1996) and

N. Phillipson, *Adam Smith: An Enlightened Life* (London: Allen Lane, 2010), 102–19.

29. Smith, *WN*, I, 377.
30. On these implications, see Istvan Hont, 'The Political Economy of the "Unnatural and Retrograde" Order: Adam Smith and Natural Liberty', in Schriften aus dem Karl-Marx-Haus (ed.), *Französische Revolution und Politische Ökonomie*, 41 vol. (Trier: Friedrich-Ebert-Stiftung, 1989), 122–49, reprinted in Hont, *Jealousy of Trade*, 354–88.
31. Smith, *WN*, II, 572.
32. Phillipson, *Adam Smith*, 228.
33. Smith, *WN*, II, 564.
34. Smith, *WN*, II, 564–5.
35. Smith, *WN*, II, 565.
36. Adam Smith, 'Early Draft of the Wealth of Nations', in R. L. Meek, D. D. Raphael and P. G. Stein (ed.), *Lectures on Jurisprudence* (Indianapolis: Liberty Fund, 1982), 579.
37. Smith, *WN*, II, 601.
38. For an examination of Locke's arguments in this regard, see James Tully, 'Rediscovering America: The Two Treatises and Aboriginal Rights', *An Approach to Political Philosophy: Locke in Contexts* (Cambridge: Cambridge University Press, 1993), 136–76.
39. Smith, *WN*, 626. This judgement is similarly extended to European conquests in Asia.
40. Smith, *WN*, II, 565.
41. Smith, *WN*, II, 565.
42. Smith, *WN*, II, 585–7.
43. Hume, 'Of the Populousness of Ancient Nations'. See also Sir James Steuart, *An Inquiry into the Principles of Political Economy* [1767], A. S. Skinner, N. Kabayashi and H. Mizuta (eds), 4 vols. (London: Pickering and Chatto, 1998), bk. I, chapter 7.
44. Smith, *WN*, II, 557.
45. As Phillipson notes (*Adam Smith*, 201), Smith had offered a 'surprisingly perfunctory reply' to an earlier inquiry from Lord Shelburne concerning the governance of Roman colonies, explaining that he had 'not found anything of much consequence'. Smith, Letter to Lord Shelburne, 12 Feb. 1767, *Correspondence*, 122–4, 123.
46. Smith, *WN*, II, 558.
47. Anthony Pagden, *Lords of All the World: Ideologies of Empire in Spain, Britain and France, c. 1500–c. 1800* (New Haven, CT: Yale University Press, 1995), 11–2 and *Passim*.
48. Montesquieu, *De l'Esprit des Lois*, in *Œuvres*, II, 612–3.
49. Hugo Grotius, in Richard Tuck (ed.), *The Rights of War and Peace*, 3 vols. (Indianapolis: Liberty Fund, 2005), I, chapter. 3.xxi; II, chapters 9 and 10. Samuel Pufendorf, *Of the Law of Nature and Nations*, Basil Kennett (trans.), 4th edn, 8 bks (London: J. Walthoe et al., 1729), bk. VIII, chapter XI. §6, 872; bk. VIII, chapter XII §5, 876–7.
50. Jean-Pierre Bougainville, *Dissertation Sur Cette Question Quels Étaient Les Droits Des Métropoles Grecques Sur Leurs Colonies, Et Les Devoirs Des Colonies Envers Les Métropoles* (Paris: Desaint et Saillant, 1743). A second edition appeared in

1745 under the title *Dissertation Qui a Remporte Le Prix de l'Académie Royale Des Inscriptions Et Belles Lettres En l'Année 1745* (Paris: Desaint and Saillant, 1745).

51. James Abercromby, *De Jure et Gubernatione Coloniarum, or An Inquiry into the Nature and the Rights of Colonies, Ancient and Modern, [c. 1774]*, in Abercromby, *Magna Charta for America*, J. P. Greene, C. F. Mullett and E. C. Papenfuse Jr. (eds) (Philadelphia: American Philosophical Society, 1986), 171–300.
52. Smith, *WN*, II, 564.
53. Smith, *WN*, II, 566–7.
54. Smith, *WN*, II, 567.
55. Smith, *WN*, II, 567.
56. Smith, *WN*, II, 582.
57. Smith, *WN*, II, 582.
58. Skinner, 'Adam Smith and the American Economic Community', 59–78.

4

Views from the South: Images of Britain and Its Empire in Portuguese and Spanish Political Economic Discourse, ca. 1740–1810

Gabriel Paquette

> 'All European nations have improved themselves through reciprocal imitation; each one carefully keeps watch over the actions taken by the others. All of them take advantage of the utility of foreign inventions'.[1]

> 'I saw at Coruña a translation of Adam Smith on the *Wealth of Nations*. What mutilations it may have undergone I know not, but surely no mutilation can prevent such a work from producing good in Spain'.[2]

In his farewell 1796 *relación* from New Granada, the departing viceroy, José de Ezpeleta, lamented that the deplorable state of Spain's colonies was attributable, in 'no small measure, to the ignorance of governors in political and economic affairs'. Guided by 'the military spirit', they treated their subjects with 'more harshness than they would have handled a regiment'. Instead, he argued, future cadres of colonial bureaucrats should be selected from the diplomatic corps, which was composed of men who were 'perspicacious in matters commerce and navigation'. Ezpeleta contended that a diplomat's exposure to 'advanced and industrious nations' would ensure that he would 'undoubtedly attempt to encourage the same ideas in America'. Furthermore, having observed firsthand the 'methods by which these nations extract great riches from their colonies', this new breed of administrator could 'raise Spain's empire to the same level of opulence' as its rivals. Men accustomed to 'observing usable roads, well-managed ports, easy navigation and flourishing agriculture', the viceroy argued, would pursue equivalent projects in the colonies which they governed.[3]

Ezpeleta's final *relación* was written in 1796, the same year in which Rodrigo de Souza Coutinho (1755–1812) was elevated to secretary of state for the navy and overseas dominions, with chief responsibility for the administration of Portugal's overseas possessions. The son of a former governor of Angola and, subsequently, Ambassador to Spain and Britain, as well as the godson of the Marquis of Pombal, Souza Coutinho's rise to ministerial power followed decades of diplomatic service in Turin at the Savoyard Court. Though they likely never met, Souza Coutinho and Ezpeleta clearly agreed on the role of the observation of foreign policies and practices on the fortunes of nations. 'Among the duties of a diplomat who resides at a foreign court', Dom Rodrigo remarked in a dispatch from Turin, 'perhaps there is none more interesting and useful than that of recording and transmitting the current state of affairs in the country, the causes which have secured its prosperity or hastened its decline'.[4]

Indeed, as Souza Coutinho suggested in another document, 'it is a just ambition of all governments to bring to their vassals the *luzes* enjoyed by more enlightened nations, recognizing that a nation's future greatness depends on the use of such principles'.[5] After 1796, when Dom Rodrigo became responsible for Portugal's ultramarine dominions, he would attempt to disseminate such insights to Brazil. Writing to the viceroy, the Count of Rezende, in 1798, he promised that the Crown would arrange for various *memorias* concerning agriculture to be translated and printed in order to 'spread to the inhabitants of Brazil knowledge which could give them considerable advantages', not least an 'increase in the number of crops cultivated there'.[6]

Bourbon ministers in Madrid and their Pombaline (and post-Pombaline) counterparts in Lisbon siphoned foreign ideas—from Britain, Naples, Denmark, Prussia, Holland, and France—and blended them with peninsular ones to produce hybrid policy prescriptions. The process was not mere copying. Critical reflection on, and a correction of, a model distinguishes emulation from mere imitation. Emulation implied admiration fused with a desire to surpass the original model.[7] Foreign ideas often were refracted and adapted according to the dictates of local circumstances and reordering, abridgement, and amplification proved inevitable.[8] As foreign models entered Spain and Portugal, they mingled with deeply-rooted Iberian traditions, producing an amalgamated ideology which was, in turn, harnessed to meet the demands of the respective reform programmes in the two empire-states.

This essay seeks to describe, analyse and compare the ways in which the example of Great Britain—particularly the principles of political economy which influenced the fashioning of its imperial policy and ultramarine institutions—was invoked and emulated, often critically, in Spanish and Portuguese reform discourses of the second half of the eighteenth century. Relying on a broad base of published as well as manuscript sources over a period of seventy years, this essay is inherently anecdotal as well as focused almost exclusively on bureaucratic discourses generated by high-ranking government officials. It seeks neither to recreate the context for each utterance it discusses nor to disguise the contradictory impulses which prompted the invocation of the British example. It is thus a small, not necessarily representative sample of a broader, multifaceted phenomenon that was pervasive across eighteenth-century Europe: fascination with Britain and its institutions. As one historian has noted: 'The English economic mind was the object of continuous investigation in eighteenth- and nineteenth-century Europe. The advantages and disadvantages of England were enumerated, evaluated, lamented over and compared'.[9] Of course, 'Britain' and 'British' hardly were static or monolithic categories; British policy was not uniformly consistent across space and time, and the variety of practices, policies, and predilections grouped under the umbrella term 'Britain' must be taken into account.

What was perhaps distinctive about interest in Britain in the Iberian world was the level of attention lavished on imperial policy, an infatuation which underscores the 'entangled histories' of each Iberian power with Britain in both Europe and America.[10] At stake in this essay, therefore, is a revision of the historiography of the eighteenth-century Iberian 'official mind'. It was England, with its North American empire and foothold in South Asia, and not France, shorn of much of its territorial empire after 1763, that was the relevant touchstone for Iberian political and economic writers seeking to 'modernize' their overseas empires. When England's role is recognised, the conventional story about the origins and scope of 'enlightened reform' in the Ibero-Atlantic world becomes less persuasive. Instead, its 'extra-European' dimensions become more compelling and central to the main story. Debates about colonial commerce, the slave trade, population promotion schemes, land tenure, labour regimes, agricultural improvement, and naval strategy, to name but a few, become imbued with new significance. Colonies were not merely laboratories where ideas generated in the metropole were clumsily applied. The colonial world was not merely a distant appendage of Europe. The world beyond Europe played an integral role in the evolution of ideas about political economy, reform, and development.

It was with regard to these topics that England's historical experience could be compared to, and contrasted with, those of Portugal and Spain. Such subjects were more often treated in official memoranda than in published tomes, partly because of their delicate connection to state security. It was in government documents—memorials, official and personal correspondence, industrial espionage reports, diaries from scientific voyages and travels abroad, and minutes of meetings—that British policy was discussed. The intellectual history of the period thus takes on an unfamiliar hue when the attitudes, anxieties, prejudices and often-unfulfilled aspirations contained in unpublished manuscript sources are integrated into the bigger picture.

During the latter five decades of the eighteenth century, both Spain's Bourbon monarchs and Portugal's Braganza rulers oversaw a comprehensive reform of their peninsular kingdoms and overseas empires. In Spain, the ministers who dominated policy making in the reigns of Charles III (r. 1759–1788) and his son Charles IV (r. 1788–1808) sought to renovate a rickety if durable state apparatus, buttressing it with a centralised bureaucracy, emanating from Madrid, outfitted with the revenue-generating mechanisms needed to restore the prestige and influence of the monarchy.[11] Repudiating the notion of Spain as an eclipsed power through bold action in Europe, Madrid also endeavoured to assert its rejuvenated sovereignty over its far-flung empire against the relentless encroachments of pesky smugglers and competitor imperial states. These low-intensity threats, along with the omnipresent spectre of war, further propelled the Crown's predilection for the concentration of power. Bourbon reformers turned away from the stable and resilient 'composite' monarchy structure bequeathed by their Habsburg predecessors.[12] In its place, they sought to erect a unified nation-state, subservient to the monarchy, and capable of inculcating a new patriotic spirit.[13]

At the end of the seventeenth century, Portugal was a relatively poor state on the periphery of Europe, notwithstanding its vast dominion of Brazil and scattered possessions on the coasts of Africa and the Indian subcontinent. The reign of Dom João V (1706–1750) coincided with Portugal's resurgence, buoyed chiefly by gold strikes in Minas Gerais during the waning years of the seventeenth century and the resulting windfall of precious metals and diamonds which were extracted from Brazil in the early decades of the eighteenth century. Dom José I's reign

(1750–1777) was dominated by the energetic and ironfisted ministry of Sebastião José de Carvalho e Mello (1699–1782), better known to posterity by his later title, the Marquis of Pombal, who rose to power in the wake of the catastrophic Lisbon earthquake of 1755.

Pombal's strident, yet efficient, emergency measures quickly stabilised the country: he brutally repressed the social anarchy spawned by the disaster, executing looters and fixing the prices of food, building materials, and rents.[14] After overseeing the reconstruction of Lisbon, his power consolidated, he shifted his reforming gaze to the Inquisition, the Jesuits and the peninsular as well as the ultramarine economy, attempting to reconfigure their relationship. After the death of Dom José, the fall of Pombal, and the accession of Dona Maria I, the pace of reforms slowed but still continued in both Portugal and Brazil in the decades preceding the court's forced migration, under British tutelage, to Rio de Janeiro in late 1807.[15]

The reformers of the Iberian monarchies shared more in common than may, at first, appear obvious. Policy makers in both Lisbon and Madrid grappled with the challenge of how to galvanise vast colonial possessions in order to raise their respective nations into the first rank of the European powers while simultaneously preventing the wealth of empire from being drained by economically more vigorous rivals and allies. If the events of 1807–1808 revealed such an aspiration to be little more than a chimera, the reforms undertaken in the final decades of the eighteenth century indicate that the dissolution of the Iberian empires was far from apparent to those who directed the metropolitan and ultramarine bureaucracies.

Though Portuguese and Spanish imperial reform possessed distinct, even idiosyncratic qualities which complicate facile comparison, one common feature that lends itself to comparative analysis is the critical emulation of the policies and practices of competitor empire-states, especially Great Britain. By studying how statesmen, political writers and colonial administrators conceived of British political economy's impact the British empire, it may be possible to understand with greater clarity the similarities and differences between Spanish and Portuguese imperial policy.

The use of foreign ideas was not mere fashion, but crucial to state survival in the tumultuous decades of the late eighteenth century. Souza Coutinho succinctly made this point when he wrote that 'given the present state of learning in Europe, with the *luzes* diffused generally throughout the continent, those states and nations which have played the most important role in politics are those which have protected and encouraged the *luzes*'.[16] By politics, of course, was meant international relations. Spain was embroiled almost continuously in global and local wars between 1759 and 1808, whereas Portugal was frequently, if less violently, sucked into conflicts due to its centuries-long alliance with Britain.[17] International conflict, paradoxically, gave impetus to the emulation of one state's institutions and policies by another. Faced with excruciating defensive and fiscal pressures, Spanish and Portuguese reformers necessarily coveted, and sought to reproduce, successfully implemented policy innovations. Policy makers thus mingled cosmopolitan sensibilities with patriotic allegiance and were committed to employing the common European stock of ideas for the improvement of their respective countries.[18]

Bourbon and Pombaline reformers emulated rival European powers in areas of administrative, fiscal or military policy in which the respective Iberian counterpart was deemed comparatively deficient. Emulation promised rapid improvement and mitigated the risk of failure associated with policy experimentation.[19] Although the emulation of successful practices of competitor states was urged, failed or misguided policy also could be invoked as an albatross, a symbol of a course of action whose replication might prove counterproductive in the pursuit of geopolitical greatness. Political writers and ministers, therefore, dissected, analysed, and either lauded or rejected, the ideas, institutions, reforms and character of rival empires. Such emulation was pragmatic, a scramble for viable models with which to compete against those same states whose policies were emulated or rejected.[20] As foreign models were encountered, modified and incorporated, both Bourbon and Braganza policy goals, content and instruments increasingly came to resemble those of its rivals.[21] Incessant war, mercantile rivalry and the drive for power resulted in policy convergence and a movement toward institutional isomorphism across Europe's Atlantic empires. Emulation could serve as a 'vehicle for *grandeza*, a quest for national pre-eminence'. It came to be viewed as a 'patriotic duty, motivated by the love of country and serving national honour'.[22]

In Portugal, the tendency to emulate other European states was prevalent. Often it was the failure to exploit a resource of considerable commercial potential that encouraged political writers to consult foreign models for inspiration. Concerning silk production, for example, Souza Coutinho noted that 'the utility to the nation, the increase of its revenue and the example of the nations of the North [of Europe] are the strongest and most decisive factors in favour of [the silk industry's] encouragement'. He lamented that 'we witness Prussia battling against the dictates of its climate, aided by its king, to produce silk which previously was deemed impossible. How can Portugal, then, with its benign climate and countless advantages not achieve the same result?'[23] In this case, then, Portugal's laggard pace, notwithstanding its natural endowment, led Souza Coutinho to invoke the example of foreign practice and hold it up as a model for emulation. Nor was this trend confined to the administrative elite. On the contrary, Brazil's viceroy, in 1783, would complain that Rio's merchants 'always embrace novelties, which are unusual and deprecate [Portuguese] products because they are not foreign'.[24] Such fashions are important because even if the mercantilist system kept, notwithstanding substantial spillage, commodities and manufactured products within each imperial system, ideas and styles moved with greater ease across national and imperial boundaries.

Spanish commentators, too, embraced emulation as a salutary or, at least, an inevitable, ubiquitous tendency. A high-ranking official argued that nations whose commerce flourished 'emulate that which is most advantageous'.[25] Spain, he implored, should 'open its eyes' and 'follow the right methods' in order to sustain its 'legitimate and lofty independence and perhaps achieve parity' with France and England.[26] An influential political economist urged the creation of learned academies modelled on English and French precedents. These institutions would, he asserted, 'enable [Spain] better to imitate the curious inventions of others, and also to make useful discoveries ourselves, of such things that are serviceable to a foreign and home trade'.[27] Count Pedro Rodríguez de Campomanes, one of the architects of reform during the reign of Charles III, concurred, pleading that 'by means of their academies, the empire of the arts has been appropriated, and the rest of the Europe merely copies their inventions'. With academies, this minister declared, Spain could 'reach the same level and, within a few years, overcome its backwardness and regain the time that it has lost'.[28] Such institutions were established gradually, but other techniques were employed in the interim, including industrial espionage. For example, when Jorge Juan made a secret mission to England in 1749–1750, he was instructed to observe practices as diverse as the use of steam power, port-sweeping methods and the design of British warships, not to mention engage in the clandestine recruitment of English shipwrights.[29]

Like their Portuguese contemporaries, Spanish political writers did not merely copy and servilely imitate, but rather engaged actively in criticising, adapting, and sometimes rejecting, foreign ideas. Campomanes contended that imitation and adaptation were potentially creative acts. He insisted that certain 'arts and professions originated in a new combination of [existing] objects, and this is what is called invention'.[30] These 'new combinations' and 'inventions' would prove vital to Spain's capacity to compete with its geopolitical rivals. In this sense, the union of cosmopolitanism and patriotism defines emulation in late eighteenth-century Spain.[31]

The preoccupation of Crown officials and political writers with colonial economy and agricultural improvement produced a deep, if often overlooked, fascination with Britain. Spain's recovery lay in following the recommendations of 'a variety of authors, both our own and foreigners, and even of our enemies'.[32] In the late eighteenth century, there was no greater threat to Spain's Atlantic empire than England, which aspired, many Spaniards believed, to be 'master of universal commerce in both hemispheres'.[33] War with England, however, whether hot or cold, was a constant factor in Spanish foreign affairs between 1713 and 1808.[34] Since the demands of geopolitical competition were one of the major spurs of Bourbon reform, it is logical that Britain, Spain's chief adversary, would profoundly impact Spanish ideas about political and economic regeneration.

Several examples furnish evidence for the pervasiveness of the images of Britain in Spanish political discourse. Colonial governance garnered approbation, for example, as British America was 'watched by all of Europe, a true theatre, in which outstanding achievements are performed'.[35] In naval affairs, Antonio de Ulloa's praised Britain's diligent, steady nurturing of its fleet: '[Britain] always attends to its navy, dedicating to it a firm determination, [an attitude] which has long been sustained.... Far from having waited for other nations to invent useful things for its use, it has hurried to make the most ingenious discoveries, to its great benefit'.[36] Even the English constitution was invoked favourably by reformers: whereas Spain and France were 'compound' monarchies and 'disconnected pieces linked to one another without mutual adhesion', it was argued, in England 'nothing is divided and, therefore, one senses the immense power of royal authority' which 'helped to form a close union between the nobility and the people'.[37] Beyond specific political, administrative and military institutions, Britain's alleged public spiritedness, which assisted in the 'triumph of its government', mesmerised Spaniards while simultaneously provoking self-pity because 'patriotism sparks in the hearts of our rivals a vigorous activity which is [still] unknown to us'.[38]

These depictions and attitudes toward Britain reveal a fascination with its enviable prosperity, stable institutions, and national character. Bourbon political writers and policy makers moved beyond the vague stereotypes sketched in the previous paragraph. They delved deeper, fully engaging with one feature of Britain's intellectual life that was especially important to their reform ambitions: political economy.

Some scholars have questioned the extent and intensity of Iberian interest in British political economy. One historian has argued that before 1760, with the notable exception of the 1753 Spanish translation of Joshua Gee's *The Trade and Navigation of Great Britain Considered* (1729), 'references to British authors were practically nonexistent and of little significance'.[39] Translations from French to Spanish of the works of Herbert (1755), Mirabeau (1764) and Forbonnais (1765), among others, it must be conceded, preceded those of Grenville (1770), Davenant (1779), Hume (1789), and Smith (1794).[40]

The absence of direct translations and the relative paucity of English books, however, did not preclude the formative influence of English ideas.[41] News concerning, and précis of, English books was widespread from the 1760s, finding expression in publications like the *Diario Estrangero* (1763) and the *Estafeta de Londres* (1762).[42] English texts often were transmitted through a third language, most commonly French.

The Bourbon reformers engaged with, and disseminated widely, works of British political economy. Representative of the policy intelligentsia, Campomanes supported the diffusion of economic knowledge, regardless of its provenance.[43] 'Academic chairs for the teaching of the true rules of commerce have been established in Naples and Milan....The reading of economic works is absolutely needed in order to learn certain cardinal rules.'[44] He informed his readers of the several 'excellent works published abroad, which recently have been translated', and reassured them that 'notes and reflections to accommodate them to our soil' would be appended.[45] He referred his audience to 'J. Child on the progress of the Spanish colonies in the Americas'.[46] Furthermore, among Campomanes's unpublished works was a translation of Davenant's 'On the Use of Political Arithmetic'.[47] English political economy was, therefore, a key source for Campomanes's proposals concerning Spain's potential regeneration.

Campomanes often extolled the utility of seventeenth-century English political economy. As early as 1761, he lauded 'this most useful calculus to compare the strength of nations with respect to one another, drawing on the principles of Petty and Davenant in England, which also were praised by our Uztáriz'.[48] In his *Industria Popular* (1774), he argued that the English 'have been those who most accurately used this type of calculation, whose books should be consulted' and, subsequently, observed that 'the study of the English language is of great importance to understand the excellent writings and insights relative to the improvement of industry'.[49] Indeed, a perusal of the catalogue of Campomanes's personal library (as of 1778) reveals multiple works by English writers in French translation, including John Cary, Josiah Child, David Hume, Joshua Gee, Bernard Mandeville, Charles King, and Arthur Young.[50]

The admiration of Britain by Spanish political writers should not obscure the critical dimension of their treatment of foreign practices. Far from a passive or derivative process, Spanish engagement with British texts and practices was highly selective. Some political writers even disagreed that emulation was a path to national regeneration. 'Every nation', Juan Sempere y Guarinos contended, 'esteems itself above the others, and believes that its land, practices and customs are better than those of the rest of the universe'.[51] He maintained that Spanish writers furnished adequate resources, making recourse to foreigners superfluous. Sempere y Guarinos argued that 'it is not necessary to turn to Montesquieu, Hume, Melon or any other foreign writers, whose ideas are suspicious for not having been careful always to unite the demands of religion with those of politics'.[52]

Hostile assessments of Britain's supposedly quintessential values percolated as well. One influential diplomat voiced suspicion of, and hostility toward, British ultramarine designs, which he claimed emerged from a combination of 'dark and hidden maxims', 'ambition' and 'excessive pride'.[53] Other commentators castigated the 'dominant character of the English, the love of liberty, its most violent passion'.[54] The future minister of the Indies, José de Gálvez, distanced himself from this 'violent passion': 'We do not aspire', he wrote, 'to entirely adapt the liberty and other maxims of the English, because we recognize of course the great differences between the two states'.[55] Such recognition of the contradictions and potential fallibility ensured that admiration for English models never became sycophantic.

The image of England also played a crucial role in the Duke of Almodóvar's *Historia Política de los Establecimientos Ultramarinos de las Naciones Europeas* (*Political History of European Overseas Settlements*), published in Madrid between 1784 and 1790.[56] He utilised contemporary reports of English atrocities in India to undermine the cultural chauvinism that he perceived permeated European accounts of the Spanish Conquest, culminating in the still ubiquitous 'Black Legend'.[57] In a voluminous appendix entitled 'The English Constitution and the Affairs of the English East India Company', Almodóvar lavished considerable attention on the Company which previously 'had conducted itself well relative to other companies, better conserving the customs, discipline and vigor than those of other nations'. In Bengal, however, this laudable conduct degenerated and had 'altered and corrupted all the sources of confidence and public happiness'. He did not refute the Black Legend explicitly, but rather tarnished England's reputation for being 'so reflexive, philosophical, generous and such a good friend of liberty'. England had, according to Almodóvar's account, 'stained its glories' by its recent reprehensible conduct in India and demonstrated itself to be 'cruel, haughty, avaricious and unjust'.[58] In this way, Almodóvar appropriated the language of the Black Legend, formerly used exclusively to denigrate Spanish colonialism, and imposed it on the British. A type of counter-emulation was urged, in which Britain's imperial excesses were impugned as conduct to be both derided and avoided.

Whether expressing approbation or opprobrium, it must be added, most Spanish political writers did not estimate Britain to be superior to Spain. It is implicit, perhaps, in all comparisons, that the gap between the prosperity and power of the two empire-states was not insuperable. In the wake of the British capture of Havana in 1762, one influential optimist, Agustín Craywinckel, compared the two empires, noting that Spain's superiority in geographical size, the fertility of its land, and the produce of its colonies should have precluded such a debacle had resources been exploited properly and allocated efficiently. Everything, he argued, suggested that Spain should be a 'great, happy and powerful' country. Britain's greater revenues, then, were attributable to 'the better disposition' of its 'arts, fishing industry, agriculture, navigation and commerce', whereas Spain remained 'quite languid'.

Craywinckel rejected the attribution of the divergence of fortunes, as many of his contemporaries did, to a 'different genius, or character', dismissing the notion of the 'laborious and diligent' Englishman and the 'lazy and distracted' Spaniard. The difference lay in government policy. 'If Spain were governed in the same way that England is', he predicted, 'within a few years it would be superior in power and wealth'.[59] Such optimism concerning Spain's future fortunes and the role of the 'British model' in bringing this result about may be found in Pablo de Olavide's agrarian reform proposals, which explicitly endorsed Spain's imitation of the historical trajectory of British agriculture as a guarantor of prosperity:

> England, that powerful and populated kingdom, was before in the same situation in which today Spain finds itself. It was devoted to the same erroneous principles and was poor, depopulated and miserable. Then a ray of light penetrated its government and transformed its

> legislation. Since then, it has protected cultivation and encouraged the employment of fallow lands. And, by changing this aspect of its legislation, it became populated and wealthy. This system is followed today by all nations that pursue the well-being of their people.[60]

But if there was little doubt, apart from its rapacity and hypocrisy in South Asia and North America, that Great Britain was a worthy model for emulation, there was significant debate concerning which lessons, precisely, should be drawn from the British experience and which policies, exactly, might be efficaciously replicated. Opinion divided most starkly, perhaps unsurprisingly, concerning the regulation of colonial commerce.

Debates concerning the relative merits of free trade and privileged companies were notably boisterous in the Spanish empire.[61] By the early eighteenth century, Spanish political economists endorsed both Spain's absolute monopoly and the virtues of privileged trading companies. They attributed Spain's economic stagnation to the composition of its foreign and domestic trade and to its poor shipping facilities, both of which precipitated otherwise reducible outflows of precious metals. These factors, among others, led Spain to fall behind its imperial rivals. One mid-century Spanish political writer noted, 'The spirit of commerce has been born and is spreading among the modern nations.... We sleep while they pass the night in fervent activity.'[62] Privileged companies, it was hoped, could help to improve Spain's lagging position, overcome the mercantile superiority of other nations, and foment commerce in less developed parts of the empire where the absence of Spanish trade had engendered rampant contraband. Campomanes, normally an ardent opponent of privileged trade, glumly credited the seventeenth-century Navigation Acts for the discrepancy between the Spanish and British empires:

> By means of [the Navigation Acts] the English violate commercial treaties.... By ill fortune Spain was oppressed by wars in all parts of the world while England prepared the foundation for its mercantile revolution; it is possible to infer that [from this point] Spain's backward slide began, ignorant as it was of the true principles of commerce.[63]

Spain, Campomanes implied, might match Britain's ascendance if its policies were underpinned by such 'true principles'. Almodóvar also praised the 'fortunate tyrant' Cromwell for his 'famous Acts of Navigation by which the commerce and marine of England flourishes even today'.

Privileged companies also were meritorious in Almodóvar's view, especially when their 'ancient relations and established credit made them indispensable'. He implored the reader, 'the man of healthy judgment', not to be seduced by the cries of '*commercial liberty* and *civil liberty*'. He warned that economic writers purveying such schemes promised advantages which often proved to be nothing but a 'chimera'.[64]

By the final third of the eighteenth century, however, Spanish opinion had turned against privileged trading companies. They had failed to lower prices, improve the quality of goods, introduce new methods or establish a stable and secure commercial system. The touted free trade (*comercio libre*) decrees of 1765 and 1778 eliminated some of the regulations constricting Spanish colonial commerce, represented a potential death knell of existing chartered companies, and appeared to prefigure an embrace of freer oceanic trade.[65]

By the mid-1780s, though, the shortcomings of the new, less regulated approach prompted Madrid's policy makers to return to the more regulated practices of the past and thus simultaneously experiment with combinations of freer trade and privileged companies in the hopes of discovering a formula for lasting prosperity. It was in the decades of the 1760s, 1770s, and 1780s, then, when the example of England became a feature of these debates and was used both by partisans of privileged trade and by apostles of less regulated commerce, on both sides of the Atlantic. In 1794, Adam Smith's Spanish translator, perhaps unsurprisingly, mocked Britain for having granted trading companies sovereign power and the right to maintain garrisons and fortifications in overseas dominions, particularly in Bengal.[66] In this way, the 'English model' was far from monolithic. Instead, several purported 'English' models percolated and were drawn upon in peninsular Spanish debates. The Navigation Acts, classical political economy, and the English East India Company could be invoked to make radically different arguments about the surest path to prosperity.

Whereas the discussion concerning the regulation of colonial commerce in peninsular Spain mainly arose from the reading of published texts, some ultramarine participants in these debates drew on firsthand observation. In particular, colonial intellectuals pointed to Britain's nine-month occupation of Havana in 1762–1763 at the end of the Seven Years' War as a case study for the benefits of less regulated trade to an rapidly expanding, slave-dependent sugar economy. In the wake of Britain's withdrawal, Madrid sent Alejandro O'Reilly to survey the damage wrought and to recommend policies for Cuba's renewal. O'Reilly, however, reported that the British conduct, far from deleterious, had amply demonstrated 'the infinite advantages' offered by the 'expansion of commerce', marvelling at the wealth accrued by the British during their nine-month occupation.[67]

In a report submitted three years later, Agustín Crame, an engineer who accompanied O'Reilly's fact-finding expedition, bluntly stated that the British occupation of Havana had 'opened [Cuban] eyes', awakening its inhabitants from their 'remarkable ignorance'. Crame clearly was referring to the 4,000 African slaves introduced during the occupation, a figure which dwarfed the total number of slaves sold into bondage in Cuba during the preceding five years, and who had supplied the forced labour necessary for the sugar industry's rapid expansion.[68] Other metropolitan voices concurred: Cuba's 'commerce would increase if it enacted policies like those of the English in the nine months that they were masters of but a single port.... If Spain were to renew this policy, there would be considerably less clandestine trade introduced in the island.'[69] While deploring the temporary loss of Havana, then, crown officials discerned its economic benefits and urged that certain British policies should be established. That the *comercio libre* decree of 1765 was issued so soon after O'Reilly's report was filed is surely more than a coincidence.

The British occupation of Havana continued to spur prospective reformers in subsequent decades. Francisco Arango y Parreño, who heaped elogiums on Britain's 'opulence', the 'beauty of its countryside', and the 'perfection of its cultivation', was more than a dilettante anglophile.[70] In his maiden speech to the *Consulado* in 1794, Arango asserted that Havana's agriculture had suffered as a 'victim of an exclusive monopoly company that shackled its industry'. While paying lip service to the 'tragic surrender' of 1762, he lauded the unintended, yet beneficent, results of the British occupation, which brought 'considerable wealth' to the island. Arango argued that, 'with their [African slaves] and free commerce, [Britain] accomplished more [in nine months] than we had in the previous seventy years'.[71]

Arango's glowing appraisal of British practices was shared by Havana's Economic Society, whose members admired the 'progress of [England's] agriculture by indefatigable constancy' and 'continued relish for the perfection of rural practices' which had brought 'abundance to that kingdom'. The Economic Society also lauded Britain's 'foreign commerce, which had increased prodigiously and [enabled England to] amass wealth and population'.[72] When Arango contended that it was necessary to 'transplant to our soil the advantages achieved by foreign nations by means of their greater knowledge', the thinly veiled allusion to British trade policy in 1762–1763 would not have been lost on his contemporaries.[73]

The preceding section has suggested the critical engagement of Spanish reformers with, and their intellectual appetite for, the political and economic practices of other European states, especially their administration of their overseas possessions and their conduct of colonial commerce. Various, sometimes clashing, images of Britain were incorporated into Bourbon political discourse and applied to contemporary policy decisions confronting Spain's empire. The Bourbon reforms were far from a derivative affair or a pale shadow of developments in France and Britain; instead, emulation was distinguished by intellectual cross-pollination, a cosmopolitanism tempered by patriotic duty and religious piety, and a conviction that rival states might furnish the insights required to propel Spain to recover its diminished geopolitical greatness.

Images of Britain were as numerous and influential in the Portuguese empire as they were in that of Spain. It could be argued that the British model, whether lauded or disparaged, had more of a directly discernible impact on policy in Portugal than in Spain due to its central place in the political and economic thought of the Marquis of Pombal. Pombal has been characterised accurately as an 'enlightened Iberian economic nationalist' who 'devised measures to retain capital within his own economic system…and to diminish the negative impact of being a producer of precious metals'.[74] It was during Pombal's ascendancy that the Luso-Brazilian commercial system was revamped: sugar, tobacco and gold were protected by legislation, new revenue-generating mechanisms were established, and long-delayed administrative reforms were undertaken.[75]

The intellectual origins of Pombal's reform programme may be traced to formative stints of diplomatic service, especially his service in London between 1738 and 1743.[76] While it remains unclear whether or not he spoke English, Pombal compiled a library of 254 English titles, including works by William Petty, Charles Davenant, William Wood, Josiah Child and Jonathan Swift. His voracious appetite for British economic tracts, supplemented by firsthand observations of policy in Britain, were decisive in the overhaul of the state apparatuses in the Luso-Atlantic world which he later undertook after 1755. The influence of his diplomatic stint in London was remarked upon by contemporary English observers. Robert Southey, for example, in his *History of Brazil* (1816), noted that 'during his residence in London and Vienna, [Carvalho] caught something of the spirit which began to infect the circles of fashionable life, and the courts of Catholic princes'.[77]

Pombal's journals from this period further substantiate the claim for the indelible impact of his diplomatic stint in London. In his words, 'as one nation's riches and forces increase, it diminishes, to the same proportion, the capacities and power of the nation with whom it trades'. Following England's example, Pombal contended, Portugal should seek to import 'raw materials to process as manufactures' instead of sending its raw materials abroad.[78] But such backwardness was not immutable, and Pombal remained acutely aware that the application of the proper policies could radically alter the fortunes of states. As he noted several decades later in a letter to Lord Chatham, '[England] cut quite a meagre figure in Europe whilst we were already a great power.... We dominated the commerce of Asia, Africa and America whilst you ruled nothing but a poor isle off the coast of Europe'.[79] Yet if Portugal were to extricate itself from its current plight and regain its former geopolitical stature, Portugal's human capital would need replenishment.

In his journals dating from the 1740s, Pombal's chief lament, therefore, was Portugal's paucity of '*homens de estado* instructed in these affairs'. He argued that if Portugal 'reduced the art of commerce to a few simple and clear principles, practices and techniques, the number of merchants would multiply and the state's revenues would increase'.[80] Portugal's fortunes, therefore, depended on providing merchants with the technical skills and mentality required to flourish in overseas markets. Reflecting on the history of the English East India Company, Pombal concluded that the 'increase or ruin of these establishments depends most essentially on the ability of the directors and merchants'.[81] Pombal almost directly translated these observations into practice: the *Junta do Comércio* (Board of Trade), founded in 1755, established a school of commerce in 1759, making Portugal the first European nation to implement a system of technical and commercial education that was widespread and accessible.[82]

But if England was to be admired and perhaps emulated for its economic ascendancy, Pombal was acutely aware that such progress had come, at least partially, at Portugal's expense. Specifically, Pombal blamed the 1703 Methuen Treaty for the 'notorious decline in our marine and in our foreign and domestic commerce', adding that even this disadvantageous treaty was further 'abused and violated' by English merchants in Portugal.[83] The Methuen Treaty enshrined British penetration of the Portuguese market, permitting the duty-free entry of woollen goods into Lisbon and Porto and offering Portuguese wine reciprocal advantages on the British market. From the early eighteenth century, the massive influx of Brazilian gold was used by Portugal to reduce deficits and purchase foreign (mainly English) goods, which effectively smothered Portugal's domestic manufactures.[84] While Pombal's policies did much to circumvent and, indeed, reverse the ill effects of the Methuen Treaty, his tendency to blame it for Portugal's economic underperformance reverberated more generally in Portugal. 'Many of the Portuguese', Southey observed in the late 1790s, 'dislike the English influence and reprobate the Methuen Treaty as the ruin of their commerce'.[85]

Although Pombal recognised that 'all business conducted in foreign countries was insecure and contingent', due to the 'ambition and greed it inspired in other countries', he did not include colonial trade in this category. On the contrary, colonial commerce was, potentially, 'secure and perpetual', so long as 'foreigners were excluded' and adequate care was taken to 'watch over the colony's commerce'.[86] Pombal was thus faced with several dilemmas, of which the most important was to balance Portugal's dependence on its military-diplomatic alliance with Britain while simultaneously circumventing the advantages enjoyed by Britain, sanctioned in the Methuen Treaty, in Portuguese markets in the Old World and the New.

The formula which Pombal struck upon to resolve the dilemma was the formation of monopoly companies and the rigorous prevention of contraband from entering Brazilian ports, policies which were taken from England's seventeenth-century geopolitical playbook, though now to be used to diminish Britain's advantages over Portugal in the eighteenth century. Pombal's preference for monopoly companies is foreshadowed in his London journals in which he had speculated on the usefulness of companies to 'fertilise' and 'sprout' colonial commerce. 'The utility of a company', he explained, 'is proven by the experience of all European states which have established them, collecting as a result great revenues'.[87] After his ascent to power, trading companies became an essential component of his political design, particularly the companies of Grão Pará and Maranhão, by which Pombal sought to develop new export commodities, such as cotton and rice, which were not affected by previous commercial treaties.[88] In 1755, Pombal would describe such companies as the 'only way to reclaim the commerce of all Portuguese America from the hands of foreigners'.[89] These trading companies remained in existence until Pombal's fall from power in 1778, after which time a freer trade regime was established.[90]

Alongside the system of monopolies for the less developed areas of Brazil, Pombal instructed the leading crown officials to vigorously repress contraband, particularly that arriving on British ships. Pombal's attitude toward clandestine trade is clearly revealed in a letter to Viceroy Lavradio: 'underlying [Britain's] pacific system of commerce is an insufferable perfidy'.[91] Furthermore, responding to Lavradio's concern that British ships were attempting to use of Brazilian ports citing the diplomatic alliance between Portugal and Britain, Pombal wrote that 'each kingdom or sovereign state, has its unique laws, regulated according to its particular interests.... It obeys such laws that conform to both natural right and international law'.[92] Pombal's attitude toward Britain, then, was highly ambivalent. Certain features of its colonial system, especially companies, were regarded as worthy of Portugal's emulation, whereas its influence on the revival of Portugal's oceanic commerce and peninsular industry was deemed deleterious.

Although Pombal's legacy has been deeply contested ever since his fall from power in the late 1770s, aspects of his policy were staunchly defended. Rodrigo de Souza Coutinho would praise the efficacy of his godfather's policies in an undated letter to the Abbé Raynal:

> In 1755, the nation was submerged in superstition and ignorance, without agriculture, industry and commerce.... In 1777, the royal treasury was full, accounts were in order, the navy could be found in a good state, and the army adhered to a new standard of discipline.... This record cannot but place [Pombal] among the first rank of ministers of state[93]

Souza Coutinho did not, of course, explicitly refer to emulation of England as a factor in the success of Pombaline reform. On the contrary, it seems, the methods of enlightened absolutist regimes seemed as meritorious as those of constitutional monarchies, including that of England. In a dispatch from 1791, Souza Coutinho remarked that 'absolutist governments can produce a level of public prosperity not inferior not merely to the absurd and unstable government of France, but also to those governments in which the principles of liberty are perfectly understood and where limited monarchy exists, as in England'.[94] Clearly, then, the English model was not deemed the only one capable achieving the ends toward which Souza Coutinho believed government should strive.

Furthermore, Souza Coutinho offered some praise for British practice and did not uncompromisingly laud Pombaline policy's anti-British orientation. For example, the monopoly system which Pombal had set up in order to regulate the post wine trade was fiercely criticised by Souza Coutinho.[95] He urged the Crown to 'destroy such a ruinous system, so absurd in every way, and substitute the system practiced in England' in its place, a curious suggestion since Britain's policy had been its original inspiration. Should such a change be adopted, Dom Rodrigo asserted, 'our sovereign would double or even triple the state's revenue and also bolster the progress of agriculture, alleviate poverty and cause the nation's wealth to increase'.[96] Nor was this emulation of Britain a limited case: Souza Coutinho commissioned a list of English books concerning agriculture to be drawn up which would 'provide the best ideas which we can take advantage of'.[97] In Souza Coutinho's thought, then, as in Pombal's, the English model was engaged with frequently, but critically, and emulation was highly selective.

The call for emulation of Britain was not limited to Pombal and Souza Coutinho. The example of Britain would be employed by political writers and administrators urging concrete shifts in the following policy areas: population, agriculture, international commerce, and financing of public works. Britain's rapid population of its Atlantic colonies impressed Portuguese observers who maintained that the same result might be achieved in Mozambique. 'England has planted thriving colonies in New England, New Georgia [*sic*] and Nova Scotia', one commentator wrote, and 'in but a few years it has filled these places with thousands of vassals whose number have aggrandised the greatness of the British Crown'.[98] With regard to agricultural prosperity, England too was a model for careful study. One political writer offered an anecdote he claimed was derived from Neapolitan policy in order to emphasise the point that 'agriculture is not something learned by chance; it is an art, even a science, and is rather difficult to master'. The same writer related that

> when the king of Naples wanted to improve the agriculture of his kingdom, he sent an intelligent man to apprentice himself to one of the most successful farmers in England, in order to learn the best techniques. Upon his return [to Naples], the king ordered that this man set up a school, and gave him land upon which he could practice, for the benefit of all, what he had learned abroad.[99]

In a similar vein, and contrary to Pombal's assessment, some commentators argued that competition with English manufactures on the Portuguese domestic market produced an overall salutary effect. As

Domingos Vandelli concluded, 'first, because the people bought goods of better quality at a lower price; second, that such competition would compel our manufacturers to perfect their products'.[100] Even British public finance garnered enthusiasm. Brazilian viceroy Luís de Vasconcellos called for a lottery to be established in order to finance public works in the infrastructure-poor capital of Rio de Janeiro, favourably invoking the example of Britain's lotteries which permitted that country to 'sustain excessive expenses in time of war'.[101]

The bevy of examples, from an array of Portuguese and Brazilian documents, both ultramarine and peninsular, suggest the robust engagement with English practices, policies and ideas, especially political economy. Yet modification, revision and selective omission were all integral aspects of this process. Portuguese reformers, like their Spanish counterparts, did not blindly follow foreign practices. Vandelli, prominent natural scientist and director of the Royal Botanical Garden at Ajuda, argued that 'we have an almost exorbitant abundance of economic books, written in many languages, but not everything contained in these books is applicable to the climate of this country'.[102] Even such an unrepentant anglophile as the Bahia-born, Coimbra-educated political economist José da Silva Lisboa was not, it must be stressed, a proponent of uncritical emulation of Britain. In fact, he repeatedly warned that blind copying could yield pernicious consequences. He therefore rejected proposals to nurture British-style manufactures in Brazil. 'If we attempt to introduce them here, solely driven by the spirit of rivalry, spurred by mere imitation of foreign precedent', he chided, 'such action would diminish our agriculture, exports and maritime trade'.[103] Similarly, he repudiated the English Navigation Acts, hailed by Pombal and many of his successors as venerable models, describing the formation of such companies as a 'great error'.[104] He warned that 'imitation would result in a sad parody of English policy, which is not a model of *liberalidade* in every respect'. The Navigation Acts, he contended, only made sense given Britain's geographic position, whereas their implementation would prove ruinous in other countries operating under different constraints. Such misapplication, he warned, 'has caused many injustices, political animosities, and wars'.[105] According to Silva Lisboa, it was late eighteenth-century Britain's turn toward less regulated trade, not seventeenth-century Britain's protectionism, that deserved emulation in the Luso-Brazilian world.

As in Spain, the mania for English institutions was derided by certain sectors in Portugal. This tendency became more pronounced after 1815 when the royal family failed to return the seat of the monarchy to

Lisbon, preferring to remain in Rio de Janeiro even after the conclusion of the French Revolutionary Wars. In 1808 and 1810, Brazilian ports were opened to British trade, and this hurt Portuguese merchants who were suddenly deprived of the advantages conferred by colonial monopoly. Anglophobia rose in response to these changing events. With his characteristic biting wit, José Agonstinho de Macedo remarked that he was 'impressed' how Portuguese who 'after taking a stroll around Falmouth or visiting the dunes, suddenly consider themselves very wise, literate, gifted, instructed, and capable of governing the world'.[106] This suspicion drew strength from mounting hostility toward Britain because of its effective military occupation of Portugal after 1814 and its decisive role in separating Brazil from Portugal. As a supporter of the pretender Dom Miguel observed in 1828, it was from English involvement in Portuguese affairs beginning in 1807 that 'we can date the beginning of Portugal's humiliation, the beginning of an era in which more was lost than during the sixty years that Portugal was under Spanish rule'.[107]

Nevertheless, though eschewing all insinuations of the derivative nature of the Luso-Brazilian enlightenment, it is equally clear that the mechanisms by which foreign ideas and models entered into the Luso-Atlantic world have been understudied and that Britain offered one possible alternative to the obstinacy of old ways. If its example inspired reformers, they proceeded cautiously and chose selectively. Like their Spanish counterparts, Luso-Brazilian engagement with foreign practices resulted not in bland copies of a British original but in complex, hybrid forms adjusted to the particular conditions encountered in the Atlantic World.

* * *

This chapter sought to make several points of interest to eighteenth-century specialists: the centrality of emulation and comparison in statecraft; imitation's role in the processes by which ideologies of development were shaped; and the intellectual repercussions of geopolitical competition. But there is a larger point of interest, perhaps, to a broader cohort of historians. Since Franco Venturi's pioneering work, historians have grown accustomed to discussing the *circulation* of ideas, their transmission and exchange across borders, oceans, and linguistic groups. By tracing footnotes, reconstructing the history of a translation of a book, or reconstructing the intellectual network of a particular traveller who helped to disseminate or popularise a certain idea, our understanding of the movement of ideas is immeasurably enriched.

But it seems to me that the *generation*, or production, of political and economic ideas has not received the attention it deserves. How were ideas reshaped, modified, and distorted/enhanced as they moved across space over time? The circulation of ideas should be seen as one aspect of a larger process of the generation of knowledge. What the study of the Iberian reformers of the late eighteenth century suggests is that the task of making English ideas and experience relevant to Spanish or Portuguese political life involved much more than translating those texts from one language into another or invoking an eminent foreign writer to bolster the authority of a claim. It was instead a process of adaptation, of manipulating insights gleaned from one national context to provoke a new debate. In some cases, the original model or inspiration was discarded or mutilated beyond recognition. In other cases, the original source's influence remained discernible. The circulation of ideas was an indispensable first step in the creation of new, hybrid forms of knowledge in the late eighteenth-century Atlantic empires. From this cosmopolitan exchange of ideas sprang resurgent imperial states whose resulting internecine conflicts would destroy everything they had sought to retain and improve upon through reform inspired by emulation of their rivals.

Notes

The author thanks the following institutions for the material support that facilitated the research upon which this essay draws: Trinity College, Cambridge; Harvard University; the British Academy; and the Portuguese Fulbright Commission.

1. Sebastião José de Carvalho e Melo [later Marquis of Pombal], *Escritos Económicos de Londres (1741–1742)* (Lisbon, 1986), 158.
2. Robert Southey, *Letters Written During a Short Residence in Spain and Portugal*, 2nd ed. (Bristol, 1799), 141.
3. B[iblioteca] del P[alacio] R[eal] (Madrid) II/2896, 'Relación del Gobierno del Exmo. Sr. D. Josef de Ezpeleta ... a su Succesor el Exmo. D. Pedro Mendinueta' (1796), fos. 321–2.
4. Rodrigo de Souza Coutinho, 'Reflexões Políticas sobre os Motivos da Prosperidade da Agricultura deste País, que Servem a Fazer Praticamente as Vantajosas Consequências dos Sábios Princípios Adoptados (1789)', in Souza Coutinho, *Textos Políticos, Económicos e Financeiros (1783–1811)*, vol. I (Lisbon, 1993), 141; Souza Coutinho held the post of Secretary for the Navy and Colonial Dominions until 1801. He later served as Secretary of State for War and Foreign Affairs, following the Portuguese Monarchy's forced relocation to Rio de Janeiro from 1808 until his death in 1812.
5. Souza Coutinho, 'Recopilação dos Oficios Expedidos de Turim no Ano de 1786', 3 January 1787, in Souza Coutinho, *Textos Políticos (1783–1811)*, vol. I, 79.

6. A[rquivo] N[acional] de R[io] de J[aneiro], Estado, Cod. 67, vol. 23, Rodrigo de Souza Coutinho to Conde de Rezende, 2 January 1798 and 2 March 1798; n.b. since Brazil had no printing press until 1808, the *memorias* either would have been printed in Portugal and shipped to Brazil or else copied by hand and circulated in manuscript within a small circle of crown officials.
7. G.W. Pigman, 'Versions of Imitation in the Renaissance', *Renaissance Quarterly* 33, no. 1 (1980): 4, 22, 25, 32.
8. Daisy Ripodas Ardanaz, *Refracción de Ideas en Hispanoamérica Colonial* (Buenos Aires, 1983), 35; for treatment of this phenomenon in another national context, see Sophus A. Reinert, 'Blaming the Medici: Footnotes, Falsification, and the Fate of the "English Model" in eighteenth-century Italy', *History of European Ideas* 32, no. 4 (2006): 430–55.
9. Emma Rothschild, 'The English *Kopf*', in Donald Winch and Patrick O'Brien (eds), *The Political Economy of the British Historical Experience, 1688–1914* (Oxford, 2002), 31.
10. Eliga Gould, 'Entangled Histories, Entangled Worlds: The English-Speaking Atlantic as a Spanish Periphery', *American Historical Review* 112, no. 3 (2007): 764–86 passim.
11. For classic overviews of the Bourbon reforms for peninsular Spain, see Richard Herr, *The Eighteenth Century Revolution in Spain* (Princeton, 1958) and Charles Noel, 'Charles III of Spain', in H. M. Scott (ed.), *Enlightened Absolutism: Reform and Reformers in Later Eighteenth-Century Europe* (London, 1990); for Spanish America, see D.A. Brading, 'Bourbon Spain and its American Empire', in Leslie Bethell (ed.), *Cambridge History of Latin America,* vol. I (Cambridge, 1984) and Stanley Stein and Barbara Stein, *Apogee of Empire: Spain and New Spain in the Age of Charles III* (Baltimore and London, 2003).
12. J. H. Elliott, 'A Europe of Composite Monarchies', *Past and Present* 137 (1992): 48–71 passim.
13. J. H. Elliott, *Empires of the Atlantic World: Britain and Spain in America 1492–1830* (New Haven and London, 2006), 307–8.
14. Kenneth Maxwell, *Pombal: Paradox of the Enlightenment* (Cambridge, 1995), 24.
15. For an overview of the Pombaline and post-Pombaline periods, in addition to the studies by Maxwell already cited, see Francisco José Calazans Falcon, *A Época Pombalina (Política, Econômia e Monarquia Ilustrada)* (São Paulo, 1982); for an intellectual history of the period in transatlantic perspective, see Maria de Lourdes Viana Lyra, *A Utopia do Poderoso Império: Portugal e Brasil, Bastidores da Política 1798–1822* (Rio de Janeiro, 1994), esp. 42–133.
16. Souza Coutinho, 'Discurso em que se Prova a Necessidade e Utilidade dos Estudos e Conhecimentos Hidrodinâmicas em Portugal (1787)', in Souza Coutinho, *Textos Políticos (1783–1811)*, vol. I, 174.
17. In the case of Spain, for example, these included: the misguided intervention in the Seven Years' War; the botched invasion of Portugal (1762); the *Monitorio* conflict with the Papacy and the protracted expulsion of the Jesuits (1766–1773) from Spanish dominions; the disastrously amateurish invasion of Algiers (1776); incessant conflict with Britain which led to intervention in the American Revolution (1779–1783), wrangling over the Mosquito Coast (until 1786), and contention over the Nootka Sound (1790–1791); a profligate war against revolutionary France (1793–1796); economically crippling wars with regicide France against Britain (1796–1802 and 1804–1808); and the eventual occupation of Spain by Napoleonic forces (1808–1814).

18. This insight is adapted from John Robertson's, 'Analysis of Franco Venturi', *The Case for the Enlightenment: Scotland and Naples 1680–1760* (Cambridge, 2005), 38.
19. This framework is adapted from contemporary political science. Kurt Weyland, 'Introduction', in Weyland (ed.), *Learning from Foreign Models in Latin American Policy Reform* (Washington D.C., 2004), 21; as Weyland indicates, imitation of foreign models is not without pitfalls: the 'desire to copy promising practices in order not to fall behind...can expose policy makers to untested "fads and fashions" that hurt the quality of policy outputs'; see Weyland, 'Introduction', 5.
20. Some scholars choose to distinguish between emulation and other types of policy or ideological diffusion mechanisms, including 'coercion', 'learning' and 'competition'. For an overview of the most recent political science literature, see Beth Simmons, Frank Dobbin and Geoffrey Garrett, 'Introduction: The International Diffusion of Liberal Ideas', *International Organisation* 60 (2006): 781–810.
21. A modification of the framework proposed by Colin Bennett, 'What is Policy Convergence and What Causes it?' *British Journal of Political Science* 21, no. 2 (1991): 215–22 passim.
22. Istvan Hont, *Jealousy of Trade: International Competition and the Nation-State in Historical Perspective* (Cambridge, MA, 2005), 120–1.
23. Souza Coutinho, 'Reflexões Políticas', 127.
24. ANRJ, Estado, Cod. 67, vol. 11, Luis de Vasconcellos to Martinho de Mello e Castro, 14 September 1783.
25. BPR II/2829, Marqués de Llanos, 'Los Medios con que Puede Conseguir la Felicidad de la Monarquía' (1755), fo. 102v.
26. Eduardo Malo de Luque [Duke of Almodóvar], *Historia Política de los Establecimientos Ultramarinos de las Naciones Europeas*, vol. III (Madrid, 1784–1790), appendix, 68.
27. Gerónimo de Uztariz, *The Theory and Practice of Commerce and Maritime Affairs*, vol. II (London, 1751), 423; the impact of French mercantilist writers in Spain is treated in Stein and Stein, *Silver, Trade and War: Spain and America in the Making of Early Modern Europe* (Baltimore and London, 2000).
28. Pedro Rodríguez de Campomanes, *Discurso Sobre la Educación Popular de los Artesanos y su Fomento* (Madrid, 1775), 79. On Campomanes's life and thought, see Vicent Llombart, *Campomanes, Economista y Político de Carlos III* (Madrid, 1992).
29. Ivan Valdez Bubnov, *Naval Power and State Modernization: Spanish Shipbuilding Policy in the Eighteenth Century* (Ph.D. Dissertation, University of Cambridge, 2005), 158–60.
30. Campomanes, *Educación Popular*, 25.
31. This fusion has been recognised in other national contexts. On Naples and Scotland, for example, see Robertson, *The Case for the Enlightenment*, 38.
32. A[rchivo] H[istórico] N[acional] (Madrid) Estado 2927, no. 271, Craywinckel 'Utilidad que Podría Sacar España', 25.
33. AGI Estado 86A, no. 2, [José de Gálvez], 'Discurso y Reflecxiones [sic] de un Vasallo Sobre la Decadencia de Nuestras Indias Españolas' n.d., fo. 3v.
34. Antonio Domínguez Ortiz, *Sociedad y Estado en el Siglo XVIII Español* (Barcelona, 1990), 53.
35. Francisco Álvarez, *Noticia del Establecimiento y Población de las Colonias Inglesas en la América Septentrional* [1778] (Madrid, 2000), 3.

36. Antonio de Ulloa, *La Marina: Fuerzas Navales de la Europa y Costas de Berberia* (Cádiz, 1995).
37. Almodóvar, *Historia Política*, vol. II, appendix, 12.
38. *Espíritu de Los Mejores Diarios Que Se Publican en Europa*, no. 88 (24 January 1788), 798.
39. Llombart, *Campomanes*, 81, 82, fn. 46.
40. John Reeder, 'Bibliografía de Traducciones, al Castellano y Catalán, durante el Siglo XVIII, de Obras de Pensamiento Económico', *Moneda y Crédito* 126 (1973): 57–78 passim.
41. To my knowledge, no scholar has assessed how many Spaniards, at least who made up the ranks of the intelligentsia, spoke English. It has been impossible for me to ascertain which of the political writers and policy makers discussed in this essay spoke or read English, though their knowledge of English books, often through French translations, is incontestable. Eterio Pajares has called French the 'authentic cultural bridge between the languages and cultures of Spain and England'; see Pajares, 'Traducción Inglés-Español en el Siglo XVIII', *El Mundo Hispánico en el Siglo de las Luces* (Madrid, 1996), 992.
42. Francisco Sánchez-Blanco, *El Absolutismo y las Luces en el Reinado de Carlos III* (Madrid, 2003), 24.
43. On Campomanes's economic thought, see Manuel Bustos Rodríguez, *El Pensamiento Socio-Economico de Campomanes* (Oviedo, 1982); Laura Rodríguez Díaz, *Reforma e Ilustración en la España del Siglo XVIII* (Madrid, 1975).
44. Campomanes, *Discurso Sobre el Fomento de la Industria Popular* (Madrid, 1774), cxlix; there were many calls for Charles III to establish a chair of commerce in Spain as he had in Naples; see AHN Estado 3188, no. 377, Eugenio de Santiago Polomares, 'Establecimiento de una Escuela de Comercio en Madrid o Valencia', July 1786.
45. Campomanes, *Industria Popular*.
46. Pedro Rodríguez Campomanes, *Reflexiones sobre el comercio español a Indias* (Madrid, 1988), 233.
47. Concepción de Castro, *Campomanes: Estado y Reformismo Ilustrado* (Madrid, 1996), 69–70; also in the Archivo del Conde de Campomanes (Madrid), 20–4, 31–1.
48. Campomanes, *Itinerario de las Carreras de Posta de Dentro, y Fuera del Reyno [1761]* (Madrid, 2002), 1.
49. Campomanes, *Industria Popular*, cxliii fn., cli fn.
50. Llombart, *Campomanes*, 329–35 passim.
51. Juan Sempere y Guarinos, *Historia del Luxo y de las Leyes Suntuarias de España*, vol. II (Madrid, 1788), 167.
52. Sempere y Guarinos, *Historia del Luxo*, vol. II, 210.
53. A[rchivo] G[eneral] de S[imancas], Estado 7005, Almodóvar to Floridablanca, 25 May 1779.
54. A[rchivo] G[eneral] de I[ndias], Santa Fe 758B, 'Idea de la Obra de los Escritos de Coronel Roberto Hodgson', 25 June 1784.
55. AGI Estado 86A, no. 2, [José de Gálvez], 'Discurso y Reflecxiones [sic] de un Vasallo Sobre la Decadencia de Nuestras Indias Españolas', n.d, fo. 33.
56. Pedro Francisco Jiménez de Góngora y Luján (1727–1796), later elevated to title of the Duke of Almodóvar, was director of the Royal Academy of History from 1791 until 1796. Almodóvar previously had served as a diplomat in the courts of various European states. For an overview of Almodóvar's work,

see Ovidio García Regueiro's, *Ilustración e Intereses Estamentales: Antagonismo entre Sociedad Tradicional y Corrientes Innovadoras en la Versión Española de la Historia de Raynal* (Madrid, 1982).

57. On the Black Legend, see J. H. Elliott, *The Old World and the New 1492–1650* (Cambridge, 1970), 94–7; Ricardo García Cárcel, *La Leyenda Negra: Historia y Opinión* (Madrid, 1992); Anthony Pagden, *Lords of All the World: Ideologies of Empire in Spain, Britain and France c. 1500–1800* (New Haven, 1995), 87; on the Spanish contestation of these images through the writing of 'official history', see Richard L. Kagan, *Clio and the Crown: The Politics of History in Medieval and Early Modern Spain* (Baltimore, 2009).
58. Almodóvar, *Historia Política*, vol. II, appendix, vii, 125, 209; additional contemporary Spanish writers criticised Britain for 'operating semi-tyrannies in its colonies... [by which Britain] has subverted its empire in the Indies'; see BPR II/2866, Josef Fuertes, 'Pensamientos, o Proyecto Sobre Volver a Reconciliar con la Madre Patria las Provincias Discolas de la América Meridional (1781)', fos., 248–9 passim.
59. AHN Estado 2927, no. 271, Agustín Craywinckel, 'Utilidad que Podría Sacar España', 7–13 passim, 17, 25.
60. Pablo de Olavide, 'Informe Sobre la Ley Agraria', *Obras Selectas* (Lima, 1987), 488–9; Olavide was a great admirer of English literature, ranking Samuel Richardson, Henry Fielding and Daniel DeFoe among his favourite authors. See Luís Perdices de Blas, *Pablo de Olavide (1725–1803): El Ilustrado* (Madrid, 1993), 45.
61. The secondary literature on Spanish economic debates is vast. Among the best treatments in Spanish include: Marcelo Bitar Letayf, *Economistas Españoles del Siglo XVIII: Sus Ideas sobre la Libertad del Comercio con Indias* (Madrid, 1968); Enrique Fuentes Quintana (ed.), *Economía y Economistas Españoles, Volume 3: La Ilustración* (Barcelona, 2000); Mariano García Ruiperez, 'El Pensamiento Económico Ilustrado y las Compañías de Comercio', *Revista de Historia Económica* 4, no. 3 (1986): 521–48; more generally, Lars Magnusson, *Mercantilism: The Shaping of an Economic Language* (London and New York, 1994).
62. BPR II/2666, Miguel Antonio de Gandara, 'Apuntes para Formar un Discurso Sobre el Bien y el Mal de España (1759)', fo. 135.
63. Campomanes, *Reflexiones*, 242.
64. Almodóvar, *Historia Política*, vol. II, appendix, 23.
65. The best analysis of *comercio libre* may be found in Stein and Stein, *Apogee of Empire*, ch. 3–7 passim.
66. Josef Alonso Ortíz, translator's preface, Adam Smith, *Investigación de la Naturaleza y Causas de la Riqueza de las Naciones* (Valladolid, 1794).
67. BPR II/2819, Alejandro O'Reilly, 'Descripción de la Isla de Cuba (1764)', fo. 334 v.; on O'Reilly's report and its impact, see Eduardo Torres-Cuevas, 'El Grupo de Aranda en Cuba y los Inicios de una Nueva Época', in Benimelli (ed.), *El Conde de Aranda y su Tiempo* (Zaragoza, 2000), esp. 330–1; and also Stein and Stein, *Apogee of Empire*, 57.
68. BPR II/2827, Agustín Crame, 'Discurso Político Sobre la Necesidad de Fomentar la Isla de Cuba (1768)', fos. 237–8; Manuel Moreno Fraginals, *El Ingenio: Complejo Económico-Social Cubano del Azúcar* (Havana, 1978), 35.

69. BPR II/2819, Manuel Leguinazabal, 'Tesoro de España: Discurso Sobre el Comercio de España con sus Americas (1763–1764)', fo. 38 v.
70. AGI Estado 5B, no. 4, 'Puntos que ha tratado en la Junta de Gobierno del Real Consulado de la Isla de Cuba ... Arango en la Relación que de su viaje ha hecho (1796)', fos. 1–5 passim.
71. Francisco Arango y Parreño, 'Discurso Sobre la Agricultura de la Habana y Medios de Fomentarla', *Obras,* vol. I (Havana, 1952), 117–8.
72. *Memorias de la Sociedad Patriótica de la Habana,* vol. I (Havana, 1836), 35.
73. Arango y Parreño, 'Reflexiones Sobre la Mejor Organización del Consulado de la Habana, Considerado como Tribunal', *Obras* (Havana, 1888), vol. I, 209.
74. Maxwell, *Pombal*, 67.
75. These policies are described in detail in Kenneth Maxwell's, *Conflicts and Conspiracies: Brazil and Portugal, 1750–1808* (Cambridge, 1973).
76. Though this essay stresses his diplomatic period in London, it is necessary to recognise the formative impact of his subsequent diplomatic service in Vienna as well (1745–1749). It was there that he met his wife, Maria Leonor Ernestina Daun, a daughter of the Austrian minister responsible to radical army reform. His connections in Vienna most likely earned the attention paid to him by Maria Ana of Austria, Dom João V's queen, who managed to have him recalled to Lisbon shortly before the king's death in 1750. See Maxwell, *Pombal*, 4–6.
77. Robert Southey, *History of Brazil*, 2nd ed., vol. I (London, 1822), 505; Falcon noted that the 'influence of English mercantile discourse' is 'quite clear' in this period. See Falcon, *A Época Pombalina*, 308.
78. Carvalho e Melo, *Escritos Económicos*, 36, 41.
79. Pombal to Lord Chatham, 'Cartas que o Marquez de Pombal, sendo Conde de Oeiras, escreveu a Lord Chatham, pedindo satisfação por ser quimada uma esquadra franceza na costa do Algarve, junta a Lagos', *Cartas e Outras Obras Selectas do Marquez do Pombal* (Lisbon, 1822), third letter, 5.
80. Carvalho e Melo, *Escritos Económicos*, 154, 150.
81. Carvalho e Melo, *Escritos Económicos*, 139.
82. José Ferreira Carrato, 'The Enlightenment in Portugal and the Educational Reforms of the Marquis of Pombal', *Studies in Voltaire and the Eighteenth Century* 168 (1977): 369.
83. Carvalho e Melo, *Escritos Económicos*, 76.
84. Maxwell, *Pombal*, 42–3.
85. Southey, *Letters Written ... Spain and Portugal*, 402.
86. Carvalho e Melo, *Escritos Económicos*, 42.
87. Carvalho e Melo, *Escritos Económicos*, 136; for a positive appraisal of the impact of the Pombaline companies, see LME Shaw, 'The Marquês de Pombal (1699–1782): How he Broke Britain's Commercial Ascendancy in Portugal', *Journal of European Economic History* 27, no. 3 (1998): 537–54; for a more critical view, see Francisco Ribeiro da Silva, 'Pombal e os Ingleses (Incidências Económicas e Relacões Internacionais)', *Actas do Congresso o Marquês do Pombal e a sua Época* (Oeiras, 2001).
88. It must be conceded that not all of these developments can be attributed directly to commercial rivalry with Britain; some were a direct response to new exigencies provoked by declining mineral yields in Brazil, plunging gold prices on the world market and the escalating costs of securing the southern

frontier with Spanish America. See Dauril Alden, *Royal Government in Colonial Brazil: With Special Reference to the Administration of the Marquis of Lavradio, Viceroy, 1769–1779* (Berkeley, CA, 1968), 353.

89. Pombal, quoted in Maxwell, *Conflicts and Conspiracies*, 19.
90. On the Pombaline companies in Brazil, see Antonio Carreira, *As Companhias Pombalinas de Grão Pará e Maranhão e Pernambuco e Paraíba* (Lisbon, 1983); the abolition of the companies did not result from anti-Pombal sentiment alone, but also from their underperformance: in 1776–1777, less than one-quarter of shipments to the colonies was composed on national manufactures and Portuguese-made textiles amounted to a mere 30 per cent of the total dispatched to the colonies. See Jorge Pedreira, 'From Growth to Collapse: Portugal, Brazil and the Breakdown of the Old Colonial System (1760–1830)', *Hispanic American Historical Review* 80, no. 4 (2000): 844.
91. Conde de Oeiras [Pombal] to Marquês do Lavradio, 14 April 1769, Marcos Carneiro do Mendonça, *O Marquês de Pombal e o Brasil* (São Paulo, 1960), 36.
92. Ibid., 77.
93. B[iblioteca] N[acional] do R[io] de J[aneiro], Coleção Linhares I-29, 13, 4. In the catalogue of the BNRJ, this letter is listed as written by Souza Coutinho to the Abbé Raynal.
94. Souza Coutinho (1791), quoted in Pedro Miguel Carvalho Alves da Silva, 'O Dispotismo Luminozo: Introdução ao Pensamento de Dom Rodrigo de Sousa Coutinho' (MA thesis, Universidade Nova de Lisboa, 1997), 86; due to the necessarily limited scope of this essay, I cannot discuss Souza Coutinho's general vision of colonies. For a full discussion, see José Luís Cardoso, 'Nas Malhas do Império: A Economia Política e a Política Colonial de D. Rodrigo de Souza Coutinho', in Cardoso (ed.), *A Economia Política e os Dilemas do Império Luso-Brasileiro 1790–1822* (Lisbon, 2001).
95. On Pombal's Companhia Geral da Agricultura das Vinhas do Alto Douro, established in 1756, see Maxwell, *Pombal*, 63, 70–1.
96. Souza Coutinho, 'Reflexões Políticas', 148; Kenneth Maxwell has situated Souza Coutinho's opposition to monopoly in a broader context: 'D. Rodrigo's...opposition to monopolies and the contracting of revenues, and his fervent support of an efficient and solvent financial administration, grew from his belief that intelligent reform was essential if Portugal were to avoid a similar collapse' as that of France. See Maxwell, 'The Idea of a Luso-Brazilian Empire', *Naked Tropics: Essays on Empire and Other Rogues* (New York and London, 2003), 133.
97. BNRJ, Coleção Linhares I-29, 16, 35, Lista de Livros de Agricultura Ingleses nos quais se encontrão as melhores idéias para se aproveitar (n.d.); It should be noted that Souza Coutinho was highly regarded by the British political writers he encountered whilst in Turin, including Arthur Young who praised him in the 1791 *Annals of Agriculture*.
98. Fritz Hoppe, 'Memorandum do Desembargador Duarte Salter de Mendança 7 December 1751', *A África Oriental Portuguesa no Tempo do Marquês do Pombal* (Lisbon, 1970), 332.
99. ANRJ, Diversos Codices 807, vol. 21, Agostinho Ignacio da Costa Quintela, 'Verdadeiro Projeto ou Breve Discurso para se Aumentar a Agricultura em Portugal' (n.d.), fo. 7.

100. ANRJ, Diversos Codices 807, vol. 25, 'Memoria de Domingos Vandelli sobre a Diplomacia Portuguesa', 10 August 1796.
101. ANRJ, Secretario de Estado do Brasil, cod. 67, vol. 9, Luis de Vasconcellos to Martinho de Melo e Castro, 15 July 1781.
102. Domingos Vandelli, 'Memória sobre a pública instrução agrária (1788)', in J. V. Serrão (ed.), *Domingos Vandelli: Aritmética Política, Economia e Finanças* (Lisbon, 1994), 131.
103. José da Silva Lisboa, *Observações sobre a franqueza da indústria e estabelecimento de fábricas no Brasil* (Rio de Janeiro, 1810).
104. Silva Lisboa, *Memoria da Vida Publica do Lord Wellington* (Rio de Janeiro, 1815), 86.
105. Silva Lisboa, *Memória Econômica*, 53.
106. José Agostinho de Macedo, 'O Espectador Portuguez', *Jornal de Litteratura, e Critico* II, no. 3 (Lisbon, 1816): 12.
107. Biblioteca da Ajuda, 54-VI-52, doc. 38, *A Conspiração contra o Principe D. Miguel* (Lisbon, 1828), fos. 49–52 passim.

5

The Empire of Emulation: A Quantitative Analysis of Economic Translations in the European World, 1500–1849

Sophus A. Reinert

The Tudor merchant George Nedham presented an unusually succinct meditation upon the problem of power in international relations in his ca. 1568 manuscript *Letter to the Earls of East Friesland*. 'Wealth and strength', he knew well, went hand in hand in the modern world, but the Dutch and, as a result, the 'empire' of Philip II, currently seemed to have a stranglehold on both. Yet Nedham argued steadfastly that English and German merchants and sovereigns still could turn the tables, and do so 'without great expense, war, trouble and bloodshed'. The key to this indirect *translatio* of empire lay in pursuing the right 'policy', the right measure for countervailing Philip II's economic superiority and, with time, achieving dominion over him in turn. The Dutch had grown wealthy and powerful by attracting foreign merchants and manufacturers to their sterile lands, and their riches had thus been 'gotten politically' rather than by natural resources and industry. 'By the like policy', Nedham reasoned, their wealth 'may be taken away from them again'.[1]

No clear vocational category yet existed for Nedham's endeavour, unless one places him in the venerable and capacious *Fürstenspiegel* tradition. The term 'political economy' would not adorn the title page of a book until the French dramaturge Antoine de Montchrétien published his *Traicté de economie politique* in 1615, and the politics of international trade would first be classified as a 'science' in the English language by the Bristol merchant John Cary in 1719. Yet Nedham's aim of encouraging trade by means of politicising expert knowledge – by deriving future policies from the study of past and present economic conditions – was the same as those of these later authors. Though their analytical vocabularies differed, their conceptual languages were remarkably resonant. They all realised that power in the modern world had come to depend on comparative wealth in international relations, and that the only means of achieving and maintaining greatness was to pursue a politics of emulation. The economies of England and Holland, Montchrétien stated paradigmatically, were objects of 'emulation' for France as clearly in 1615 as the 'republics of Genoa and Venice' had been for their 'ancestors'. And although he subsequently was shot, quartered, and incinerated, he bequeathed subsequent scholars and statesmen one of *the* defining concerns of modernity, 'political economy', and delineated some of its basic tenets: emulation, industry, and empire.[2]

Montchrétien's example, though, was only symptomatic of how emulation and an acute awareness of political economy's agonistic nature drove early modern economic theory and policy – from Nedham to Veit Ludwig von Seckendorff, who inaugurated the 'science' of cameralism in his 1665 *Additiones* to the *Teutcscher Fürsten-Staat* following a formative sojourn in Holland, to Alexander Hamilton, who described the glory of industry in his 1781 *Report on the Manufactures* in Philadelphia after surveying the factory systems of the Old World. As many lacked the resources of these luminaries for international travel, a principal vehicle of emulation became textual translation.[3] Though unable to convey the sights and impressions of other countries firsthand, one could nonetheless render understandable the words of those who were, and translations gradually became a key to erecting, imitating, and countervailing the economic structures of empire. Indeed, some works of political economy, in that and in later periods, became far more influential in new contexts abroad than they ever were in the place and time of their writing.

So though the practice of economic espionage was widespread in the early modern world, this chapter will focus on the concomitant and much broader form of emulation taking place at the time through the translation of economic texts, first widely practicable with the emergence of political economy as an institutionalised subject of inquiry and of a public sphere in which economic concerns could be debated and eavesdropped upon.[4] What mattered, in this case, was not simply the translation and transmission of an individual text but rather its promulgation through printed media in a new cultural and economic context. The emergence of such a commerce of economic texts was by no means a uniform process across the European world, and it was intrinsically linked to the gradual freeing of speech and expression from the strictures of sacred and secular censorship.[5] Traditionally, economic policies such as those discussed by Nedham had been safely confined to the secret sphere of early modern statecraft, the realm of reason of state and Tacitus' *arcana imperii*.[6] It was in this tradition that a Venetian spy in England reported to the Doge:

> It has always been difficult to understand commerce thoroughly and at the present time especially it has become a secret, for everyone applies himself to it devotedly, and the powers take an interest in the matter because of the immense advantage to be derived for their territories and subjects.[7]

As the importance of commerce grew in the world, so did the imperative to safeguard its secrets and monopolise on its benefits. And even as late as 1750, Dutch diplomats feared that Prussia might learn 'the most hidden secrets of commerce' and that way beat them at their own game.[8] Yet the European situation did change, and a continental discourse of political economy eventually wrested itself loose from the restrictions of the Old Regime, incrementally and, on occasions, in leaps and bounds. Despite the idiosyncrasies of early modern European censorship, the trend in the grand history of the continent was clear.[9] As the Milanese statesman and political economist Pietro Verri noted in an early 1760s manuscript, 'now' one could 'find the true interest of States, and their real and physical force, in bookshops'. Mysteries of state were a thing of the past: 'Governing a nation is no longer a magical art, but rather a published science subject to the laws of reason'.[10] And there could be no doubt that 'enlightened emulation' was a historical necessity, for, as his brother and colleague Alessandro Verri put it around that time, 'no nation has become excellent on its own'.[11]

The old world was that of the Count de Perron, who in 1751 sent manuscript translations of British economic pamphlets to Turin for circulation in the Savoy administration hoping to encourage emulation with the motto *Cherchez de bon modèles, et imitez-les*.[12] The new was represented by men like Peter Christian Schumacher, former Kammerherre to the king of Denmark–Norway, who embarked on a Grand Tour in the 1780s to study European political economy and brought back select texts not only for translation but for publication and widespread dissemination.[13] Something akin to a market for economic ideas was being woven into existence in the eighteenth century, its threads delineating a transnational civil society of political economists that, though generally conversant in French, translated texts into the European vernaculars as a means of encouraging widespread enlightenment. While this system of learning drew on many of the habits and institutions of the republic of letters (Schumacher's ritualised visits to eminent statesmen in Germany and Italy being a case in point), it differed considerably from it. The imagined community of early modern political economy was less concerned with the general learning of the few than with the technical expertise of the many, less with Wunderkammern than with agricultural output and manufacturing innovations; and ultimately driven less by a disinterested quest for knowledge than by the ruthless exigencies of economic competition, exigencies which could galvanise national animosities even in its most cosmopolitan participants.[14] For every mild-mannered David Hume preaching peace and welfare for all, there were countless writers like Gaetano Filangieri demanding *'vendetta'* for Britain's Cimmerian economic policies.[15] It was in effect competition, not concord, which united subjects of this empire of emulation, a quixotic community unified by the sovereign power of economic expediency and justified by the promise of perpetual civil war.[16]

What follows is an attempt to map this empire of emulation through a quantitative analysis of economic translations as they contributed to 'enlightened emulation' in the European world, roughly from the Renaissance through the Industrial Revolution. While the great question of how economic texts travelled as vehicles of emulation, both in terms of macro numbers and micro histories, has only begun to be studied, the case can be made that changing patterns of economic translations convey powerful insights into the dynamics of power in early modern and modern history. Daniel Milo proposed in an 1984 article in *Annales* that translations perhaps could serve as a 'cultural barometer'; using UNESCO's *Index translationum* to chart the shifting 'global stock market [*bourse*] of translation' in the twentieth century, he showed how the most culturally valuable authors, in terms of volume of translations, shifted from Leo Tolstoy, Charles Dickens, and Honoré de Balzac to Agatha Christie, Walt Disney, and Jules Verne in the decades after World War II.[17] Besides the change in translation patterns shown by Milo, it is worth noting that the most translated authors in the period remained strictly limited to the realm of fiction, and that the changes he documented in the end measured cultural and literary rather than political and economic desirability.

While there certainly exist pertinent relations between cultural preferences and economic forces, this chapter will narrow the problem down by limiting this study to translations of what can broadly be considered 'economic' works. It will argue that a quantitative study of translations of political economy in early modern Europe can serve as something like a barometer of economic success, measuring the fluctuating values assigned, for whatever reason, to national economies by their allies and competitors. This, in turn, can inform us about the changing relations of power in the early modern world and their echoes to this day. Applying Milo's method to the economic, rather than more general cultural sphere, and throwing the net backwards in time to the early modern period, however, poses the problem of providing an enormous data set for a period long before that covered by UNESCO, and one for which we simply do not have accurate information about total numbers of books published. To complete a perfect data set of all early modern translations of economic works between all European languages is in fact impossible, no different from the utopian visions of universal libraries proposed by the bibliophiles of the time.[18] Similarly, the very term 'economic' is itself open to different interpretations, for where does agriculture end, and botany begin?[19] Needless to say, it is a problem for which no certain lines can ever be drawn, and about which any suggested solution by necessity must be nebulous and, to some, inadequate.

Yet, thanks to an ongoing collaboration with Kenneth E. Carpenter, who came close to this ideal of completeness during his long tenure as curator of the Kress Collection at Harvard Business School's Baker Library, it is now possible to analyse a set of more than two thousand 'economic' translations, consisting of a critical mass housed in the world's mayor collections of economic literature.[20] While a work in progress and not complete – and this cannot be emphasised enough – the current data set we have put together is considerable enough to draw some conclusions regarding the dynamics of early modern economic translations and what they tell us about the agonistic interactions of the rising and declining empires of the period. The early modern European overseas empires indeed matured alongside the codification of political economy as a self-confessed 'science' from which practical economic policies could be derived, and key attempts to formalise this 'science' in different countries were derived explicitly from increases in the absolute volume of economic translations, themselves inexorably intertwined with the most dramatic changes in the constellations of power in eighteenth-century Europe, like the Treaty of Aix-la-Chapelle and the French Revolution. Successful empires, it was thought, rested on practices that, like those of the paradigmatic eighteenth century pin factory lionised by the *Encyclopédie* and by Adam Smith, could be codified, transmitted, and emulated through the translation of books and pamphlets.

So if the reflections resulting from the following analysis by necessity are based on a cliometric approximation, they can nonetheless suggest new ways of considering the relation between economic power, empire, and intellectual history in the early modern period. 'We know', as Raynal wrote, 'that the jealousy of commerce is nothing more than a jealousy of power'.[21] If power is *imperium*, that axiomatic Machiavellian liberty which expands at the expense of that of others, and it is vied for through an economic competition for world trade shaped and informed by emulation, then the study of changing patterns of economic translation can indeed shed light on the nature of freedom, the changing constellations of power, and the larger translation of empire from 1500 to 1849. As can be seen from Figure 5.1, however, such translations are few and far between in the earlier centuries.

There is a modest increase in the second half of the seventeenth century that intensifies further in the opening years of the eighteenth. The high point before 1750 measured in sheer volume was the first decade of that century, with a relatively modest 18 translations. A very sudden break therefore occurs in the mid-eighteenth century, when the total number rises to 123, and again in the 1760s, when the total peaks at 323, before again declining to 154 in the 1770s. If the anonymous English translator of Tommaso Campanella's *Discourse Concerning the Spanish Monarchy* could declare in 1654 that 'we are fallen into an Age of *Translations*', the

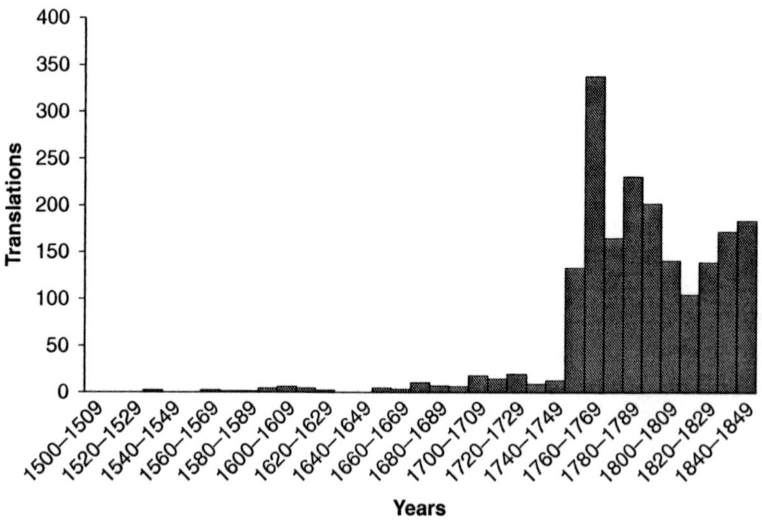

Figure 5.1 Total European economic translations per decade

more specific age of translations of political economy happened to coincide, in the 1750s, with the period in which English technologies seriously began to be transferred to the continent through emulation and conscious acts of industrial espionage.[22] With the exception of a trough during the Napoleonic Wars in the 1810s, in fact, economic translations then remained at a permanently high plateau throughout the period under analysis.

The changing pattern of translations in early modern Europe, and particularly the peak in the 1750s and 1760s, could conceivably reflect a general trend of publishing – more works of political economy being translated and published simply as a corollary of some overall expansion of the book trade and the emergence of a continental civil society more generally, a republic of translations, if not Latin letters. Yet, the aggregate data on the development of the European book industry between 1454 and 1794 shows that no such massive percentage increase in general publications took place on a European scale in the 1750s and 1760s. The Swedish book trade was exploding in those decades, and there was an upwards trend throughout the eighteenth century generally, but no spikes or sudden market movements can be identified in the decades in question looking at the continent as a whole. Such deviations from a state of steady increase are, however, readily observable around the time of the English civil war, with the decline of Italian publishing towards the late seventeenth century and with the advent of the French Revolution.[23] The sudden spike in the number of translations of political economy evident in the 1750s and 1760s, then, reflects an absolute increase with respect to the overall output of books in the period. Simply put, the translation of works of political economy came to occupy a larger share of the eighteenth-century book trade and of the market for knowledge at the time.

While changing censorship practices well might be part of the explanation, the radical increase in the total number of translations observable in the 1750s is not surprising given the European political and economic context of the time, in which different national discourses of political economy were evaluated very differently on the international stock market of translations suggested by Milo.[24] Though the data set underlying the present study would enable such studies, it has here been impossible, for the sake of comparative macro-studies of economic performance, to really differentiate between, say, Naples and Venice or London and Bristol. This is, for a bibliophile or someone interested in specific histories, an unthinkable omission, but it simply proved unfeasible to do elegantly and would have required the comparison of so many interconnected graphs that any explanatory value the exercise might have had in this context would have dissolved in the acidity of the reader's impatience. Future studies will highlight this data set's heuristic value at the regional rather than linguistic level, but the present perspective is very much a bird's-eye view of the history of economic translations.

Furthermore, to appreciate the tremor that shook the market of economic translations in the 1750s, one must momentarily leave the empirical study of translations behind. A millennial perspective on the world economy recently published by the Organisation for Economic Co-Operation and Development (OECD) can shed important light on the dynamics of early modern economic translations. As shown in Figures 5.2 and 5.3, in the year 1500, when the gaze of the world still rested safely on Renaissance Italy, the gross domestic product of the Atlantic archipelago now called the United Kingdom was nearly $3 billion (or $714 per capita in 1990 USD). By comparison, the Netherlands reached $716 million ($754 per capita), Norway $192 million ($640), and the Italian peninsula a staggering $11.5 billion ($1 100). By the year 1700, however, the gross domestic product of the United Kingdom had reached $10.7 billion while Italy had experienced only a moderate increase to $14.6 billion.

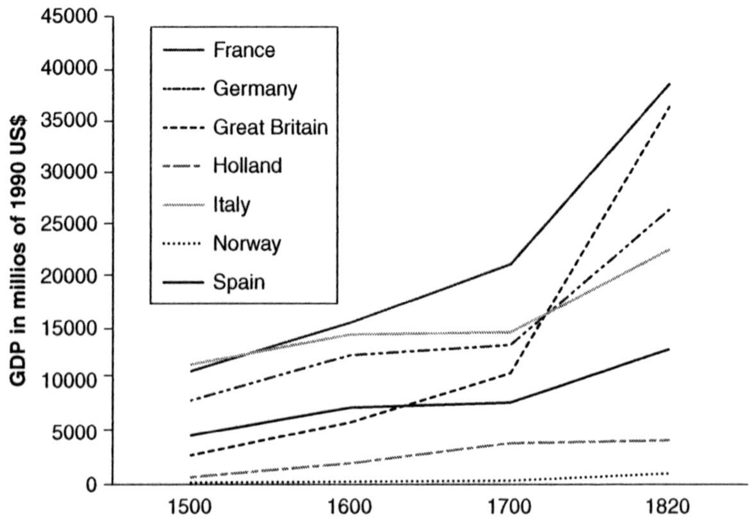

Figure 5.2 Economic development in Europe, 1500–1820
Source: Based on Maddison (2006, 244–7, 263–5).

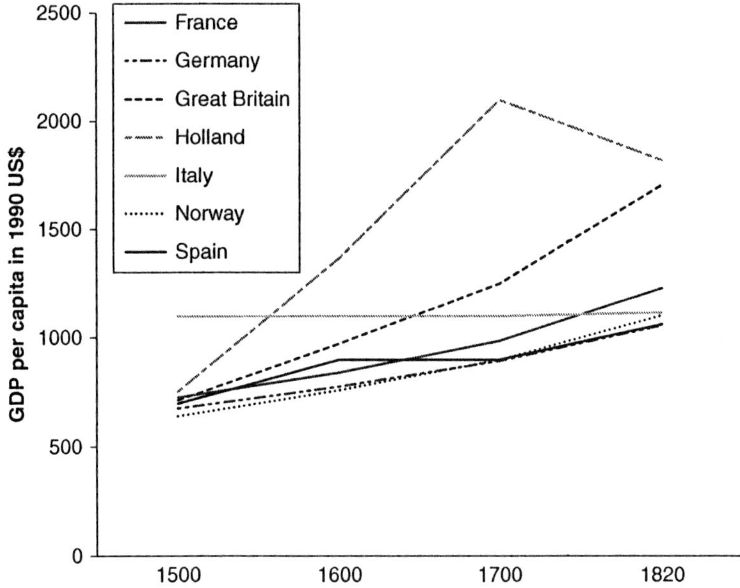

Figure 5.3 Per capita development in Europe, 1500–1820

Source: Based on Maddison (2006, 244–7, 263–5).

In terms of per capita distribution during the same period, that of the United Kingdom had reached $1,250 while that of Italy tellingly had remained stagnant at $1,100. By 1820, the gross domestic product of the United Kingdom had reached $36.2 billion, that of Italy only $22.5 billion. In other words, the economy of the United Kingdom had almost tripled between 1500 and 1700, while that of Italy had increased only by a mere 27 per cent. *The mean rate of economic growth in the period was therefore more than ten times higher in the United Kingdom than in Italy*. This takeoff continued into the eighteenth century, for by 1820 the economy of the United Kingdom had grown by a staggering 1287 per cent since the year 1500, while that of Italy had only grown by 95 per cent. Whereas the United Kingdom's percentage share of world GDP had risen from 1.1 to 5.2 in the period, that of Italy had sunk from 4.7 to 3.2.[25] A very similar story emerges from existing demographic data. In 1500, 22 per cent of the population of Italy was urban, and 16 per cent were rural nonagricultural. Three centuries later, the percentages were 22 and 20. In England, on the other hand, which only enjoyed a meagre 7 per cent urbanisation ratio in 1500, with 18 per cent employed in nonagricultural rural activities, this had risen to 29 per cent and 36 per cent respectively by 1800. Whereas England had been the most agricultural nation in Europe West of the Rhine in 1500, by 1800 it was the least so by a wide margin.[26] Even more striking are the changing structures of British trade during its period of intensifying industrial policies. From importing 34.7 per cent of raw materials and 31.7 per cent of manufactured goods in the period 1699–1702, England imported 62.3 per cent of raw materials and a mere 4.3 per cent of manufactured goods in the 1840s.[27]

While the data for GDP is conjectural, it is clear that the most radical changes in the early modern European economic theatre were the relative declines of Italy, Spain, and Holland and the industrialisation of Great Britain. While France's enormous population made it enjoy the highest GDP in Europe at the time for demographic reasons, England was far wealthier per capita, and a variety of well-known factors contributed to its eventually acknowledged dominance in world affairs. From being a peripheral exporter of raw wool in the sixteenth century, England had conquered its surrounding Celtic crescent and had, through ruthless reason of state and aggressive economic policies like the Navigation Acts, become a proverbial workshop of the world under the moniker of Great Britain. It had then shocked Europe through a series of unforeseeable military victories during the Nine Years' War and the wars of Spanish and Austrian Succession, the last of which culminated in the 1748 Peace of Aix-la-Chapelle. As Great Britain asserted itself as a great, if not *the* great power, the status of the English language in Europe consequently rose hand in hand with the positive balance of its trade. Just as Great Britain went from being an exporter of raw materials to one of manufactured goods in the early modern period, the English language in fact went from being an importer of foreign vocabulary in the sixteenth century to become a net exporter in the eighteenth.[28] A concomitant change would soon be evident in its balance of economic translations, for, as the Castilian scholar and grammarian Antonio de Nebrija had explained to Queen Isabella of Spain already in 1492, language was not only itself a 'tool of conquest', but had 'always been the consort of empire, and forever shall remain its mate'.[29]

The rampant successes of Great Britain's credit-based war financing had invalidated the venerable trope of political philosophy that virtuous men rather than money were the 'sinews of war', and all over Europe, statesmen were forced to reconsider many of their most basic assumptions and prejudices. It was acutely evident that the mechanisms of commerce now posed both clear limits and provided pertinent possibilities for national as well as international politics.[30] Whether one lived in

Stockholm, Leipzig, or Milan, there was a pressing need to understand the intertwined phenomena of wealth, war, and public happiness, and it was also increasingly obvious that lessons of political economy were taught best by observing and emulating more successful economies.[31] The radical increase in the total number of translations observable in the wake of the Treaty of Aix-la-Chapelle is therefore not surprising given the European political and economic context of the period. The boom in translations observable in Figure 5.1 in fact corresponds to the period immediately following the Treaty of Aix-la-Chapelle, whereby Great Britain for the third time that century demonstrated its economic and military superiority. As the balance of economic translations between English and the continental languages in Figure 5.4 shows, this boom can in large parts be explained by the wish to emulate the successes of Great Britain, which had succeeded Venice and the Low Countries as the centre of economic gravity in Europe.[32] With the considerable number of English economic works arriving in various European countries through an intermediary French translation, the role of Great Britain became even more domineering.[33]

It is evident from a conjoined reading of the above figures that a positive balance of trade – and the structural transformation from being an exporter of raw wool to one of manufactured goods – and the military might this ensured was followed by a positive balance of economic translations, and, ultimately, by a positive linguistic and cultural balance first seriously evident in the 1750s. Even though English only broke even consistently from the 1740s onwards, the net balance of translations for the entire period from 1550 to 1849 was an unparalleled 615 exports to

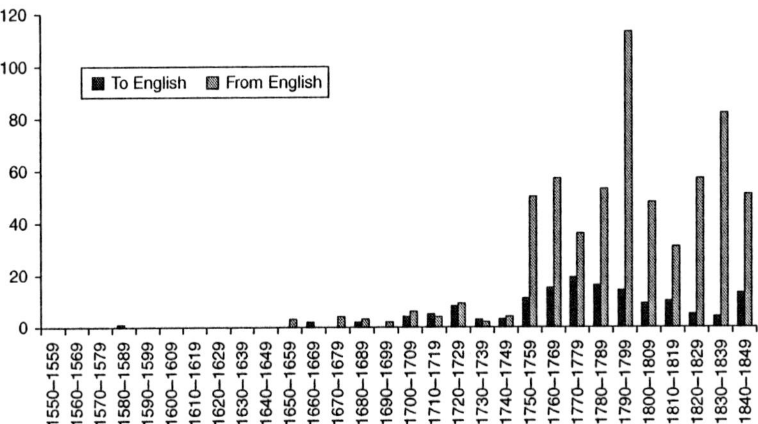

Figure 5.4 English balance of economic translations, 1550–1849

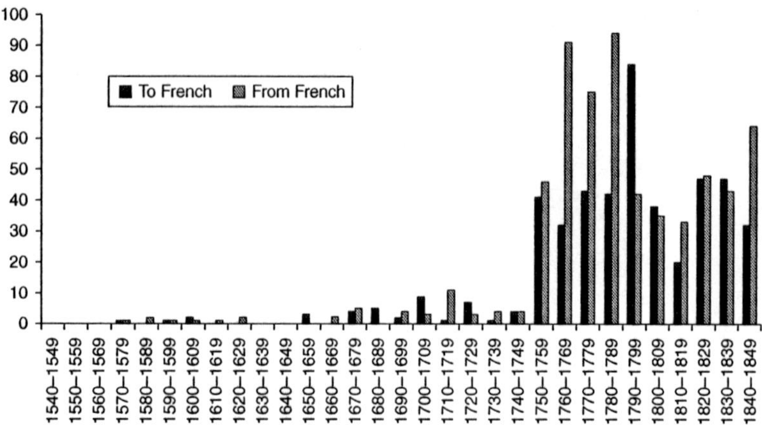

Figure 5.5 French balance of economic translations, 1550–1849

144 imports. While French, as a *lingua franca* of the eighteenth century, in total seems to have exported the same number of economic works (well within the vague margin of error inherent in the data set), the English balance of translations was far better than that of any other language because it imported far fewer translations than its main comparable economic rival France (615 to 464).[34]

Although it is not surprising that the insularity of English is reflected also in this, it is almost unimaginable that it nearly surpassed French in the total number of exported economic translations, and likewise striking that Great Britain remained a net importer of economic works as late as the 1730s, only breaking even in the 1740s. The dramatic increase did not reflect changes in the long-term comparative economic development of Europe, nor the gradual growth of the European book trade, but rather the impact, on the Braudelian level of the event, of Britain's somewhat shocking victory in the War of Austrian Succession and its following arms race for trade and empire leading up to the Seven Years' War.[35] This is of course not to say that some people did not foresee the coming turning of the tables. Daniel Defoe joined a venerable tradition of interpretation when, in his important but never translated 1737 *Plan for the English Commerce*, he mused on the historical cyclicality of emulation:

> Most of our great Advances in Arts, in Trade, in Government, and in almost all the great Things, we are now Masters of, and in which

> we so much exceed all our Neighbouring Nations, are really founded upon the Inventions of others.... Now we see the World ambitious of imitating us in the same Manner, and to rival our Manufactures, are obliged to hire Instructors from hence, and to learn of those who were but Learners before.[36]

Inexorably intertwined with the rise of England, the second important piece of information revealed by the OECD statistics is the relative decline of Italy and the Spanish dominions, areas where the shift in the European centre of economic gravity did not go unnoticed either. While the former had botched the political transition from city-states to nation-state in the late Renaissance and had stagnated economically thereafter, no country in Europe had suffered from the dark side of early modern political economy more than Spain, whose enormous influx of gold and silver from the New World in the end had paid only for mercenary armies and foreign manufactures.[37] Their empire, once almost universal in scale and scope, had seemingly failed to adapt to the exigencies of commercial society.[38] This was the reality to which Juan Enrique de Graef reacted when, in his 1752–1756 journal *Discursos mercuriales*, he sought to encourage a renewal of the empire by translating and 'compiling what foreigners write on the principal matters of commerce, cultivation and exercise of the arts'.[39] As a Spanish translator of Dangeul's fake translation of John Nickolls emblematically wrote in his 1771 preface, 'it seems to me that our language, arts, and Muses will extend their empire, and take the tribute of commendation from the emulating nations, which until this point they scornfully have denied us'. This was why he hoped 'the translation of a book' could 'contribute to the realization of many maxims which your highness hopes to establish' by demonstrating the 'commerce undertaken by two rival nations, and the way in which they have arrived at the opulence they have acquired'.[40]

The *abbé* Antonio Genovesi presented a complimentary analysis when, in the 1750s, he set out to render a series of English works on political economy in Italian to use as textbooks at his newly established chair of political economy at the university of Naples. Noting the irony that Italians now were forced to emulate the English model as the English had once emulated Italy, he translated authors like John Cary and Thomas Mun to communicate to as wide an audience as possible the 'springs and levers' Great Britain 'had operated to lift itself, in all parts of its economy, to greatness'.[41] As Figure 5.6 demonstrates, Italy remained a net exporter of economic works throughout the

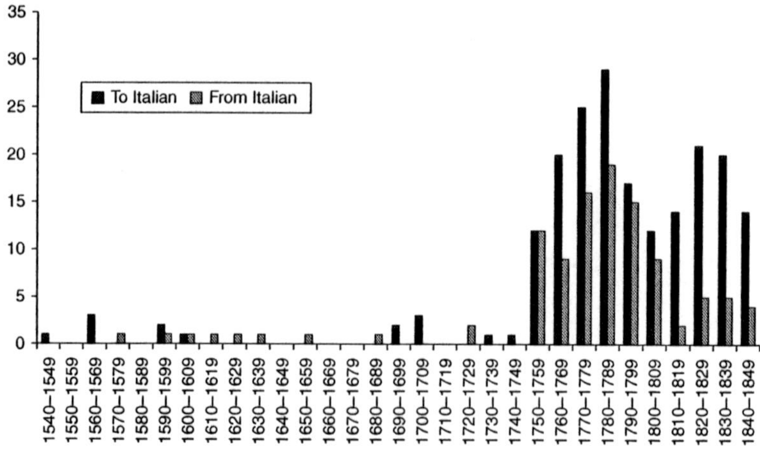

Figure 5.6 Italian balance of economic translations, 1540–1849

sixteenth and seventeenth centuries, a trend that becomes even more pronounced if one ignores Italian translations of classical authors and works by Italians originally written in Latin. From the 1730s onwards, however, and dramatically so from the late 1750s, Italy would suffer from a vertiginous translation imbalance with the rest of Europe, and mainly with England and France.

And if the Scandinavian countries never had reached the peaks of Italy and Spain, the same principle of emulation, and the same anxieties, guided attempts there to catch up with or at least countervail the growing dominance of England and France.[42]

Although it is evident that the French empire, as the greatest exporter of economic works in the period, proved to be a model for most European countries to emulate, and although it remained unclear at mid-century whether control of the seas and of the New World in the end would fall to it or to Great Britain, contemporaries believed that French political economy emerged as a discipline in the 1750s almost entirely through the mediation of English works from the previous century. As the January 1756 issue of the *Journal Oeconomique* emblematically asserted, *the Ardour, with which the English apply themselves to all that can make commerce flourish, should no doubt excite our emulation.*[43] Yet translations never made up a large percentage of the total number of all broadsides, pamphlets, brochures, and works on the subject widely conceived.[44] Perhaps the solution to this conundrum is simply the extraordinarily coherent program undertaken by the group of *philosophes*, statesmen, and former merchants gathered around the previously mentioned figure of Vincent de Gournay, *intendant du commerce* under Louis XV in the 1750s. What mattered was not merely the *quantity* of works on political economy. By publishing a critical mass of interrelated works on the subject, Gournay's circle in effect created a field from scratch, a field in which books making different but interrelated arguments – Cary's history of English manufactures, Ustàriz's history of Spanish industrial decline, and Coyer's eulogy of commercial nobility – could refer to each other synergetically in the act of weaving together a new economic ideology for France. Individually, these books were mere strands of thought. Together, they formed a thick web of political economy strong enough to support a lively culture of public debate and informed reforms alike.[45]

Their adopted program of translation included not only the greatest English works of political economy, but tellingly also those of Spain, a fact that poses difficulties for the hypothesis that translations can be studied as a measure of the relative economic successes of nations. The contrasting economic experiences of the two empires clearly taught important and complementary lessons for European statesmen in the period leading up to the Seven Years' War, but whereas British works were translated as 'how to' guides for the political economy of empire, Spanish works might well have been translated as 'how not to' guides, as examples of which policies might work to reverse a relative decline in economic affairs.[46] As one work of English political economy published under Gournay's aegis put it, 'nothing contributes advantage in sustaining our emulation' more than 'contemplating the acts of our enemies' precisely through such economic translations.[47]

The French illness that contemporaries dubbed *Anglomania*, which manifested itself through the imitation of English gardens, institutions, and apparel, was one of the principal reasons for the dramatic change in translation patterns observable in the second half of the eighteenth century.[48] As the British envoy Edward Gibbon noted in the wake of the Seven Years' War, at a time when the Atlantic archipelago had become the greatest imperial power the world had ever seen, 'the name of Englishman inspires as great an idea at Paris, as that of Roman could at Carthage, after the defeat of Hannibal'.[49] The importance of English works in the French balance of translations is even more clearly observable in Figure 5.7, charting the balance of translations between the two countries only.

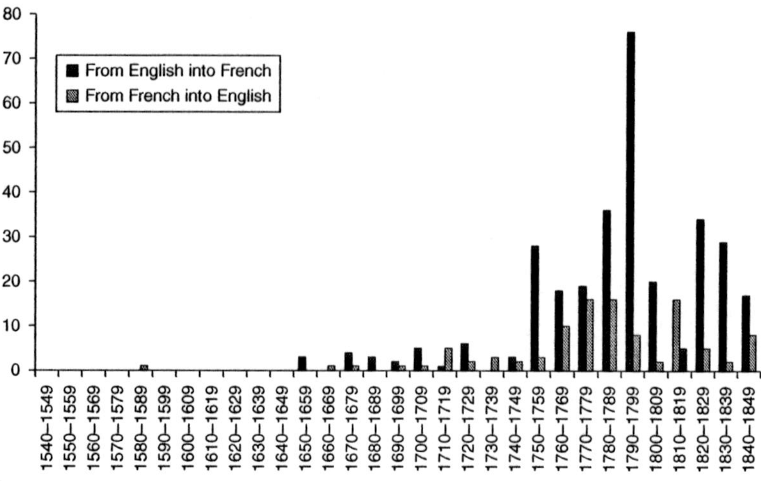

Figure 5.7 English–French balance of economic translations, 1540–1849

Although the numbers for the early centuries are too small to warrant sweeping generalisations, it is observable that English and French vied for a positive balance of translations until the 1740s, at which point a century of *Anglomanie* set in that, not surprisingly, would peak in the years surrounding the French Revolution. France was nonetheless Great Britain's main rival at the time, and charting the balance of economic translations between English and other continental languages shows an even more marked discrepancy. Compared to 173 direct German translations of English economic works, only 15 German works had made their way to Great Britain by 1849. And the 1750s were again a turning point, the decade in which English books for the first time began to vie with French imports at the Easter book fair in Leipzig.[50] Germany was in fact the clear loser in the European balance of translations in absolute terms, importing 776 works but only exporting 197.[51] Although the argument could be made that a laggard area like the German states simply had nothing to offer in terms of early modern economic writings, the first chairs of political economy in the world were established in early eighteenth-century Germany, and the now dated *Bibliographie der Kameralwissenschaften* covers thousands of entries for the period in question.[52] Different national or regional cultures of political economy were characterised by evidently different degrees of openness to foreign ideas and practices, and on the macro-level of translation data it is obvious that, though a continuous circulation of economic texts in translation existed in continental Europe, the English language gave far more than it received on the subject.

Translations of economic works were so symptomatic of these larger changes in European economic and linguistic relations because they represented an ideal case of emulation. They were both themselves emulative acts *and* the foundation for further and more widespread emulation of theory and practice. And, in terms of the overarching development of European commercial society at the time, it was obvious that the English polity became a unique repertoire of political and economic ideas for the eighteenth century. An English–German dictionary exemplified these general changes towards the end of the century: 'As the English Nation is taking the Lead in almost every Art and Science, so it is become necessary to Foreigners aiming at Perfection in any Branch of Business the English chiefly excel in, to gain a proper Knowledge of the English Tongue'.[53]

Widely circulated and translated in his lifetime, Josiah Child knew the cyclical nature and double-edged power of such emulation all too well. The first edition of his *Discourse on Trade*, a work famous for emphasising the need to lower the rate of interest, repeatedly argued that England should look towards the economic successes of the continent for inspiration, not only in terms of interest rates, but also industry: '*If we intend to have the Trade of the World*', he maintained emblematically, '*we must imitate the* Dutch, *who make the worst as well as the best of all Manufactures, that we may be in a capacity of serving all Markets, and all Humors*'. England, in other words, should indulge in its economic nationalism by copying the more varied and inclusive Dutch industrial practices.[54] Child's own caveat to the fourth edition of his *Discourse* is thus particularly striking:

> Before I conclude, I think it necessary, for caution to my Countrymen, to let them know what effects these discourses have had on others. When I wrote my first treatise, interest was in the Island of Barbados at 15 *per cent.* where it is since by an Act of the Country brought down to 10 *per cent.* a great fall at once, and our weekly Gazettes some months past informed us, that the Swedes by a law had brought down their interest to 6 *per cent.* neither of which can have any good effects upon us, but certainly the contrary, *except by way of emulation they quicken us to provide in time for our own good and prosperity.*[55]

Observing that his ideas had been implemented abroad, Child's only succour was the 'good and prosperity' that would result from the ongoing struggle between successful nations. By creating a permanent state of precarious competition, Child and his contemporaries across Europe came to consider economic emulation a constructive, if nerve-wracking phenomenon that ultimately would make everyone better off, fuelling a virtuous circle of one-upmanship.[56]

This insight regarding the mechanisms of emulation through translation also came to inform the theory of language itself. As a result of the very specific political context of the European system of states after the War of Spanish Succession, what J. G. A. Pocock has called the 'Utrecht Enlightenment', the myth of Babel was in fact inflected to the point where the separation of languages surprisingly came to be evaluated positively. The Peace of Utrecht of 1713 brought the confessional anarchy and the subsequent Wars of Religion that had dominated politics on the continent since the Reformation to a momentary close, inaugurating a period when the European order of states was linked by the mutual emulation of commerce and manners.[57] This was the context in which the a*bbé* Pluche published his *La Mécanique des langues et l'art de les enseigner* in 1751, as the volume of translations in Europe was about to explode as a cause and effect of the reciprocal process of emulation and development observed by Child. In it, he radically delineated the positive consequences of the fall of Babel in light of this new world order, arguing that civilisation and the beneficial advances of the nation-state were made possible only by the forced subdivision of men occasioned by the episode of the tower, by the concentration and internal development enforced by the isolation of linguistic communities.[58] Translation, it followed, was far more important than questing for a universal language, as it had been for magicians and polymaths like Ramon Llull and Athanasius Kircher, for it was the competitive interaction of nations which begat civilisation and development, and only through translation could one hope to emulate the achievements of others.[59]

While the historiography of economics now generally relegates the dawn of political economy as a 'science' to William Petty's *Political Arithmetick*, its cockcrow to François Quesnay's *Tableau économique*, and its glorious daybreak to Adam Smith's *Wealth of Nations*, approaching the development of political economy in Europe from the perspective of translations delineates an alternate picture. Different economic works were of course qualitatively different carriers of influence in translation, but those that emerge as particularly important seldom correspond to the canon of political economy established in the nineteenth and twentieth centuries. Where numerous articles and volumes on the physiocrats for example now appear on a monthly basis, it is beyond doubt that the anti-physiocrats won the day at the time as the system erected by Quesnay's men degenerated into dearth and famine.[60] Three translations of Voltaire's attack on physiocracy in fact appeared in London and Ireland before any physiocratic text was translated into English, and Ferdinando Galiani's scathing critique of them similarly reached most of Italy before they did. The anti-physiocrat Necker's three best-selling works went through at least 60 editions, selling more than 120,000 copies across Europe only in the 1770s and 1780s. He might have been the best-selling political economist in history well into the nineteenth century, yet his work on the subject is rigorously neglected in the Anglophone world.[61]

Similarly, the most studied 'British' economic writers of the late seventeenth century – pamphleteers like Nicholas Barbon, Dudley North, the early Henry Martyn, Charles Davenant, and Andrew Fletcher of Saltoun – were remarkably uninfluential in terms of editions and translations. Although the current fame of some authors like Thomas Mun does reflect a wide readership in early modern Europe, this is an exception that proves the rule. Not only do digital tools like *Early English Books Online* and *Making of the Modern World* show that North and Martyn were hardly ever referenced by their contemporaries in England, but they were *never* republished, *never* translated, and practically never read before McCulloch rediscovered them in the 1850s. Instead, continental translators looked to authors and pamphleteers that were deemed more in line with actual British policy at the time: currently neglected 'mercantilists' like John Cary, the authors of the *British Merchant*, and later Joshua Gee, all men of practice rather than moral philosophers who momentarily turned their gazes to worldlier concerns. The economic policies spearheaded by these writers – in a few words, pursuing profits through armed coercion, freeing internal trade, and encouraging domestic industry with high tariffs on the exportation of raw materials and the importation of manufactured goods – are a far cry from those proposed today by mainstream economists. A bias in the secondary literature towards 'precursorism', towards charting the genealogy of current ideas and ideologies rather than studying ideas in their own contexts (what Quentin Skinner has called the 'mythology of prolepsis'),[62] has profoundly skewed our understanding of the history of political economy in the European world.

If one's interest is in ideas and their repercussions in their historical context rather than ideas as they seem immediately applicable to current concerns, a study of the history of economic texts in translation suggests that a fundamental revision of the established canon might not only be possible but indeed absolutely necessary. J. G. A. Pocock long ago called for a more thorough history of translations, arguing that 'we must consider what happened when Grotius was read in London or Hobbes in Leiden, Locke in Naples or Montesquieu in Philadelphia'. He concludes that the Dutch reading of Hobbes meant 'no more than that *Leviathan* has many histories, and figures in the creation and diffusion of languages through many kinds of contexts,' but one must push beyond this to get at the core of the problem.[63] For, if one truly respects contexts, the question cannot simply be how Locke's economic works were read in Casalpusterlengo or how Quesnay was appropriated in Skiippagurra, a method which reproduces all of the prejudices and none of the pleasures of teleology. This is to put the cart before the horse. We should study the canon historically, not history canonically. A serious engagement with the history of economic translations demonstrates that authors such as Locke, North, and Quesnay were not read as widely and religiously as one might have imagined, and the striking question is really what people might have read instead. The 'canonical' authors of British political economy were simply not the same in Europe as in Britain, or even in Britain then as in Britain now.

The international economic rivalry of the early modern period contributed to the creation of a widespread market in Europe for the translation of works on political economy widely considered, a vast and varied market that historians too long have ignored. For while Nietzsche remarked in the *Gay Science* that 'translation was a form of conquest' in Roman times, when poets such as Horace and Propertius absorbed Greek texts for the Roman present as part of a protocol of cultural annexation, economic translations have historically served precisely the opposite purpose.[64] Resisting a conquering economy required countervailing its measures and emulating the instruments of its empire; occasionally before, and systematically after 1750, translations became the principal catalyst of this process. Whether the context was the explosive rivalry between giants like France and Great Britain or the more anxious attempts by new nations like Naples to find a place under the already crowded sun, translation was, as Goethe would write to Carlyle in July of 1827, 'one of the most important and valuable concerns in the whole world of affairs'.[65]

Notes

Though embarked upon long before, this chapter reworks parts of Sophus A. Reinert, *Translating Empire: Emulation and the Origins of Political Economy* (Cambridge, MA, 2011), ch I.

1. G. D. Ramsay (ed.), *The Politics of a Tudor Merchant Adventurer: A Letter to the Earls of East Friesland* (Manchester, 1979), 92.
2. Antoine de Montchrétien, in Th. Funck-Brentano (ed.), *Traicté de L'oeonomie Politique: Dedié En 1615 Au Roy Et À La Reyne Mer Du Roy*, (Paris, 1889), 44, 134–7, 141–3; John Cary, *An Essay towards Regulating the Trade and Employing the Poor of this Kingdom* (London, 1719), 1. On emulation and political economy, see Istvan Hont, *Jealousy of Trade: International Competition and the Nation-State in Historical Perspective* (Cambridge, Mass., 2005), 115–22 and Sophus A. Reinert, 'Emulazione E Traduzione: La Genealogia Occulta Della *Storia Del Commercio*', in Bruno Jossa, Rosario Patalano and Eugenio Zagari (eds), with the collaboration of Marina Albanese and an introduction by Rosario Patalano, *Genovesi economista* (Naples, 2007), 155–92.
3. On the importance of translation for European civilisation see George Steiner, *After Babel: Aspects of Language & Translation*, 3rd edn (Oxford, 1999).
4. On such espionage, see also Sophus A. Reinert, 'Another Grand Tour: Cameralism and Antiphysiocracy in Baden, Tuscany and Denmark-Norway', in Jürgen Georg Backhaus (ed.), *Physiocracy, Antiphysiocracy and Pfeiffer* (Dordrecht, 2011), 39–69.
5. See for example James van Horn Melton, *The Rise of the Public in Enlightenment Europe* (Cambridge, 2001).
6. On which see Jacob Soll, *The Information Master: Jean-Baptiste Colbert's Secret State Intelligence System* (Ann Arbor, 2009).
7. Girolamo Alberti to the Doge and Senate, 16 September 1672, in *Calendar of State Papers Relating to English Affairs in the Archives of Venice*, vol. 37, Allen B. Hinds (ed.) (London, 1939), 282–3.
8. In Florian Schui, *Early Debates about Industry: Voltaire and His Contemporaries* (Basingstoke, 2005), 68.
9. E.g. the curious case of Denmark–Norway, on which see Lars Berge (ed.), *Å Beskrive Og Forandre Verden: En Antologi Tekster Fra 1700-Tallets Dansk-Norske Tekskultur* (Oslo, 1998), 9–10; Svend Bruhns, *Bibliografiens Historie I Danmark, 1700- Og 1800- Tallet* (Aalborg, 2004), 31, 162–3.
10. Pietro Verri, *Considerazioni Sul Commercio Dello Stato Di Milano*, C. A. Vianello (ed.) (Milan, 1939), 202.
11. Alessandro Verri, 'Dei Difetti Della Letteratura E Di Alcune Loro Cagioni', in Gianni Francioni and Sergio Romagnoli (eds), *Il Caffè: 1764–1766* (Turin, 1998), 543.
12. Archivio di Stato di Torino, Turin, Italy, *Materie di Commercio*, 3° Categoria, Mazzo 3, n°4, 1751, [Comte Perron], 'Pensèes diverses sur les moïens de rendre le Commerce florissant En Piemont…'.
13. Christian Schumacher to Ove Høegh-Guldberg, 12 August 1784, *Ove Høegh Guldbergs og Arveprins Frederiks brevveksling med Peter Christian Schumacher 1778–1807*, J. O. Bro-Jørgensen (ed.) (Copenhagen, 1972), 288; Rigsarkivet, Copenhagen, Denmark, 06312, *Schumacher, Peter Chr., 1762–1817 Breve, kopibøger, optegnelser m.m.*, 7: *Breve fra private V-Æ*, A. I. 3: *Breve fra Christian August Wichmann, Leipzig*.
14. See, on the old republic of letters, Anthony Grafton, 'A Sketch Map of a Lost Continent: The Republic of Letters', in id., *Worlds Made by Words: Scholarship and Community in the Modern West* (Cambridge, Mass., 2009), 9–34. There were of course also examples of eminently erudite political economists

straddling both traditions, see Sophus A. Reinert, 'Lessons on the Rise and Fall of Great Powers: Conquest, Commerce, and Decline in Enlightenment Italy', *The American Historical Review* 115, no. 5 (2010): 1395–425.

15. David Hume, *Political Essays*, Knud Haakonssen (ed.) (Cambridge, 1994); Gaetano Filangieri, *La Scienza Della Legislazione*, Vincenzo Ferrone et al. (ed.), 7 vols. (Venice 2004), II, 156–7.
16. On the propensity of emulation to degenerate into envy, see Reinert, 'Emulazione E Traduzione'.
17. Daniel Milo, 'La Bourse Mondiale de La Traduction: Un Baromètre Culturel?' *Annales: Économies, Sociétés, Civilizations* 29 (1984): 93–115.
18. On which see Roger Chartier, *The Order of Books* (Stanford, 1994).
19. Richard Drayton, *Nature's Government: Science, Imperial Britain and the 'Improvement' of the World* (New Haven, 2000).
20. In many ways, this current project began with Kenneth E. Carpenter, *Dialogue in Political Economy: Translations from and into German in the 18th Century* (Boston, 1977). On the Kress collection see Ruth R. Rogers, 'The Kress Library of Business and Economics', *The Business History Review* 60, no. 2 (1986): 281–8. Methodologically, in what follows, editions of works count as 1 'translation'.
21. Guillaume-Thomas Raynal, *Philosophical and Political History of the ... East and West Indies*, 6 vols. (London, 1798), 368.
22. Anonymous translator's introduction to Tommaso Campanella, *A Discourse Touching the Spanish Monarchy...* (London, 1654). On industrial espionage, see J. R. Harris, *Industrial Espionage and Technology Transfer: Britain and France in the Eighteenth Century* (Aldershot, 1998), 544.
23. Jan Luiten van Zanden, *The Long Road to the Industrial Revolution: The European Economy in a Global Perspective, 1000–1800* (Leiden, 2009), 185.
24. Geneviève Roche, *Les Traductions-Relais En Allemagne Au XVIIIe Siècle: Des Lettres Aux Sciences* (Paris, 2001), 21 argues that the 1750s experienced a general increase in the volume of translations.
25. Calculations are based on Angus Maddison, *The World Economy* (Paris, 2006), 244–7, 263–5, numbers are in 1990 US$ and are historical projections of the performance of current regions.
26. Robert C. Allen, *The British Industrial Revolution in Global Perspective* (Cambridge, 2009), 17.
27. Joseph E. Inikori, *Africans and the Industrial Revolution in England: A Study in International Trade and Economic Development* (Cambridge, 2002), 362.
28. On England's interconnected imperial and linguistic expansion, see Peter Burke, *Languages and Communities in Early Modern Europe* (Cambridge, 2004), 13, 80–1; Bernhard Fabian, *The English Book in Eighteenth-Century Germany* (London, 1992), 110.
29. In Robert Phillipson, *Linguistic Imperialism* (Oxford, 1992), 31. On the deep historical relation between language and power, see David W. Anthony, *The Horse, the Wheel, and Language: How Bronze-Age Riders from the Eurasian Steppes Shaped the Modern World* (Princeton, 2007), 464.
30. Hont, *Jealousy of Trade*.
31. Reinert, 'Emulazione e traduzione'..
32. On this transition, see Patrick O'Brien, 'Inseparable Connections: Trade, Economy, Fiscal State, and the Expansion of Empire, 1688–1815', in P. J. Marshall

(ed.), *The Oxford History of the British Empire, vol. 2: The Eighteenth Century* (Oxford, 1998), 53–77; Robert C. Allen, 'Britain's Economic Ascendancy in a European Context', in Leandro Prados de Escosura (ed.), *Exceptionalism and Industrialisation: Britain and its European Rivals, 1688–1815* (Cambridge, 2004), 15–34.

33. On this phenomenon in general, see Roche, *Les Traductions-Relais.*
34. On the emulation of English theories and practices see Emma Rothschild, 'The English *Kopf*', in Donald Winch and Patrick K. O'Brien (eds), *The Political Economy of British Historical Experience* (Oxford, 2002), 31–60 and my 'Blaming the Medici: Footnotes, Falsification, and the Fate of the English Model in 18th-Century Italy', *Journal of the History of European Ideas* 32, no. 4 (2006): 430–55.
35. On this context see Bob Harris, *Politics and the Nation: Britain in the Mid-Eighteenth Century* (Oxford, 2002).
36. Daniel Defoe, *Plan for the English Commerce* (London, 1737), 300–1 and similarly Voltaire, *Letters on the English Nation* (London, 1733), 222. See on this phenomenon Christine MacLeod, 'European Origins of British Technological Predominance', in Prados de Escosura (ed.), *Exceptionalism and Industrialisation* (2004), 111–26.
37. See my 'The Italian Tradition of Political Economy: Theories and Policies of Development in the Semi-Periphery of the Enlightenment', in Jomo K. Sundaram and Erik S. Reinert (eds), *The Origins of Development Economics: How Schools of Economic Thought Have Addressed Development* (London, 2005), 24–47.
38. See, however, on the sophistication of Spanish economic thought, Cosimo Perrotta, 'Early Spanish Mercantilism: A First Analysis of Underdevelopment', in Lars Magnusson (ed.), *Mercantilist Economics* (Boston, 1993), 17–58.
39. Juan Enrique de Graef, *Discursos Mercuriales Económico-Políticos (1752–1756)*, Francisco Sáncez-Blanco (ed.) (Seville, 1996), 130–2. See similarly Gabriel Paquette's rich essay in this volume.
40. D. Domingo de Marcoleta, *Observaciones Sobre Las Ventajas, Y Desventajas de La Francia, Y La Gran Bretaña* (Madrid, 1771), 6–7, 9–10.
41. Antonio Genovesi, *Storia Del Commercio Della Gran Brettagna Scritta Da John Cary*, 3 vols. (Naples, 1757–1758), vol. I, ii. On this see my 'Emulazione e traduzione'.
42. See for example the first Dano-Norwegian journal of political economy *Danmarks og Norges Oeconomiske Magazín* (1757–1764) and C. K., *Davenants Afhandling, Angående Sætt och Utvægar, Hvarigenom et Folk kan Winna uti Handels-Wågen* (Stockholm, 1756), A2r.
43. *Journal Oeconomique*, January 1756, 16.
44. Christine Théré, 'Economic Publishing and Authors', in Gilbert Faccarello (ed.), *Studies in the History of French Political Economy: From Bodin to Walras* (London, 1998), 1–56; see also John Shovlin, *The Political Economy of Virtue: Luxury, Patriotism and the Origins of the French Revolution* (Ithaca, 2006), 2.
45. See on this circle, among others, Michael Sonenscher, *Before the Deluge: Public Debt, Inequality and the Intellectual Origins of the French Revolution* (Princeton, 2007).
46. Niccoló Guasti, 'Forbonnais e Uztariz: Le Ragioni di una Traduzione', *Cuadernos aragoneses de economia*, 2° epoca, vol. 8, no. 1 (1998), 125–41.

47. Anonymous, *Le people instruit* (N.P., 1756), ii.
48. Josephine Grieder, *Anglomania in France 1740–1789: Fact, Fiction, and Political Discourse* (Geneva–Paris, 1985).
49. In J. G. A. Pocock, *Barbarism and Religion*, 4 vols. (Cambridge, 1999–2005), vol. I, 241.
50. Fania Oz-Salzberger, *Translating the Enlightenment: Scottish Civic Discourse in Eighteenth Century Germany* (Oxford, 1995), 59.
51. See, on translation in Germany at the time, Thomas Huber, *Studien zur Theorie des Übersetzens im Zeitalter der Deutschen Aufklärung 1730–1770* (Meisenheim am Glan, 1968) and Oz-Salzberger, *Translating the Enlightenment.*
52. Magdalene Humpert, *Bibliographie der Kameralwissenschaften* (Cologne, 1937). On the origins of political economy in Germany see Jürgen G. Backhaus, 'The German Economic Tradition: From Cameralism to the Verein für Socialpolitik', in Manuela Albertone and Alberto Masoero (eds), *Political Economy and National Realities* (Turin, 1994), 320–56.
53. In Fabian, *The English Book*, 77.
54. Josiah Child, *A New Discourse of Trade* (London, 1690), 131, 42.
55. Josiah Child, *A New Discourse of Trade* (London, 1740), 85–6; Emphasis added.
56. See similarly Hont, *Jealousy of Trade.*
57. Pocock, *Barbarism and Religion*, vol. III, 206.
58. Nöel Antoine Pluche, *La Mécanique Des Langues Et L'art de Les Enseigner* (Paris, 1751); Umberto Eco, *La Ricerca Della Lingua Perfetta Nella Cultura Europea* (Bari, 1993), 364–5.
59. See on this tradition Paolo Rossi, *Clavis Universalis: Arti Della Memoria E Logica Combinatoriale Da Lullo a Leibniz* (Bologna, 2000) and Eco, *La Ricerca.*
60. On which see Steven L. Kaplan, *Bread, Politics and Political Economy in the Reign of Louis XV* (The Hague, 1976).
61. Kenneth E. Carpenter, 'The Economic Bestsellers before 1850', *Bulletin of the Kress Library of Business and EconomicsI*, no. 11 (Boston: Harvard Business School, 1975).
62. Quentin Skinner, *Visions of Politics*, 3 vols. (Cambridge, 2002), vol. I, 73.
63. J. G. A. Pocock, 'The Concept of Language and the *Métier d'historien*: Some Considerations on Practice', in Anthony Pagden (ed.), *The Languages of Political Theory in Early-Modern Europe* (Cambridge, 1987), 19–38, 20, 37.
64. Friedrich Nietzsche, *The Gay Science*, Walter Kaufman (trans) (New York, 1974), 173.
65. Johann Wolfgang von Goethe and Thomas Carlyle, *Correspondence between Goethe and Carlyle*, Charles Eliot Norton (ed.) (London, 1887), 26.

Part II

Imperial Experiences

6
War, Peace and the Rise of the London Stock Market

Giles Parkinson

The stock market which arose in London toward the end of the seventeenth century emerged from a confluence of political, social, economic and cultural processes. The focus of this chapter is on the extent to which England's participation in continental war between 1689 and 1697 called the nascent market in securities into being and, furthermore, conditioned its early development. The argument will develop as follows. To begin, the case for war as a catalytic effect upon the stock market is presented; consideration is also given to the future role the capital market in securities would play in financing the wars against France over the course of the long eighteenth century. Next, an historical question is posed: how was it that contemporaries came to identify fluctuations in abstract share prices as real changes in the national fortunes of their country? Answers are sought in two places. First, it is noted that the forts and ships of overseas trading companies were especially vulnerable to attack during periods of episodic warfare: profits would slump, dividends were suspended, and the share price would tumble. Second, attention is given to the value of securities issued to fund the conflict; they are seen to rise and fall in response to news of events affecting the survival of the Glorious Revolution because, ultimately, their worth depended upon the promises of future payments made by the regime.

I

The decade of the 1690s was a period of great change and ferment in the London stock market. For years the aggregated total number of shareholders had remained steady at around 700.[1] There was little investment choice beyond the East Indian, Royal African, and Hudson's Bay companies; only eleven other enterprises were incorporated as

Table 6.1 Annual numbers of transfers of stock, 1688–1698

Year	Bank of England	East India Company	Royal African Company	Hudson's Bay Company	Estcourt's Lead Mine
1688		624*	101	24	
1689		X	81	22	
1690		X	38	67	
1691		3139*	928	92	
1692		X	487	92	
1693		X	391	81	99
1694	880*	2426*	207	50	105
1695	1371	X	194	52	30
1696	1322	X	129	21	
1697	2082	X	195	21	
1698	2477	1158*	734	14	

Sources: see Parkinson, 'London stock market', 'Table 2.1: Annual numbers of transfers of stock, 1688–1698', p. 73.

Note: An asterisk (*) denotes proportional extrapolation from incomplete data to arrive at an annual figure, a cross (X) that data does not survive for that year.

joint-stock companies with transferable shares by 1688.[2] Liquidity was thin. During the 1680s the annual number of share transactions in these three trading companies ticked over at around three or four hundred transfers per year.[3] Then, sometime around 1690–1691 – the data are patchy – the number of share transactions ballooned (see Table 6.1). Part of this sudden increase in share activity was caused by new investors rushing to participate in the market; the number of stockholders rose by eightfold during the decade to approximately 5,000.[4]

What changed? The explosion in market activity has been attributed in part to the lubricating effect of the large 'scrip dividends' – 'stock splits' in modern parlance – issued by two companies in these years.[5] That is, in September 1690 each stock owner of the Hudson's Bay Company had the number of his shares tripled, while the Royal African Company quadrupled the size of existing holdings in July 1691.[6] There are several flaws with this argument, however. First, increasing the number of shares available in a market does not stimulate demand in and of itself since potential investors are not compelled to buy the stock on offer. Moreover, the East India Company did not issue a scrip dividend at this time, and yet it can be seen that the number of annual transactions in this stock increased fivefold in just three years. Finally, focusing on internal changes in preexisting companies does not explain why new enterprises, such as the Bank of England and Estcourt's Lead Mine, should be founded at this particular time. Rather than looking to scrip dividends to account for the dramatic changes of the 1690s, the dominant factor lies elsewhere.

A contemporary explanation for this prodigal expansion is offered by John Houghton, a Londoner prominent in the history of the early stock market.[7] During the decade he peddled share tips and brokering services from his business behind the Royal Exchange and published *A Collection for Improvement of Husbandry and Trade*, a periodical which discussed aspects of the fledgling stock market.[8] In the summer of 1694 he ran a series of essays exposing the inner mysteries of the stock market to his readers and wrote,

> A great many Stocks have arisen since this war with France; for Trade being obstructed at Sea, few that had Money were willing it should be idle, and a great many that wanted Employments studied how to dispose of their Money, that they might be able to command it whensoever they had occasion, which they found they could more easily do in Joint-Stock, than in laying out the same in Lands, Houses or Commodities, these [shares] being more easily shifted from Hand to Hand.[9]

According to Houghton, normal capital flows were disrupted as a result of England's entry into the War of the League of Augsburg in 1689; capital found an outlet in the London stock market because of the fungibility provided by shares, they 'being more easily shifted from Hand to Hand' than investments in property or commercial assets.[10]

As well as being illiquid, the declining profitability of traditional investment classes further encouraged capital to be diverted into equities. In April 1694 Samuel Jeake, a nonconformist provincial merchant from the Sussex town of Rye, recorded in his diary that the 'war having spoiled all [his] Trade' he was now making 'but 5 per cent of my money at Interest upon Mortgages & Bonds, upon which I could but barely maintain my family'. Looking for a higher return, 'to venture & try to advance my income', 'several Projects... began to run in my mind', such as buying tickets in the Million Lottery, investing in East-India stock, and 'putting in moneys upon... the Bank of England'.[11] Wider empirical evidence suggests that overseas merchants were motivated by similar considerations. D. W. Jones, for example, has found that London merchants (especially wine importers) sought alternative forms of profitable yet liquid investment at this time; they were therefore prominent subscribers of capital to the Bank of England.[12] Certainly, if we examine the occupations of known shareholders, we find that a significant proportion identified themselves as 'merchants' during the 1690s.[13]

As well as stimulating the rise of the stock market at this particular time, war guided the direction which the new developments took. During the 1690s the stock market grew in size by the expansion of existing enterprises and the incorporation of new ones. The great trading companies sought to increase their market capitalisation through reorganisation of the capital structure and through secondary share issues. While the Hudson's Bay Company tripled and the (Old) East-India Company quadrupled in size between 1690 and 1700, the Royal African Company ballooned tenfold to over £1 million.[14] The stock market grew further through the diverse array of joint-stock companies founded at this time. Between July 1691 and October 1693, peak numbers of patents were enrolled, and many of the new ventures begun during the decade were incorporated to exploit one of these new inventions.[15] Take, for example, the Company for the Sucking-Worm Engine of Mr John Loftingh, Merchant, at Bow Church Yard, Cheapside, which was chartered to manufacture and market a patented design of fire engine.[16] Such was the flurry of activity that estimating the number of new companies is fraught with difficulty. Counting the scattered references from a variety of printed sources, William Robert Scott has identified the names of approximately 100 English joint stocks in existence by the end of 1695.[17] About fifty of these received periodic coverage by Houghton in the share tables he printed in each issue of his *Collection*.[18] The influence of the war upon these new companies becomes apparent when their names and charters are examined: many were founded in order to either supply war material (such as armaments, mines, and other heavy industries) or manufacture those traditionally French-produced commodities (such as paper, glass, linen, and silk) whose supply was disrupted by the hostilities.[19] Take, for example, 'The governor and company for casting and making guns and ordnance in moulds of metal' of 1693 or 'The company of the glass makers in and about the cities of London and Westminster' of 1691.[20]

A third group of enterprises connected with the war were those established to finance the conflict. Of the various funds and schemes, the most significant and enduring was the Bank of England, called into existence in 1694 through the provision of a £1.2 million loan to the government.[21] Annual payments of 8 per cent were guaranteed through an act of Parliament and backed by reserving portions of future tax revenue: the shareholders who subscribed capital to the loan were therefore relieved of the precarious uncertainty that the monarch could default on payments at will. For example, in 1672 Charles II suspended all capital repayments to his creditors in an infamous incident remembered as the 'Stop of the Exchequer'.[22] But two decades later, Samuel Jeake believed that buying shares in the Bank of England automatically bought him a guaranteed yield of '8 per cent perpetual Interest' on the investment.[23]

The founding of the bank marked the beginning of a quiet transformation in the English system of public credit and has been identified as a turning point in the creation of John Brewer's 'fiscal military state'.[24] The history of England's long eighteenth century is dominated by the wars against France which began after the Glorious Revolution. In terms of population and natural wealth, the advantage lay with the French; English resources were limited and inadequate to sustain the crippling cost of the conflict. However, through a system of long-term public borrowing, so greatly superior to that of the French, it was possible for the English government to tap the country's wealth for war purposes far more effectively than could have been achieved by taxation alone. England could now spend out of all proportion to her tax revenue and mobilise her smaller reserves of blood and treasure to greater effect, so the argument goes. Military success, in its turn, led to the expansion of economic empire and, therefore, the domination of overseas markets which, had they fallen to the French, might have seriously impaired England's economic growth. The function of the Bank of England, then, was to mobilise wealth and connect it to the making of war, financing the capture of empire.

During the 1690s the stock market expanded dramatically by every measure: joint-stock companies increased in both size and number, common and preference shares were traded with greater frequency, and thousands of new investors entered the market. They were attracted by the fungibility and potential for profit offered by equities amid the uncertain wartime economic climate which was depressing foreign trade. As well as stimulating new growth, the conflict also affected the direction of the changes by diverting capital toward those companies connected to the war economy. Beneath these developments, the beginning of a well-organised system of public credit was taking place in the form of the Bank of England.

II

The changes in the nature of the stock market just described affected the way that contemporaries thought about the shares which they bought and sold in increasing volumes. Toward the end of Anne's reign, Jonathan Swift bemoaned that 'the Wealth of the Nation, that used to be reckoned by the Value of Land, is now computed by the Rise and Fall of Stocks'.[25] Thomas Baston, publishing his *Thoughts on Trade* in 1716, wrote that most people now took stocks 'to be the Weather Glass of the State...so that they judge the Health or Sickness of the Publick'.[26] Comments such as these suggest that sometime around 1700 the rise and fall in stock prices came to be identified with the fortunes of the (Protestant) nation. How was such an astonishing connection made?

Ever since the 1680s, share prices had appeared in the London business press as a permanent feature of agricultural and industrial commodity price lists.[27] Price lists were precisely that: specialist publications aimed at a narrow mercantile audience, with limited appeal to outsiders. Readership, accordingly, was low. The only relatively reliable data for newspaper print runs in this period are based on records generated in connection with the Stamp Act of 1712; they show that at this time price lists typically paid duty on around sixty to seventy issues each week.[28] Although the earliest example of a share price reported by an ordinary newspaper comes from the *Flying Post* of 25 June 1695, financial 'gossip columns' were not common until the summer of 1696.[29] The inclusion of price data at this time, and not during the boom earlier in the decade, can be attributed to the increasing proportion of passive stock holdings in a cooling market.[30] Following the fortunes of a stock in the press would titillate the armchair investor, yet the knowledge was too dated to be of practical use to the hour-by-hour speculator.[31]

In general, newspapers restricted their share reports to the same stocks covered by the price lists: namely, the Royal African, East-India and Hudson's Bay companies, and the Bank of England.[32] Together the value of these four enterprises commanded the dominant share of the aggregate market. Likewise, contemporaries also focused their attention on the same narrow range of stocks when writing about the movements of shares.[33] For example, the diarist Narcissus Luttrell gave a running commentary on a reversal in the fortunes of the East-India Company during the autumn of 1695. On 5 September he wrote that the price of stock had risen to £94 after the arrival of a ship bearing cargo worth £25,000.[34] The press expected the shares to rise still further.[35] The following week, however, they slumped to £74 when news arrived of the loss of two ships.[36] Then, in mid-October, the price collapsed to £54 with the announced loss of a further three vessels.[37]

Bad news from abroad broke abruptly and brought sudden ruin, but the building anticipation of positive news was crucial in talking up the price of a stock. This was especially true for the trading companies since news of the impending arrival of a ship often outpaced its return to port from the far corners of the globe. Investors flocked to buy shares in the hope that the profits of the cargo would be redistributed through a special dividend. For example, on 29 April 1696, Houghton quotes the price of East-India stock at £54.[38] Two weeks later, *The Protestant Mercury* publicised the contents of a letter the company had received from 'Mr Viccars, Master of the Packet Boats in Dublin', warning that ships were soon expected to arrive in London.[39] The price of the stock began to nudge upward to reach £58 on 13 May.[40] When the ships arrived, as the *Flying Post* reported on 21 May 1696, the shares leapt to £67.[41] A week later, *The Post Boy* was gamely describing how 'the Actions of the East-India Company advance daily, and I hear they expect 5 ships before Winter'.[42]

Although the foreign trading companies were given a monopoly position within England to carry on a particular trade, their charters did not protect them against depredations and encroachments from outsiders. As one pamphlet explained, 'East Indian, Affrican and Hudsons Bay Companies are...affected by the War with private Traders, their present Importations and Exportations are attended with greater Risques, higher Fraight and new Duties'.[43] Especially, the trading companies were vulnerable to attack by the French. For instance, John Evelyn noted in his diary that, following a run of military setbacks in West Africa, the price of shares in the Royal African Company had collapsed to £30 in 1694 from £173 in 1689.[44] Throughout the decade the Hudson's Bay Company faced low-level economic rivalry from French traders in Canada which often erupted into an open conflict of tit-for-tat raids and counter-raids, depressing share prices and interrupting regular dividend payments.[45]

From the mid-1690s, then, the publication of share prices was increasingly prevalent, and attention tended to concentrate on the fortunes of the main trading companies. Connections were being made, moreover, between the shipping news of safe arrivals or losses at sea and fluctuations in the price of the stock. In particular, it was recognised that the success or failure of an individual overseas trading company was bound up with the wider narrative of England's successes and failures as a corporate body in the wars against France. This association, it will be argued in the next section, was especially strong with connection to the Bank of England, the other stock which contemporaries paid particular attention to.

III

The financial interdependence of rulers and ruled has been coined the 'Eumenes effect'.[46] Eumenes of Cardia was one of Alexander the Great's generals who survived the initial power struggle following the death of Alexander because he was so heavily indebted to the other generals: his rivals had a vested interest in keeping him alive in the hope of repayment! If creditors have a general self-interest in maintaining the ability of debtors to repay their financial obligations, by the same principle lenders to the post-1688 Crown acquired a political interest in the survival of the sovereign regime, principally against the Franco-Jacobite threat. The founding of the Bank of England in 1694 institutionalised the new relationship between nation and monarch by acting as a financial mediator: contemporaries recognised that the bank, 'like the other Publick Funds, ty[ed] the People faster to the Government'.[47] Indeed, it can be contended that a purchase of government debt bought with it a stake in the post-Revolutionary nation and its anti-Catholic principles. As such, investment in the funds became a patriotic gesture.[48] This observation goes some way in explaining the disproportionate number of Huguenot names which are found on shareholder lists, especially within the Bank of England.[49]

The other 'public fund' of significance established at this time was the Million Adventure. Designed by Thomas Neale to raise a quick £1 million in 1694, 100,000 lottery tickets were sold at £10 each, the proceeds going to the government.[50] Unlike most modern lotteries, after the initial draw, non–prize winning (or 'blank') tickets were not worthless but rather yielded an annuity of £1 per annum for sixteen years. A secondary market in these tickets immediately sprang up to cater to those who did not wish to wait for sixteen years to elapse before realising their full investment.[51] Of course, if King William was toppled by a Jacobite coup or French invasion before the sixteen-year period was over, then the tickets really would be worthless, as would shares in the Bank of England.

If the 'Eumenes' hypothesis is correct, any change in the probability of a Jacobite restoration or French victory over England should be reflected in the financial markets.[52] Any Franco-Jacobite activity that altered the possibility of a Stuart restoration would have an immediate and predictable effect. Specifically, the perceived worth of securities which depended upon payments by King William's government – such as the price of Bank of England shares and the resale value of 'blank' tickets in the Million Lottery – would rise or fall in proportion to the changing likelihood of the survival of the Glorious Revolution, since any change in the regime would automatically lead to a default on annuity payments (for lottery tickets) and dividends (for bank shares). On 3 January 1695, for example, John Freke – broker to John Locke – wrote that 'on the Queens death the Bank Actions fell from 76 to 72 but are now got up again'.[53] Throwaway comments such as these are not convincing when taken in isolation, but empirically the evidence for the 'Eumenes' hypothesis is much stronger. Figure 6.1 shows the price of shares in the Bank of England and the resale value of 'blank' tickets in the Million Lottery from 1695 to 1697. It can be seen that the two data series move in tandem with one another, and mathematically they show a high degree of correlation.[54]

Correlation is not causation, however; the intimate relationship between European military events and the price of securities is best

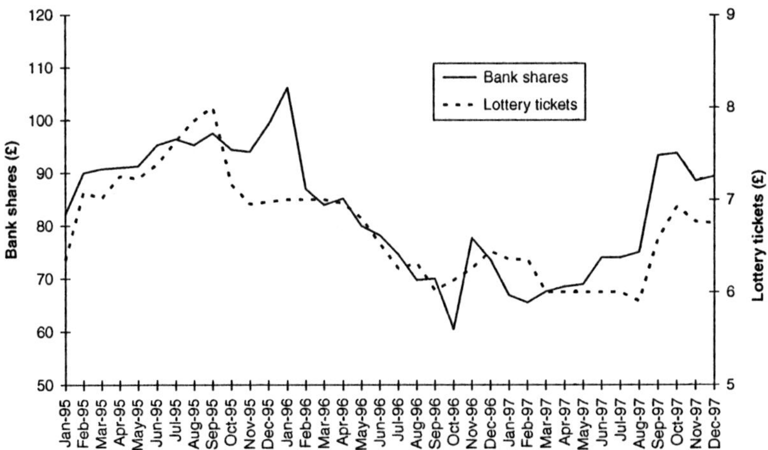

Figure 6.1 Average monthly prices for Bank of England shares and value of 'blank' million lottery tickets, January 1695–December 1697

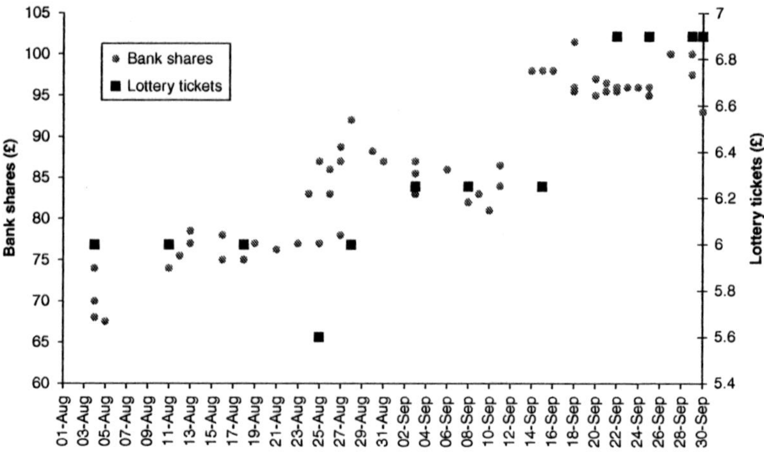

Figure 6.2 Spot data for Bank of England shares and value of 'blank' million lottery tickets, August–September 1697

demonstrated by a micro-examination of the financial impact of the Treaty of Ryswick. Again, as with news of arriving trading ships, anticipation was important. Toward the end of July, hopes of a tangible victory began to rise; Luttrell wrote in his diary that the price of Bank of England stock was up at £72 from the level of £60 where it had lingered for the last few months.[55] In Figure 6.2, securities price data were extracted from a variety of sources – including newspapers, diaries, price currents, diplomatic correspondence, and Houghton's *Collection* – and plotted as a time series.[56] Where two different prices are given for the same day, both are included without attempting to reconcile them. For much of August the price of bank shares and lottery tickets was around £75 and £6 respectively. Then, in the fourth week, there appears to have been an episode of speculation in bank stock: on 28 August the excitable *Post Boy* reported that 'the Auctions or Stocks of the several Companies advances daily, the People being convinced that the Peace is as good as concluded'.[57] Samuel Jeake hastened to London in order to monitor the situation and made a purchase of £100 nominal in bank stock at £85 10s on 6 September.[58] The miniature bubble deflated, however, and a correspondent wrote on 10 September that the share price, which had peaked at £92, had now slumped back to £80/82.[59] It remained around this level for the next two weeks, while the resale value of a 'blank' lottery ticket edged upward to £6 5s. When news arrived that the peace had been signed, the impact upon the securities market was electric: the terms not only ended the Nine Years' War but also included an explicit recognition by Louis XIV of William as king of England and, further, a renunciation of his support for the Stuart restoration. As the *Post Boy* reported:

> On the 11th early in the morning we received the agreeable News of the Conclusion of the Peace.... Upon notice of this News the Bells were rung in all parts of this City, the great Guns were fired round the Tower, and at night we had Bonefires and Illuminations, with other Demonstrations of Joy suitable to the occasion: In a word, it has already such Effect on affairs, that the Bank Stock advanced 10 per Cent the first day.[60]

And, as well as the price of bank shares shooting up to £98, the value of 'blank' lottery tickets rose to £6 18s.

By every indicator, the London stock market underwent a period of quantitative and qualitative change during the 1690s. The number of investors rose eightfold; approximately one hundred new companies were listed; existing enterprises increased their market capitalisation; stock prices were reported more often in the press; and shares changed hands with greater frequency. A new generation of investors was encouraged to enter the capital market by the fungibility which shares offered and a decline in the returns they were receiving from other assets such as bonds, property and commodities. But as well as increasing the attractiveness of the stock market, England's military campaign against France affected the direction of growth in the burgeoning capital market. In amongst the new gunpowder and glass-making companies a system of public credit was taking shape around the Bank of England and other government-backed securities. Since future payments on this quasi-national debt depended upon the survival of the Glorious Revolution, the value of bank stock and lottery tickets rose and fell in accordance with the likelihood of the Stuart restoration. Contemporaries, who noted that the price of East-India stock fell whenever news arrived that a ship had been sunk, and that lottery tickets rose with an English victory, naturally made the association between fluctuations in share prices and the changing fortunes of the nation. Moreover, those with a vested interest in preserving the post-Revolutionary religious settlement against a Catholic France – such as nonconformists and Huguenots – had every reason to invest in those public funds which were, indirectly, defending the realm.

Notes

1. K. G. Davies, 'Joint-Stock Investment in the Later Seventeenth Century', *Economic History Review*, n.s., 4, no. 3 (1952): 297.
2. These were as follows: 'the Mines Royal, the Mineral and Battery Works, the New River, the York-buildings, and the Shadwell Waterworks, the Fire-insurance company, that for making Salt Water fresh, the Convex Lights, the White Paper Makers, the Royal Lustring company, and lastly a provincial water supply undertaking at Newcastle'. William Robert Scott, *The Constitution and Finance of English, Scottish and Irish Joint-Stock Companies to 1720*, 3 vols. (Cambridge, Cambridge University Press, 1910–1912), I: 327.
3. Ann M. Carlos, Jennifer Key and Jill L. Dupree, 'Learning and the Creation of Stock Market Institutions: Evidence from the Royal African and Hudson's Bay Companies, 1670–1700', *Journal of Economic History* 58, no. 2 (1998), 'Table 1: Royal African Company. Annual Transactions by Balue and Bolume', 326; Peter Loughead, 'The East India Company in English Domestic Politics, 1657–1688' (unpublished DPhil dissertation, University of Oxford, 1981), 151; Ann M. Carlos and Jill L. Van Stone, 'Stock Transfer Patterns in the Hudson's Bay Company: A Study of the English Capital Market in Operation, 1670–1730', *Business History* 38, no. 2 (1995), 'Table 1: Annual Transactions by Value and Volume', 21.
4. G. D. B. Parkinson, 'The London Stock Market in the 1690s' (unpublished MPhil thesis, University of Cambridge, 2006), 'Table 3.2: Estimates of Investment Community Size in 1690, 1695, 1700', 105.
5. Davies, 'Joint-Stock Investment', 292. In 1682 the East India Company issued a scrip dividend of 100 per cent, with a similar stimulating effect upon the annual number of share transfers. Loughead, 'East India Company', 151. For a discussion of the blend of politico-economic motives which prompt a scrip dividend, see Parkinson, 'London Stock Market', 128–9, 129 n18.
6. A 1/12, Fair copies of Governor and Committee minutes (1689–1690), f. 30v; T 70/188, Stock Journal (1691–1693), ff. 1–6, 14–20.
7. The entry in the *Oxford Dictionary of National Biography* serves as an excellent introduction to this personality of the proto-Enlightenment, but see also D. T. O'Rourke, 'John Houghton (1645–1705): Journalist, Apothecary and F. R. S.', *Pharmaceutical Historian* 9, no. 1 (1979): 2–3.
8. The entire series of the *Collection* has been reprinted in full. John Houghton, *A Collection for Improvement of Husbandry and Trade*, 20 vols. (30 March 1692–24 September 1703; repr. 4 vols., Westmead, Farnborough: Gregg International, 1969) [cited as Houghton, *Collection* throughout]. Houghton, *Collection*, 96 (1 June 1694); see also ibid., 104 (27 July 1694). He moved from Bartholomew Lane to Grace Church Street in 1694. Ibid., 124 (14 December 1694).
9. Houghton, *Collection*, 98 (15 June 1694).
10. This is not, however, to dismiss the extent to which the changes in London's capital market during the 1690s were built upon preexisting foundations, nor to exclude all influences upon these developments other than that of war. See, for example, the discussion in Parkinson, 'London Stock Market', 11–4, 16–8.
11. Samuel Jeake, *An Astrological Diary of the Seventeenth Century*, Michael Hunter and Annabel Gregory (eds) (Oxford: Clarendon Press, 1988), 233 (16 April 1694).

12. D. W. Jones, *War and Economy in the Age of William III and Marlborough* (Oxford: Basil Blackwell, 1988), 249–50.
13. See, for example, Parkinson, 'London Stock Market', 119, 'Table 4.3: Occupations of Owners of Hudson Bay Stock, 1692–1698', 145; Anne L. Murphy, 'Society, Knowledge and the Behaviour of English Investors, 1688–1702' (unpublished PhD thesis, University of Leicester, 2005), 144, 'Table 5.5: Social Status/Occupation of Original Subscribers to the Bank of England', 147, 'Table 5.7: Social Status/Occupation of Subscribers to the Bank of England, 1697', 150. It should be remembered that occupational labels need to be used with caution. For a discussion of the problems, see James Alexander, 'The Economic and Social Structure of the City of London, c. 1700' (unpublished PhD thesis, London School of Economics, 1989), 24–8.
14. On capitalisations, see Scott, *Constitution and Finance*, passim.
15. Christine MacLeod, *Inventing the Industrial Revolution: The English Patent System, 1660–1800* (Cambridge University Press, 1988), 150. See also Christine MacLeod, 'The 1690s Patents Boom: Invention or Stock-Jobbing?' *Economic History Review*, 2nd series, 39, no. 4 (1986): 549.
16. Scott, *Constitution and Finance*, II: 481.
17. Scott, *Constitution and Finance*, I: 327.
18. Houghton, *Collection*, passim. See the reproduction of *Collection*, 111 (7 September 1694) in Scott, *Constitution and Finance*, 'Types of the Quotations of Stocks and Shares from *Collections* [sic] *for Improvement of Husbandry and Trade*, by John Houghton', I: 351.
19. Scott, *Constitution and Finance*, I: 328, 330–1. On the impact of the war upon patenting, see Macleod, '1690s Patents Boom', 557–62.
20. These were printed in Houghton's list as 'Saltpetre – Dockwra' and 'Glass' respectively. Scott, *Constitution and Finance*, II: 473; III: 109, 111.
21. Although the Bank of England survives to this day, it was originally granted a twelve-year charter and operated from a property leased for just eleven years. See Murphy, 'Society, Knowledge, Behaviour', 68–9.
22. For further discussion, see J. Keith Horsefield, 'The Stop of the Exchequer Revisited', *Economic History Review* 35, no. 4 (1982): 511–28.
23. Jeake, *Diary*, 233 (16 April 1694). Technically, the payments were more akin to that of preference share dividends rather than bond coupons since there was only an implicit understanding, rather than the obligation, that the Bank would pass through the 8 per cent interest it received on the loan made to the Crown.
24. John Brewer, *The Sinews of Power: War and the English State, 1688–1783* (London: Unwin Hyman, 1989). See also P. G. M. Dickson, *The Financial Revolution in England: A Study in the Development of Public Credit, 1688–1756* (London: Macmillan, 1967).
25. *The Examiner*, 14 (2 November 1710); repr. Frank H. Ellis (ed.), *Swift vs Mainwaring: The Examiner and the Medley* (Oxford: Clarendon Press, 1985), 7.
26. Baston, *Thoughts on Trade, and a Publick Spirit* (1716), 8.
27. Whitson, *The Merchants Remembrancer* (16 February 1680) [later, *Whiston's Merchants Weekly Remembrancer*]. No mention of share prices is made in an early surviving issue of *The Prices of Merchandise in London*, 2082 (25 March 1674).
28. Henry L. Snyder, 'The Circulation of Newspapers in the Reign of Queen Anne', *The Library* 23, 5th series, no. 3 (1968): 213; Henry L. Snyder, 'A Further Note

on the Circulation of Newspapers in the Reign of Queen Anne', *The Library* 31, 5th series, no. 4 (1976): 388–9; J. M. Price, 'A Note on the Circulation of the London Press, 1704–1714', *Bulletin of the Institute of Historical Research* 21 (1958): 221. It should be noted that many of these newspapers went overseas and consequently were exempted from the tax. John J. McCusker and Cora Gravesteijn, *The Beginnings of Commercial and Financial Journalism: The Commodity Price Currents, Exchange Rate Currents, and Money Currents of Early Modern Europe* (Amsterdam: Neha, 1991), 297.

29. *Flying Post*, 17 (25 June 1695). This, then, places the newspaper reportage as starting several years before that implied by Murphy. Murphy, 'Society, Knowledge, Behaviour', 96. Moreover, contrary to Smith, newspapers did not discontinue the practice of quoting changes in prices after the dislocations of 1696–1697, but rather included them with increased frequency. C. F. Smith, 'The Early History of the London Stock Exchange', *American Economic Review* 19, no. 2 (1929): 212.
30. Murphy, 'Society, Knowledge, Behaviour', 94–6, 159–61.
31. Larry Neal, 'The Rise of a Financial Press: London and Amsterdam, 1681–1810', *Business History* 30, no. 2 (1980): 163–4.
32. Newspapers sourced their share data from price lists on occasion. See Parkinson, 'London Stock Market', 57–8.
33. Parkinson, 'London Stock Market', 58–9.
34. Narcissus Luttrell, *A Brief Historical Relation of State Affairs from September 1678 to April 1714*, (6 vols.) (Oxford: Oxford University Press, 1857), III: 520 (5 September 1695).
35. *The Flying Post*, 48 (5 September 1695).
36. Luttrell, *Brief Historical Relation*, III: 524–5 (12 September 1695).
37. Luttrell, *Brief Historical Relation*, III: 540 (22 October 1695).
38. Houghton, *Collection*, 196 (29 April 1696).
39. *The Protestant Mercury*, 28 (11 May 1696). Some merchants established their own express news service between Ireland and London because of the advance warning it afforded. Murphy, 'Society, Knowledge, Behaviour', 123.
40. Houghton, *Collection*, 198 (15 May 1696).
41. *Flying Post*, 159 (21 May 1696). The same share price was quoted by Houghton. Houghton, *Collection*, 199 (22 May 1696).
42. *The Post Boy*, 165 (28 May 1696).
43. *Dealing: In a Dialogue between Mr Johnson and Mr Wary* (1691), 3.
44. John Evelyn, in E. S. de Beer (ed.), *The Diary of John Evelyn: Now Printed in Full from the Manuscripts Belonging to Mr. John Evelyn*, 6 vols. (Oxford: Clarendon Press, 2000), V: 174 (22 April 1694); *Whiston's Merchants Weekly Remembrancer* (17 June 1689).
45. On the armed struggle for mastery in the bay, see William Thomas Morgan, 'A Crisis in the History of the Hudson's Bay Company, 1694–1697', *North Dakota Historical Quarterly* 5, no. 4 (1931): 197–218. The rivalry ceased only when the bay was finally designated as Britis by the Treaty of Utrecht in 1713. See E. E. Rich, 'The Hudson's Bay Company and the Treaty of Utrecht', *Cambridge Historical Journal* 11, no. 2 (1954): 183–203.
46. Bruce Carruthers has written a paper entitled 'Eumenes and the Generals: Public Debt as a Hostage Strategy', but the contents could not be consulted.
47. [Michael Godfrey], *A Short Account of the Bank of England* (London 1695), 1–2.

48. Anne L. Murphy, 'Dealing with Uncertainty: Managing Personal Investment in the Early English National Debt', *History* 91, no. 302 (2006): 208.
49. A. C. Carter, 'The Huguenot Contribution to the Early Years of the Funded Debt, 1694–1714', *Proceedings of the Huguenot Society* 19, no. 3 (1955): 21–41 [reprinted in *Getting, Spending and Investing in Early Modern Times: Essays on Dutch, English and Huguenot Economic History*, Alice Clare Carter (ed.) (Assen: Van Gorcum, 1975), 76–90]; W. Marston Acres, 'Huguenot Directors of the Bank of England', *Proceedings of the Huguenot Society* 15, no. 2 (1933–1937): 238–48. See also Bruce G. Carruthers, *City of Capital: Politics and Markets in the English Financial Revolution* (Princeton, NJ: Princeton University Press, 1996), 193.
50. As well as orchestrating the Million Adventure, Thomas Neale played a disproportionate role in the rise of the early stock market. For a biography, see J. H. Thomas, 'Thomas Neal, a Seventeenth-Century Projector' (unpublished PhD thesis, University of Southampton, 1979). For an account of the Million Adventure and other lottery schemes of the period, see Anne L. Murphy, 'Lotteries in the 1690s: Investment or Gamble?', *Financial History Review* 12, no. 2 (2005): 227–46.
51. Murphy, 'Society, Knowledge, Behaviour', 43–4.
52. The methodology of linking Jacobite activity with price changes in capital markets was first proposed by John Wells and Douglas Wills in an empirical test of the North and Weingast thesis. John Wells and Douglas Wills, 'Revolution, Restoration and Debt Repudiation: The Jacobite Threat to England's Institutions and Economic Growth', *Journal of Economic History* 60, no. 2 (2000): 418–41. North and Weingast have argued that it was removal by Parliament of the sovereign's arbitrary power to renege on debts which led to the dramatic rise in capital markets after 1688. Douglass C. North and Barry R. Weingast, 'Constitutions and Commitment: The Evolution of Institutions Governing Public Choice in Seventeenth-Century England', *Journal of Economic History* 49, no. 4 (1989): 803–32.
53. E. S. de Beer (ed.), *The Correspondence of John Locke*, (8 vols.) (Oxford: Clarendon Press, 1976–1989), V: 248. Queen Mary died of smallpox on 28 December 1694.
54. The coefficient of determination (R^2) for the regression is 0.68. For an explanation of these terms, see Damodar Gujarati, *Essentials of Econometrics* (New York: McGraw-Hill, 1992), 163.
55. Luttrell, *Brief Historical Relation*, VI: 259 (31 July 1697).
56. Price data for Bank of England stock was taken from: *The Post Boy*, 354 (12 August 1697); 357 (19 August 1697); 360 (26 August 1697); 361 (28 August 1697); 362 (31 August 1697); 367 (11 September 1697); 370 (18 September 1697); 371 (21 September 1697); *Flying Post*, 370 (25 September 1697); *Foreign Post*, 32 (4 August 1697); 36 (13 August 1697); 37 (16 August 1697); 38 (18 August 1697); 42 (27 August 1697); 45 (3 September 1697); 50 (15 September 1697); 52 (20 September 1697); 53 (22 September 1697); 54 (24 September 1697); 56 (29 September 1697); *The Post Man*, 353 (5 August 1697); 354 (7 August 1697); 357 (14 August 1697); 359 (19 August 1697); 360 (21 August 1697); 362 (26 August 1697); 363 (28 August 1697); 364 (31 August 1697); 366 (4 September 1697); 367 (7 September 1697); 368 (9 September 1697); 369 (11 September 1697); 371 (16 September 1697); 372

(18 September 1697); 373 (21 September 1697); 373 [*sic*] (23 September 1697); 374 (25 September 1697); 375 (28 September 1697); 376 (30 September 1697); Luttrell, *Brief Historical Relation*, VI: 269 (26 August 1697, 28 August 1697); VI: 270 (18 September 1697); *Whiston's Merchants Weekly Remembrancer* (16 August 1697); Add. 17677 RR Netherlands transcripts, 'N. de l'Hermitage to the Staten-Generaal' (August–September 1697), ff. 420, 424, 433, 438, 453; Houghton, *Collection*, 262–70 (6 August 1697–1 October 1697). Price data for Million Lottery tickets was taken from *The Post Man*, 374 (25 September 1697); 376 (30 September 1697); *Foreign Post*, 45 (3 September 1697); Houghton, *Collection*, 262–70 (6 August 1697–1 October 1697); Luttrell, *Brief Historical Relation*, VI: 270 (28 August 1697).

57. *The Post Boy*, 361 (28 August 1697).
58. Murphy, 'Dealing with Uncertainty', 209.
59. Add. 17677 RR f. 438r.
60. *The Post Boy*, 369 (16 September 1697).

7

The Impact of Gifts and Trade: Georgia Colonists and Yamacraw Indians in the Colonial American Southeast

Claire S. Levenson

In the summer of 1734, a remarkable encounter took place in Kensington Palace: an elderly American Indian chief named Tomochichi attended an audience held by King George II of England and his wife Queen Caroline. Tomochichi was the leader of the Yamacraws of southeastern North America, and he had come with his wife and a delegation of Indians to cement a budding alliance between his people and the monarchs of Britain. During his meeting with the king, Tomochichi presented George II with a stick adorned with eagle feathers and proclaimed through an interpreter, 'These are the Feathers of the Eagle, which is the swiftest of Birds, and who flieth all round our Nations. These Feathers are a Sign of Peace in our Land, and have been carried from Town to Town there; and we have brought them over to leave with you, O Great King, as a Sign of everlasting Peace'.[1] In the middle of his speech, Tomochichi laid two animal skins at the king's feet. George II replied solemnly that he accepted these gifts 'as an Indication of their [the Yamacraw's] good Disposition to me and my People. I shall always be ready to cultivate a good Correspondence between them and my own Subjects, and shall be glad of any Occasion to shew [*sic*] you a Mark of my particular Friendship and Esteem'.[2] Several weeks later, the Indians dined with the Earl of Egmont, a prominent member of the British government. Egmont recounted that after the dinner and festivities had concluded, he presented Tomochichi 'with a guilt [*sic*] carved Tobacho [*sic*] box, who on receiving it Said, he would get a ribband [*sic*] and hang it at his breast next to his heart. At parting, he told me that he came down to See me with a good will, and return'd [*sic*] in friendship'.[3]

The two scenes illuminate a central act of diplomacy that pervaded relations between American Indians and Europeans in the sixteenth, seventeenth, and eighteenth centuries: the exchange of gifts. According to traditions shared by Native groups across North America, custom demanded that gifts be exchanged whenever any agreement was entered into or transaction completed. These peoples exchanged gifts not simply to acquire scarce or useful items, but, as importantly, to demonstrate feelings of benevolence and a desire to maintain peaceful relations. When one examines these gift exchanges, two important elements become apparent. First were the symbolic, metaphorical meanings surrounding gift exchange, including the goodwill, reciprocity, and obligation that gifts signified and engendered. Second was the concrete, material side of gift giving, embodied in the use-value of the objects and the tangible political and economic benefits both sides derived from their mutual alliance. The exchange of gifts in the spirit of reciprocity and generosity established trust among Indian peoples, and the Europeans who settled in the New World were compelled to respect and adapt to these Native traditions if they hoped to forge and maintain meaningful relationships with the Indians of North America.[4]

This chapter examines a series of gift exchanges and diplomatic interactions in the mid-eighteenth century, in what is now the southeastern United States, between the Yamacraw Indians and the British colonists of Georgia. The aim is to shed light on the motivations and strategies of these peoples. Why did they forge an alliance, how did they sustain it, and what did they hope to gain from it? Underpinning every aspect of this relationship were the desires of both groups to promote the political and economic interests of their peoples, and they understood that the survival and sovereignty of their communities depended on this alliance. In the end, the ways in which they forged and sustained a complex but mutually beneficial relationship offer significant insights into larger questions of colonial and indigenous diplomacy that extend well beyond the confines of eighteenth-century North America.

The Southeast was an unstable region during this period, dominated by the struggle for power among British settlers, Spanish explorers, French colonists, and American Indians. The British settlers who founded Georgia in 1733 understood that in this unpredictable world, Indians were necessary allies, for they provided land on which to settle, intelligence information, and military aid.[5] Indeed, British settlement in Georgia would have been difficult if not impossible had the Indians reacted with hostility to the newcomers. The Yamacraws were likewise aware of the many benefits the white settlers could offer, including political influence with other Indian peoples in the Southeast and access to much-desired European goods like metal tools, guns, and cloth.[6]

In the Southeast, gift giving formed part of the backbone of the relationship that developed between the Yamacraws and the British because it was a powerful means through which the two groups could interact and bond.[7] In the context of European and Indian relationships, gifts helped build alliances because the fundamental, peaceful messages that they communicated were understood across cultural and linguistic boundaries.[8] However, there were severe limits to that comprehension, because gifts also signified a range of other messages and obligations that were not always immediately apparent to both sides. Alliances were often in jeopardy, for behind the ostensibly benevolent face of gifts and pledges of friendship, two sovereign peoples shrewdly sought to further their own political, economic, and territorial goals. To take just one example, the gifts of land that the Indians gave to the British throughout this period served a variety of ends for both sides. They were demonstrations of goodwill, gestures that engendered obligation, and transfers of power.[9]

Relations between the British colony of Georgia and the Yamacraw Indians formally began in January 1733 when James Oglethorpe led a small group of about a hundred British settlers across the Atlantic to the North American Southeast. Oglethorpe was a prominent British politician who had begun his political life in the House of Commons. He was one of the principal architects of Georgia, and it was largely through his lobbying efforts that the British government had authorised the colony's establishment.[10]

Oglethorpe and his small group landed on the banks of the Savannah River in the northeastern section of the present-day state of Georgia, just inland from the Atlantic coast. These settlers had sailed from England to establish a charitable colony, whose ostensible purpose was to provide a home for the 'worthy poor' of Britain.[11] This venture was undertaken by a group of prominent politicians, including Oglethorpe, who called themselves the 'Trustees for Establishing the Colony of Georgia'.[12] Both the Trustees and the British government hoped that Georgia's strategic location between British South Carolina and Spanish Florida would make it a buffer between the two rival colonies. They also wanted to counteract the growing power of France's Louisiana settlements, located to the west of Georgia in the Gulf of Mexico.[13]

The Indians in the southern interior were not encountering Europeans for the first time when the British arrived. These peoples had been in contact since the sixteenth century with Europeans, from the Spanish in Florida to the British in South Carolina to the French in Louisiana. Many Indian groups had developed long-standing alliances or enmities with their European neighbours through a variety of networks, notably the deerskin trade and the trade in enslaved Indians.[14] Even those communities that did not interact regularly with Europeans, it is now clear, had for centuries endured the devastating onslaught of European diseases. Never having been exposed to illnesses like smallpox, measles, and yellow fever, the Indian communities had developed no immunities to these deadly viruses.[15] However, because Europeans did not settle in the Southeast until the seventeenth century, the Indian peoples of the region dealt with the devastation brought by European diseases in the sixteenth century before they had to handle the stresses of regular contact with European people on their land. These Indian groups thus 'had already weathered demographic crises, recreated themselves politically, innovated culturally, and gained varying degrees of knowledge of Europeans and some of their goods'. Unlike their northeastern counterparts, these Indian nations had been able to regroup and readjust to the presence of Europeans before they were confronted with direct encroachment by the immigrants.[16]

The Yamacraws were one of the first groups of southeastern Indians with whom the Georgia settlers established relations. The Yamacraws were a small group with close ethnic ties to the powerful Creeks, or Muskogee people. Spread out over the land west of Georgia to the Mississippi River, the Creeks formed a very powerful yet loose confederation of a number of different ethnic groups. One estimate has placed their numbers at about 20,000 men, women, and children in the late eighteenth century.[17] They had been classified by South Carolina traders in the previous century into the Upper and Lower Creek peoples, based upon the relative positions of each village in relation to the two main 'upper' and 'lower' trade paths that linked the Creeks with South Carolina. The people of the Upper Creek were the Abeikas, Alabamas, Tallapoosas, and Okfuskees; among the more important Upper towns were Muccolossus, Tuckbatchee, Little Tallassee, Okfuskee, and Okchai. The majority of the people of the Lower Creek towns were Cowetas, and their most politically dominant towns were Coweta and Cussita.[18]

The Yamacraws had split from the confederacy following the devastating Yamasee War (1715–1717), a conflict between the British colonists in South Carolina and an alliance of powerful Indian groups in the Southeast, led by the Yamasee Indians and supported by the Creek Indians. Though the precise causes of the war have been much debated, it is clear that a series of offenses perpetrated by British traders against their Indian clients, repeated breaches of Indian customs and diplomatic protocols by the South Carolina government over trade regulations, and a significant trade in enslaved Indians exacerbated latent tensions. The war, which claimed the lives of countless American Indians and over four hundred colonists, ended when a group of Coweta Creek Indians broke with the Yamasee Indians and negotiated a treaty settlement with South Carolina, a conclusion to the conflict that some Creeks accepted and others rejected.[19]

The Yamacraw Indians were among the groups of Creek Indians who disagreed with the peace negotiated between the Coweta Creeks and South Carolina, and they split from the confederacy and created a separate community. The diffuse nature of authority in Creek political institutions meant that these relocated groups were not coerced into accepting the Coweta position and thus were independent from, but not enemies of, the Coweta Creeks and their confederates.[20] However, according to one Creek leader, the Yamacraws had been 'banished' from the Creek confederacy, suggesting that some latent tensions remained between the two groups.[21]

The Yamacraws were a small group of predominately Lower Creek people, led by a chief, or *mico*, named Tomochichi.[22] He had relocated his family and a group of followers to the bluffs overlooking the Savannah River in the years before Oglethorpe and his party landed in the area.[23] The reasons behind the split between the Yamacraws and the Lower Creeks remain uncertain. Julie Anne Sweet has argued that many Creek leaders resented Tomochichi because they suspected that his decision to form his own community might have been a political power play.[24] However, the Yamacraws and the Creeks never severed ties completely, and their ambivalent and competitive relationship helped shape the political and economic landscape of the region in subsequent decades.[25]

From the beginning, gift giving had an essential role in establishing and strengthening the British and Yamacraws relationship. Soon after the British landed in early 1733, Tomochichi and a delegation of Yamacraw Indians paid them a series of visits. During one of the first of these meetings, Tomochichi offered Oglethorpe a buffalo skin with a picture of an eagle painted on the inside. According to Oglethorpe's account, Tomochichi gave a speech explaining,

> The eagle signified speed and the buffalo strength. That the English were as swift as the bird, and as strong as the beast; since like the first, they flew from the utmost parts of the earth over the vast seas, and, like the second, nothing could withstand them. That the feathers of the eagle were soft, and signified love; the buffalo's skin warm, and signified protection; therefore he hoped that we would love them and protect their little families.[26]

Oglethorpe, in many of his accounts of interactions with the Yamacraws, portrayed them as very receptive to Christianity, presumably because he knew that such a portrayal would appeal to the Trustees, who had settled the colony as a charitable venture. The feelings of 'love', 'warmth', and 'protection' communicated by Tomochichi could thus have been embellished by Oglethorpe to project a comforting, Christianised image of the Yamacraws. Tomochichi's declaration offers a very powerful metaphor for the British and Yamacraws relationship. Scholars have argued that for many American Indian peoples, gifts connoted 'words', meaning that the kind of present or the amount of presents given carried specific significance.[27] The eagle feathers and the buffalo skin were likely intended to flatter the British as symbols of their power and of the protection they brought to the alliance. The white colour of the eagle feathers additionally signified peace, for eagle feathers were often given by Indians of the Southeast to demonstrate friendly intentions. The gift was a tangible symbol of the alliance Tomochichi hoped to cultivate with the Georgia colonists.

Other significant gifts were exchanged during the course of this initial series of talks. In one meeting, Tomochichi presented deerskins to Oglethorpe. In return, Oglethorpe, 'after having assured them [the Yamacraws] of his friendship, and utmost assistance and protection, made them some presents with which they were very much pleased'.[28] While there is no description of the precise goods Oglethorpe gave to Tomochichi on this particular occasion, the items most often presented to the Indians by the British were cloth, metal tools, and guns.[29] Like the buffalo hide given to Oglethorpe by Tomochichi, these goods were exchanged to cement publicly the friendship between the British and the Yamacraws.

The items typically given as gifts between the Indians and the Georgia settlers reveal a great deal about the relationships between those who exchanged them. The Indians generally offered tokens of peace, like white wings, and items of monetary value, like deerskins.[30] As for the British, the items shipped from England to Georgia to be distributed as gifts to the Yamacraws and the Creeks included deeply coloured cloth, guns, and ammunition, which were purchased in large numbers.[31] Metal tools, ornaments, and paint were also common.[32] These items were distributed as gifts to the Indians because they were the most coveted. Most cloth was either deep red or deep blue, probably in part because of the native taste for bright colours. Vermillion and indigo, the dyes used on these cloths, were also given to the Indians, who mixed them with water or bear fat to make war paint. All of these items, whether practically useful or not, were greatly prized by the Indians for their symbolic, friendly meaning in the context of diplomatic interactions. Although over time intrinsically useful goods like guns, tools, and cloth came to dominate Anglo-Indian exchanges, the figurative significance of gifts, whether they were feathers or cloth, never lost its importance.[33]

The centrality of such goods to the Georgia and Yamacraws relationship was evident in the first recorded treaty council among the British, the Yamacraws, and the Creeks in May of 1733.[34] James Oglethorpe and Tomochichi had organised the council as a forum in which the delegates could discuss the territorial boundaries of the newly established Georgia settlement. The Creeks confirmed the cession of a portion of coastal land that had already been discussed and agreed to by the Yamacraws.[35] Additionally, according to a transcript of the meeting, the Indians announced that they reserved the land below the Savannah River for their use but 'gave up freely, their Right to all the Land which they did not use themselves'.[36] The language of this additional offer of land was very imprecise, probably because it was meant to be a gift rather than a formal agreement to transfer land. Additionally, whereas the British understood these treaty council agreements to be permanent, the Indians saw them as temporary arrangements that were binding until conditions or leadership changed.[37] The Indians accompanied this declaration with a gift of eight bundles of deerskins to Oglethorpe. They explained that these bundles represented the goodwill of the eight Creek towns present at the treaty council.

Several days later a formal treaty of peace was signed among the delegates, the terms of which the British cemented by presenting the Indians with an elaborate gift of European goods. They offered 'a laced Coat, a laced Hat and a Shirt... to each of the *Indian* Chiefs, and to each of the Warriors a Gun, a Mantle of Duffils [*sic*], and to all their Attendants coarse Cloth for cloathing [*sic*]'.[38] They also gave the Indians a substantial supply of bullets, gunpowder, tobacco pipes, and cloth to bring back to their villages for their people. By giving gifts to each chief and warrior, the British made the items more than general demonstrations of generosity to the Indians. They made them personal gestures of friendship. By accepting the gifts, each Indian demonstrated his acceptance of the treaty and of the British as allies.

The events of the first official treaty council among the British, the Creeks, and the Yamacraws highlight a crucial element of their relationship: the connection between gifts and land. For the English, a cession of territory normally meant an agreement that definitively transferred authority from one sovereign group to another.[39] However, the English believed that the British Crown and not the Indians had ultimate sovereignty over all Creek land. Therefore, as John Juricek has argued, when land was transferred from the Indians to the British, it could not be formally sold but was given as a gift to the British Crown. This conception of land transference fit in well with how the Indians viewed the land grants. They saw them as gifts, which they gave to the British in exchange for items like European goods. Typically, during the treaty conferences, the Indian land cessions preceded European gifts of goods, and the European goods were not seen as payment for the land. Often the value of the goods was far less than that of the land given. The Indians saw these exchanges in the context of the long-term reciprocal relationship that they were trying to forge with the British. They expected that the British would continue to give them valuable goods in the future. Remarkably, in the late eighteenth century, these land cessions turned into a means through which the British were able to wrest land from the Indians. What started as a series of gifts became a demolition of sovereignty.[40]

The relationship between gifts and land is one example of the ways in which gift giving formed an essential part of the Yamacraws and British alliance in the Southeast. In 1736, Tomochichi and his wife Senauki met with the British missionaries Benjamin Ingham, John Wesley, and Charles Wesley. After Tomochichi proclaimed that he would welcome the men in his town, Senauki reaffirmed his declaration by giving the missionaries a number of gifts. She presented them with 'two large Jars, one of Honey, and one of Milk, and invited them to come up to their new Town at *Yamacraws*, and teach the Children there; and told them, that the Honey and Milk was a Representation of their Inclinations'.[41] According to Benjamin Ingham, Senauki explained that she gave the milk, 'that we [the British] might feed them [the Indians]' and the honey, 'that we might be sweet to them'.[42] This scene echoes other Yamacraws–English gift exchanges and demonstrates the ways in which the Indians offered the English items whose intrinsic characteristics communicated political messages. In an earlier encounter, Tomochichi had offered a buffalo skin to Oglethorpe to ask for warmth and protection. The overall political meaning of both gestures is clear: they were offering goods that symbolised the military, economic, and spiritual alliance they hoped to establish with the British.[43]

Additionally, Senauki's words, as well as the nature of the gifts, underscore the ostensibly submissive role the Indians adopted in their dealings with the English. Tomochichi's desire for the British to teach his people and Senauki's plea that the colonists 'be sweet' to the Indians convey an image of the Indians as children eager for the nurturing guidance of their British friends. The British were content to have the Indians adopt this seemingly submissive role because it enhanced their image of themselves as the stronger partner in the alliance. The Yamacraws must have recognised that they were in fact significantly weaker than the Georgia colonists, who though small in number were members of an empire with powerful outposts in North America. Additionally, it was a common tactic in southeastern Indian diplomacy to portray oneself as weak and submissive when approaching an ally for aid. The Creeks and the Choctaws addressed the French on numerous occasions by lamenting that they were poor and asking the French for goods to alleviate their suffering. According to historian Gilles Havard in his study of Franco-Iroquois relations in Canada, the Indian chiefs' purposes in these instances were to 'describe the destitution of their people symbolically in order to elicit compassion from the French and encourage them to be generous in trade'.[44]

Furthermore, it was common practice among the American Indian peoples of the Southeast, well before the arrival of Europeans, to create fictive kinship ties with their allies, and they would often figuratively adopt important chiefs or diplomats of an allied group into their nations to seal an alliance. Though there is no evidence that the British understood enough about Indian diplomacy to participate fully in this kind of fictive kinship, they nonetheless tried to adopt a kind of kinship rhetoric. They referred to their relationship with the Yamacraws and the Creeks as that of parents and children or of brothers who shared the same father, that is, the king of England. The Indians echoed this rhetoric in their speeches to the British at numerous conferences. Scholar Patricia Galloway has deconstructed the role of this kind of kinship rhetoric in the context of the relationship between the Choctaws and the French in Louisiana during the same period. Her arguments shed light on the relationship between the Yamacraws and the English, for the Choctaws and Yamacraws had close ethnic ties and shared many diplomatic traditions.[45]

Galloway has concluded that when the Choctaws referred to the French as their 'fathers', they were not accepting the Europeans as authority figures but rather as kind and nurturing older relatives. In matrilineal societies like those of the Choctaws and the Yamacraws, the maternal uncle rather than the father was the male authority figure in a child's life. Galloway has determined that in the case of the Choctaws, the father was the indulgent, spoiling parent. It therefore seems very likely that when the Yamacraws were calling the English king their 'father' and asking the colonists to 'be sweet to them' and protect them, they were not categorically accepting British authority, for only maternal uncles could command such power. The British may thus have thought they were being conceded a level of authority over the Yamacraws that the Yamacraws did not intend.[46]

In return for their allegiance as 'children' of the British, the Yamacraws were looking for economic and political rewards and influence. Up to a certain point, the British were ready to help, for they were eager to take advantage of the ties that still existed between the Yamacraws and the Lower Creek. In an early conference between Oglethorpe and the Lower Creeks, with Tomochichi present, the Creek orator Oueckachumpa of the Oconas affirmed his kinship with the Yamacraws. He remarked that though Tomochichi had been 'banished' from the Creeks, 'he was a good Man ... and it was for his Wisdom and Courage, that the banished Men chose him King.'[47] The Creek chief's favourable depiction of Tomochichi suggests that the Yamacraws leader still held influence with some of the Lower Creek Indians. Though relations between the Yamacraws and the Creeks remained ambivalent, the Georgia colonists must have hoped that the Yamacraws could nonetheless provide them with a link to the Creeks and the lucrative Creek deerskin trade.

Thus, in the mid-1730s, the Yamacraws and the British both sought to enhance the status of the Yamacraws with regard to the Creek confederacy. In 1735, the Trustees sent a shipment of gifts to be delivered to the chiefs among the Lower Creeks by Patrick Mackay, the man appointed agent to the Creek Indians. Mackay wrote of his visit to Coweta, 'I took Occasion to tell them then that the King of Britain, and his greatly beloved men had sent presents afresh to them by Tomochichi as a further Indication of their Esteem & friendship for them'.[48] Though the British distributed the gifts to promote their own friendship with the Creeks, Mackay was clearly identifying Tomochichi as the one responsible for the coveted items. The letters exchanged among the Georgia leaders reveal that Tomochichi was on numerous occasions given gifts to distribute to the Creek chiefs as well as to the prominent men in his village. One letter even contains a detailed list of a series of Creek headmen to receive gifts that was 'from Tomochichis [*sic*] own Mouth'.[49] Evidently the settlers were giving Tomochichi credit for, and influence over, the distribution of gifts.

Due to the centrality of gift exchanges to Indian diplomacy, Tomochichi's role as the man responsible for allocating presents gave the Yamacraws leader considerable power. Historian Richard White has determined that among the Choctaw Indians, the centrality of gift giving reflected the importance the Indian nation placed on the virtue of reciprocity. In fact, 'a chief's practical influence in large measure depended on what he gave away. They [the chiefs] maintained power not by hoarding goods but rather by giving them away'.[50] Therefore, by giving Tomochichi a steady supply of goods to distribute, the British were increasing his ability to demonstrate his generosity, which in turn would elevate his stature within a confederacy from which he had been exiled. After all, the Indian chiefs to whom he presented the gifts would, on some level, be indebted to him. The British seem to have been eager for their Yamacraws allies to rebuild old ties with the Creeks. Tomochichi had made his allegiance to Georgia clear from his first meeting with Oglethorpe, and since the British were responsible for providing him with the goods to acquire the authority he sought, Tomochichi was in their debt. Having such a strong ally in a position of some influence among the Creeks would be of great benefit to the British.

Though beholden to the British leaders for his increased influence among the Creeks, Tomochichi clearly had his own agenda as well. Patrick Mackay complained in 1735 to the Georgia bailiff Thomas Causton of Tomochichi's distribution of the English presents, claiming that the Yamacraws leader was giving the gifts to his own friends, 'and not the Leading men, for which reason I forbid him to Invite any [Indians] without my knowledge.... I hope you'l [*sic*] Cause take Care that none of these presents be Lavished away by Tomochichi'.[51] It seems unlikely that Tomochichi, whose close relationship with the British was due largely to his considerable diplomatic skills, was 'lavishing' away the gifts. Perhaps he was distributing them to further his own goals, which did not necessarily coincide with those of the British.[52] Perhaps he was giving the presents to his own supporters among the Creeks, who may not have been the 'leading men' the British were targeting.

The efforts of Tomochichi and Oglethorpe to forge a lasting alliance between their peoples paid off in the spring of 1734, when Oglethorpe, Tomochichi, and a delegation of colonists and Indians journeyed to London.[53] The Indians came to England to be presented to the Trustees and the king and queen and to confirm the alliance they had made with the British. Oglethorpe and the colonists, however, clearly had additional motives for the voyage. According to the Earl of Egmont, the president of the Trustees, Oglethorpe wanted the Yamacraws to 'See the Magnificance [*sic*] wealth and Strength of England'.[54] Oglethorpe was trying to dazzle the Yamacraws with the grandeur of metropolitan England, impressing upon the Indians the prominence and wealth of their British allies. The Indians were also using the voyage to ingratiate themselves with the British. By undertaking the long and somewhat risky journey across the Atlantic, the elderly Tomochichi and his group were demonstrating their commitment to their friendship with the British.

In the first meeting between Tomochichi and the Trustees in July of 1734, both sides expressed their commitment to the alliance they had established. Tomochichi proclaimed that he had come to London 'for the Good of his Posterity... [and] hopes, When he is gone they [his people] and the English in his Country may live together in Peace'.[55] He declared that his coming to England was a display both of the trust he had in the friendship of James Oglethorpe and of his wish to extend that bond to the leaders of the British government in London. The president of the Trustees, the Earl of Egmont, then responded, 'The Trustees will endeavor to cement a strict Alliance and Friendship with You, Your Children shall be Ours, and Ours shall be Yours, And We are all under one God'.[56] During his stay in London, Tomochichi met with various important leaders, including, as described earlier, the king and queen, as well as the archbishop of Canterbury. In each meeting, the participants demonstrated their devotion to a strong Yamacraws and British alliance by using the same kinship rhetoric.[57]

The Indians' visit to England was more than a gesture of goodwill, however. It gave both the British and the Indians the opportunity to further the political and economic interests of their communities. First and foremost, the very presence of the Yamacraws in England proved to the Trustees and the Crown the successful inroads the Georgia settlers were making among the Indians. Furthermore, the colonists were probably hoping that their 'New World' guests would intrigue the English public. According to an English eyewitness, the Indians were dressed in a vivid combination of English and American Indian attire. They wore red, blue, and yellow vests and painted their faces in red and black, 'so thick that at a little distance they looked like masks'.[58] Tomochichi's wife wore an English dress without a corset, but by far the most noteworthy was her son, who 'was very well dressed in the English fashion, from top to toe, with waistcoat of silver tissue, silk stockings, etc.'.[59] By providing both a spectacle and proof of the colony's auspicious recruitment of Indian allies, Oglethorpe must certainly have been hoping to stimulate further political and economic support in London for his colony.[60]

The Indians, particularly Tomochichi, also had a concrete economic agenda for their visit to London. In August 1734, at the end of the Indians' stay in England, the Trustees convened a meeting to address some of the Indians' most pressing concerns, which centred on trade. According to the Earl of Egmont, the delegates spent the meeting trying to settle 'the weights, measures, goodness, Species and prices of commodities to be traffick'd [*sic*] in, wherein we found them reasonable and Sagacious'.[61] The Indians were particularly concerned about trade exchange rates. Tomochichi stated 'that they [the traders] are used to give 12 Ounces to the pound, but at other times but 8'.[62] The rates at which the British traders sold their goods fluctuated, resulting in unfair prices for the Indians. The Indians lamented that 'in England they Saw nothing was done without money, but with them, if they had but two mouthfulls [*sic*], they gave one away'.[63] They were complaining that while the British people were, at their core, inspired by profit, the Indians were motivated by reciprocity and obligation. Unfortunately for the Yamacraws, the Trustees declared that they were unable to settle on a set list of prices 'for what we Shall Send passes thro many hands, before the goods are made, each of whom must be gainers'.[64] In essence, the Trustees claimed that they did not have sufficient control over the movement of goods in the trade and were thus unable to guarantee exchange rates.

However, Tomochichi was successful in getting the Trustees to agree to his requests that they regulate the behaviour of their traders. Tomochichi and his delegation were greatly concerned with limiting the number of traders allowed to barter with their people. They 'desired there might be but one English dealer to every town, and he to be licensed [*sic*], that they might know who to complain of, and be Sure of redress if ill used, for multitude of Traders only bred confusion and misunderstanding'.[65] The Trustees had already expressed their desire to limit the number of British traders in the Indian towns, and thus they were amenable to Tomochichi's request.[66] The Trustees then discovered that one unscrupulous trader had been charging the Indians 160 pounds of leather for a quantity of blankets he was buying in Charleston for only 80 pounds. As it turned out, the Indian measure of a pound was in fact a pound and a half in English measurements, which meant that the Indians were actually paying 240 pounds for the blankets. The Trustees acknowledged the discrepancy and asked two British traders who had accompanied the Indians from North America to lower their prices significantly. The traders agreed, and though it is not clear how exactly these demands would be implemented, the Indians had at least been heard by, and obtained some relief from, the committee with the power to enact changes in the trade.

Although Tomochichi's trip to London and the trade negotiations in which he participated reflected the considerable authority the Indian leader had accumulated, the visit also foreshadowed tensions, particularly over land, which would plague Georgia–Indian relations throughout the rest of the eighteenth century. When Tomochichi met the king and queen, he presented them with a present of white eagle feathers, proclaiming, 'I am come for the good of the whole Nation called the Creeks, to renew the Peace which was long ago had with the English'.[67] With this statement, Tomochichi was saying that he was the representative of the entire Creek nation. However, as everyone present was well aware, whatever agreements he made with the English on behalf of the Creeks were not valid until they were ratified by the Creek people.

Nonetheless, the British do not appear to have questioned his authority, presumably because they knew it was in their best interest to negotiate with an Indian ally whose loyalty they enjoyed. The British had already demonstrated their eagerness to empower Tomochichi with considerable authority. They had given him gifts to distribute among the Indians and had invited him to come to London as their primary Indian ally. Coming from a centralised monarchical government, the British were at a significant disadvantage when dealing with the Creeks. Though the Creeks appeared to be a united confederacy, authority was centred in the village. According to the American chronicler William Bartram, who visited the Indian nations of the Southeast in the 1790s, 'Every town & village is considered as an independent nation or tribe, having their Mico, or King'.[68] The village was the primary political, social, and military entity for both the Upper and Lower Creek people.[69] The British had therefore learned that to gain allies and make agreements with the Creeks, they had to send emissaries to each individual town and cultivate relationships with each Creek leader. They were thus trying to promote Tomochichi, a leader already in their debt, in the hope that he might influence the other Creek leaders on their behalf. They likely thought that once Tomochichi had made an agreement with the British, the Creeks would be inclined to ratify it.

Therefore, since the British were eager to negotiate with Tomochichi, when the Yamacraws leader made agreements with the British, they had lasting consequences for both the Yamacraws and the Creeks. During his London visit, in a private, unrecorded meeting with Oglethorpe, King George II, and the secretary of state the Duke of Newcastle, Tomochichi appears to have agreed to cede a significant portion of land to the British. The Lower Creeks and the Yamacraws had already agreed to cede territory to Georgia in an earlier treaty with the colony. This London arrangement went far beyond that original agreement. According to Oglethorpe, this territory included 'all the Lands held by their Nation, from this Island to the Spanish Frontiers. There are three beautiful Islands upon the Sea Coast'.[70] Oglethorpe knew that any land grants beyond what had already been ratified would have to be confirmed by the Creeks.[71] However, Oglethorpe was clearly eager to acquire the land, and he thus did not question Tomochichi's power to give the British the territory. He wrote to his superiors in London of the verbal agreement that he had made with Tomochichi, presumably to reinforce the authority of the arrangement.[72]

However, the private meeting proved to have consequences that were far more profound than a questionable conferral of title to a piece of land. According to scholar John Juricek, Tomochichi appears to have made some kind of statement or gesture that his British hosts interpreted as a recognition not only of British ownership, but also of British sovereignty over all of the Creeks' land. In other words, the British appear to have believed, or at least allowed themselves to believe, that Tomochichi had not just made them owners of Creek land but that he had effectively transferred political control of all of the Creeks' lands to the British.

The details of exactly what Tomochichi said or how it was interpreted remain unclear. However, it seems very unlikely that Tomochichi intentionally relinquished Creek sovereignty over Creek land or that he was even aware of how the British had chosen to interpret his actions. Furthermore, the gesture would have been meaningless unless confirmed by the Creeks, which was exceedingly unlikely. Though Oglethorpe must have been eager to persuade the Yamacraws and the Creeks to accept British sovereignty over their lands, he kept this part of the meeting secret for years. He must have known that his conclusions were dubious and would receive no endorsement from the Creeks.[73]

This situation illustrates the clashing Indian and British understandings of politically charged gifts, land ownership, and reciprocity. If Tomochichi had in fact made some kind of gesture indicating that he accepted British sovereignty over Indian land while in England, the Indian leader likely intended it to be a gift of rights to use the lands, a gesture of goodwill that would cement the trade agreements he had made with the Trustees. In subsequent treaties signed between the British and the Creeks, the Indians repeatedly pledged to give the British use of lands that they were not currently using. These lands were often Creek hunting grounds devoid of permanent Creek settlements. The language of the treaties suggests that these gifts of land were often given as demonstrations of trust intended to oblige the British to reciprocate with concessions like favourable trade terms. They did not indicate Creek acceptance of British dominion over Creek lands.

By the end of the trip to London by Tomochichi and Oglethorpe in 1734, the Georgia and Yamacraws relationship had developed into a critical alliance that influenced the political, social, and territorial landscape of the Southeast. Oglethorpe and his Georgia settlers gave Tomochichi and the Yamacraws a bond with the British Empire, a tie that took the Indian leader to London and anointed him as a central political figure among the Indians of southeastern North America. The Indians, in turn, offered the British something equally valuable, a Native ally who recognised and legitimised their colony in a region inhabited by powerful indigenous groups wary of and often hostile to European settlement. The Yamacraws also provided their British friends with a link to the powerful Creek people, which brought physical security and access to a lucrative trade network.

Just as the rise of the Yamacraw's influence in the Southeast was quick, their decline was equally swift. Over the course of the next decade, the Yamacraws faded from view. In 1739, Tomochichi died, and no other Yamacraws emerged to take his mantle in the Georgia and Yamacraw alliance. The Yamacraws subsequently ceased to be mentioned regularly in the colonial record; most likely, they simply retreated from view or were folded into the Creek confederacy.

Although the Yamacraws lost much of their prominence, their influence could still be felt in the powerful Georgia and Creek alliance that came to dominate politics in the Southeast in the latter part of the eighteenth century. The Yamacraws, of course, had been instrumental in strengthening the Georgia and Creek alliance during its early years. That relationship, like the Georgia-Yamacraw alliance, was remarkable in its ability to remain peaceful in a turbulent region. This stability was largely the result of careful manoeuvering on the part of the Indian and British leadership, who remained committed to friendly relations for a variety of reasons, including the desire to avoid another costly and bloody conflict like the Yamasee War. Large-scale wars did break out between England and Spain in the 1730s, between England and France in the 1750s, and between the Cherokee Indians and South Carolina in the late 1750s. However, despite a series of trade disputes, conflicts over land sovereignty, and small-scale outbreaks of violence, the Georgia alliance first with the Yamacraws and then with the Creeks remained intact. The relative stability of these alliances helps explain how Georgia's relationships with the other Indian groups in the region, including the Choctaws, the Chickasaws, and the Cherokees, also remained reasonably peaceful throughout the mid-eighteenth century. The one exception was the war between South Carolina and the Cherokees, which briefly spread into Georgia. However, Georgia was able to use its relationship with the Creeks as a kind of buffer and prevent the war from engulfing the colony. Thus, at least in part, Georgia's relatively successful relationship with the Yamacraws and the Creeks arguably helped the English navigate the volatile terrain of relations with the rest of the Indians of the Southeast.[74]

The influential relationships among Georgia, the Yamacraws, and the Creeks were alliances forged and sustained by the exchange of politically and economically charged gifts. These gifts were exchanged as symbolic, political gestures of alliance and as concrete, practical items of intrinsic value. The goods were strategic tools that bound both sides in a complex web of alliances and reciprocal obligations that had its roots in the political landscape of precontact indigenous North America. Although the Georgians belonged to a powerful empire, the world of the Southeast that they encountered was, and for some time remained, profoundly Indian. The British were compelled to observe rituals, including the exchange of gifts accompanied by lengthy and deliberative speeches, before entering into agreements with the Indians. In this early period, the Indians did not generally speak English, forcing the British to learn Indian languages and supply interpreters for the treaty conferences. Finally, the British were forced to follow the language of Indian rhetoric, and British leaders often spoke in kinship metaphors and the highly symbolic language typical of Indian orations.

Gift giving in the context of Yamacraws, Creeks, and British relations also helps illuminate one central issue that came to dominate European and Indian relations throughout the late eighteenth and nineteenth centuries: land.[75] When Tomochichi, according to Oglethorpe's account, offered Creek land and Creek sovereignty to the British while in London, he ignited a struggle that came to dominate Georgia and Creek relations. Over the next three decades, the British waged a slow but steady campaign to secure not only a significant land base for their colony, but also British sovereignty over all Creek lands. Oglethorpe even resorted to trickery, fabricating a document that held that the Lower Creeks had agreed to relinquish sovereignty over their lands to the British Crown. Luckily for the Creeks, at the time the English did not have the power to enforce this document, and the struggle over land and land sovereignty remained locked in a relative stalemate throughout most of the eighteenth century.[76]

The Creeks never intended for their treaties with the British to sanction English encroachment onto vast quantities of their land. They were well aware that the British wanted land. Consequently, from their first treaty with the Georgians in 1733, the Creeks repeatedly affirmed their land rights in the region and were careful to keep the portions of land they ceded small and limited to coastal areas.

Unfortunately for the Creeks, their position became much more precarious following the French and Indian War, for the expulsion of the French removed a critical check on the political and territorial expansion of the English. In the 1760s and 1770s, the Creeks were forced to negotiate several significant cessions of land, the most notable of which occurred in 1773 when the British demanded land in exchange for debts that numerous Creeks had accrued with British traders.[77] However, these transfers included just a fraction of the vast landholdings of the Creek people at the time. It was only after the American Revolution that Creek sovereignty began to decline significantly. Thus, in the early 1770s, the Creeks were still very much an economically, politically, and territorially powerful nation whose authority and demands the British were compelled to respect. In the end, it took an event as violent and transformative as the American Revolution to remove the British from North America and dissolve the Anglo-Creek alliance through which the Creeks had amassed so much power.

Gift giving in the context of Yamacraws, Creeks, and British relations in eighteenth-century southeastern North America was ultimately a display of power. Overall, both sides derived a measure of mutual authority from their alliance, one that sustained their settlements in an unstable and often violent region. Throughout most of the sixteenth, seventeenth, and eighteenth centuries, much of the political, economic, and territorial power in the region rested with the Indians. As a result, they dictated many of the terms of their interactions with the British, including the regular exchange of gifts, which took the form of symbolic white feathers, cloth, metal tools, and land. In fact, one could argue that from the Creek perspective, providing the English with land for settlement put the colonists firmly in their debt from the moment the British arrived in the Southeast.

Land became an increasingly critical issue in the late eighteenth and nineteenth centuries, as the British and then the Anglo-Americans came to dominate the region and acquire significant tracts of Indian territory. While English conceptions of land rights are well known, the Indian understandings of land ownership and land sovereignty are much more ambiguous, as the vague wording of the Anglo-Creek land agreements of the early 1730s illustrates. These gifts of land, given when the Creeks were still very much in a position of power, contributed to the weakening of Creek sovereignty that later occurred. However, what is not clear is the role that differing Creek and British notions of land ownership played in that erosion.

In the end, the eventual dominance of the English depended more on historical developments than on the significance of the gifts of land. As the British grew in numbers and the colonial wars pushed out rival European colonies, the balance of power in the Southeast gradually shifted in favour of the English. Over time, the Indians began to lose their sovereignty in the wake of British and American encroachment. The gift relationship that demanded reciprocity gave way to a colonial relationship that insisted on subjugation.

Notes

1. 'Tomochichi's Audience with King George II and Queen Caroline', 1 August 1734, in John T. Juricek (ed.), *Early American Indian Documents: Treaties and Laws, 1607–1789, Volume XI, Georgia Treaties, 1733–1763* (Frederick, MD: University Publications of America, 1989), 21. Henceforth referred to as *Georgia Treaties*.
2. 'Tomochichi's Audience with King George II and Queen Caroline', 1 August 1734, *Georgia Treaties*, 21.
3. Robert G. McPherson (ed.), *The Journal of the Earl of Egmont, 1732–1738* (Athens: University of Georgia Press, 1962), 61–2.
4. Daniel H. Usner Jr., *Indians, Settlers, & Slaves in a Frontier Exchange Economy: The Lower Mississippi Valley before 1783* (Chapel Hill: University of North Carolina Press, 1992), 26. Kathryn E. Holland Braund, *Deerskins and Duffels: The Creek Trade with Anglo-America* (Lincoln: University of Nebraska Press, 1993), 27. Gilles Havard, *The Great Peace of Montreal of 1701: French-Native Diplomacy in the Seventeenth Century* (Montreal: McGill-Queen's University Press, 2001), 16–7.
5. Historian John Juricek has argued that the use of the word 'alliances' to describe the relationships that developed between the English and their Indian friends is problematic. The two groups never behaved toward each other as allies normally do. The English did not consider the Indians to be sovereign nations, and the two groups rarely assisted each other militarily. John T. Juricek, *Colonial Georgia and the Creeks: Anglo-Indian Diplomacy on the Southern Frontier, 1733–1763* (Gainesville: University Press of Florida, 2010), 83–4.

6. For in-depth discussions of Anglo-Indian relations in the Southeast in the eighteenth century, see Edward J. Cashin, *Lachlan McGillivray, Indian Trader: The Shaping of the Southern Colonial Frontier* (Athens: University of Georgia Press, 1992); Steven C. Hahn, *The Invention of the Creek Nation: 1670–1763* (Lincoln: University of Nebraska Press, 2004); Joshua Piker, *Okfuskee: A Creek Indian Town in Colonial America* (Cambridge, MA: Harvard University Press, 2004); and Julie Anne Sweet, *Negotiating for Georgia: British-Creek Relations in the Trustee Era, 1733–1752* (Athens: University of Georgia Press, 2005).
7. For discussions of European and American Indian gift-giving practices in other regions of North America and in the Southeast in the sixteenth and seventeenth centuries, see Cornelius J. Jaenen, 'The Role of Presents in French-Amerindian Trade', in Duncan Cameron (ed.), *Explorations in Canadian Economic History: Essays in Honour of Irene M. Spry* (Ottawa: University of Ottawa Press, 1985), 231–50; Wilbur R. Jacobs, *Diplomacy and Indian Gifts: Anglo-French Rivalry along the Ohio and Northwest Frontiers, 1748–1763* (Lincoln: University of Nebraska Press, 1950); Seth Mallios, *The Deadly Politics of Giving: Exchange and Violence at Ajacan, Roanoke, and Jamestown* (Tuscaloosa: University of Alabama Press, 2006); and Joseph M. Hall, *Zamumo's Gifts: Indian-European Exchange in the Colonial Southeast* (Philadelphia: University of Pennsylvania Press, 2009).
8. Gift giving and other customs of obligation were critical facets of early modern European culture as well as American Indian culture. For a discussion of gift giving and other customs in Europe, see Natalie Zemon Davis, *The Gift in Sixteenth-Century France* (Madison: University of Wisconsin Press, 2000) and Felicity Heal, *Hospitality in Early Modern England* (Oxford: Clarendon Press, 1990).
9. An extensive body of scholarly literature has accrued around the subject of gift exchange. In his influential work, *The Gift*, anthropologist Marcel Mauss refuted the notion that gifts were simple gestures of generosity. He argued that in many 'archaic' societies, 'exchanges and contracts take place in the form of presents; in theory these are voluntary, in reality they are given and reciprocated obligatorily'. The cycle of giving and receiving gifts binds the members of these societies together in a web of obligations. This structure functions as a means of achieving law, order, and economy in these so-called 'archaic' societies. According to Marshall Sahlins' reading of Mauss, gifts are the 'primitive' way of achieving peace that in 'modern', 'civil' societies is secured by the state. Marcel Mauss, *The Gift: The Form and Reason for Exchange in Archaic Societies*, W. D. Halls (trans), foreword by Mary Douglas (New York: Norton, 1990), 3, 5, 70. Marshall Sahlins, *Stone Age Economics* (London: Tavistock Publications, 1974), 169.Mauss and other scholars, including Sahlins and C. A. Gregory, have also made sharp distinctions between gift and commodity exchanges. They have argued that a gift exchange results in an unequal relationship in which the receiver is indebted to the donor, whereas in an exchange of commodities, independence and equality are maintained between the transactors. Gifts establish a relationship between the subjects, while commodity exchanges establish a relationship between the objects exchanged. C. A. Gregory, *Gifts and Commodities* (London: Academic Press, 1982).Scholars have since argued that Mauss exaggerated the distinction between gifts and commodities.

Additionally, according to anthropologist Nicholas Thomas, it is impossible to speak generally of a gift or commodity economy. Indigenous and Western economies are simply too complex to be categorised so rigidly, and the lines between them become distorted in the context of cross-cultural contact. Nicholas Thomas, *Entangled Objects: Exchange, Material Culture, and Colonialism in the Pacific* (Cambridge, MA: Harvard University Press, 1991), 33. Nonetheless, most scholars agree that the terms 'gift' and 'commodity' are useful concepts through which to analyse these interactions. They also concur that, in the words of Joseph Hall, 'bonds within and between societies depend in some part on individuals' spirit of giving, their willingness to seal intangible relationships with material exchanges'. Hall, *Zamumo's Gifts*, 13. See also David Murray, *Indian Giving: Economies of Power in Indian-White Exchanges* (Amherst: University of Massachusetts Press, 2000).Though the economies of the British and the Yamacraws were too complex to be categorised exclusively as either 'gift' or 'commodity', the approach developed by Mauss and the anthropologists who succeeded him does facilitate the analysis of these peoples and their methods of exchange. In this context, gifts can best be seen as tools of diplomacy that bound the participants in an intricate web of political alliances and material exchanges that, in turn, helped shape the struggle for power in the colonial American Southeast.

10. Larry E. Ivers, *British Drums on the Southern Frontier: The Military Colonization of Georgia, 1733–1749* (Chapel Hill: University of North Carolina Press, 1974), 11–3; Sweet, *Negotiating for Georgia*, 12; Juricek, *Colonial Georgia and the Creeks*, 34–6; Edwin W. Jackson, 'James Edward Oglethorpe (1696–1785)', *The New Georgia Encyclopedia* (www.georgiaencyclopedia.org).
11. The charitable aspect of this mission was never fully realised, and it soon became clear that Georgia was most valuable to the colonial enterprise initially as a buffer colony.
12. These Trustees included ten members of the House of Commons, two members of the House of Lords, and five ministers of the Church of England. Ivers, *British Drums on the Southern Frontier*, 11–3. Harold E. Davis, *The Fledgling Province: Social and Cultural Life in Colonial Georgia, 1733–1776* (Chapel Hill: University of North Carolina Press, 1976), 7–9.
13. Allan D. Candler, Lucian L. Knight, Kenneth Coleman and Milton Ready (eds), 'Charter of the Colony', *The Colonial Records of the State of Georgia*, vol. 1 (New York: AMS Press, 1970), 12–26. Cited hereafter as CRG.
14. For in-depth discussions of the Indian slave trade in the Southeast, see Alan Gallay, *The Indian Slave Trade: The Rise of the English Empire in the American South, 1670–1717* (New Haven, CT: Yale University Press, 2002); Robbie Ethridge, 'Creating the Shatter Zone: Indian Slave Traders and the Collapse of the Southeastern Chiefdoms', in *Light on the Path: The Anthropology and History of the Southeastern Indians* (Tuscaloosa: University of Alabama Press, 2006) and Christina Snyder, *Slavery in Indian Country: The Changing Face of Captivity in Early America* (Cambridge, MA: Harvard University Press, 2010).
15. Usner, *Indians, Settlers, & Slaves*, 16–7. Also see Peter H. Wood, 'The Changing Population of the Colonial South', in Peter H. Wood, Gregory A. Waselkov and M. Thomas Hatley (eds), *Powhatan's Mantle: Indians in the Colonial Southeast* (Lincoln: University of Nebraska Press, 1989), 57–132.

16. Joel W. Martin, 'Southeastern Indians and the English Trade in Skins and Slave', in Charles Hudson and Carmen Chaves Tesser (eds), *The Forgotten Centuries: Indians and Europeans in the American South* (Athens: University of Georgia Press, 1994), 311. Joel W. Martin, *Sacred Revolt: The Muskogees' Struggle for a New World* (Boston: Beacon Press, 1991), 47.
17. This is Braund's estimation of the Creek population on the eve of the American Revolution. Braund, *Deerskins & Duffels*, 9. The name 'Creek' was bestowed on this group of people by British traders in the late seventeenth century. The Indians never used the term Creek and instead generally referred to themselves by their village or tribal affiliation. They also sometimes used the term 'Muskogee' to refer to their people as a group.
18. Braund, *Deerskins & Duffels*, 7. Gregory A. Waselkov and Marvin T. Smith, 'Upper Creek Archaeology', in Bonnie G. McEwan (ed.), *Indians of the Greater Southeast: Historical Archeology and Ethnohistory* (Gainesville: University Press of Florida, 2000), 244. Joshua Piker, '"White & Clean" & Contested: Creek Towns and Trading Paths in the Aftermath of the Seven Years' War', *Ethnohistory* 50, no. 2 (Spring 2003): 320–1.
19. See William L. Ramsey, '"Something Cloudy in Their Looks": The Origins of the Yamasee War Reconsidered', *Journal of American History* 90, no. 1 (June 2003) and William L. Ramsey, *The Yamasee War: A Study of Culture, Economy, and Conflict in the Colonial South* (Lincoln: University of Nebraska Press, 2008) for a thorough discussion of the debate surrounding the causes of the Yamasee War. Ramsey, '"Something Cloudy in Their Looks"', paragraphs 1–5. Coweta refers to both an influential Creek town and an influential group of Creek Indians. Sweet, *Negotiating for Georgia*, 19–20. Capt. Thomas Nairne, *Nairne's Muskhogean Journals: The 1708 Expedition to the Mississippi River*, Alexander Moore (ed.) (Jackson: University Press of Mississippi, 1988) 39, 47.
20. Sweet, *Negotiating for Georgia*, 20–1.
21. One source describes the Yamacraws as having been 'banished' from the Creek confederacy. The reasons behind this banishment are not entirely clear. One reference states that they were exiled from the confederacy for destroying a French chapel. *Georgia Treaties*, 2. For a further discussion of the reasons behind the Yamacraws and Creeks split, see Sweet, *Negotiating for Georgia*, 21, n. 26. See also Georgia Historical Society, Chekilli Paper, ca. 1729–1734, for an eighteenth-century Creek description of the Yamacraws and Creeks relationship.
22. John Juricek argues that they were a mixed band of refugees and outcasts and that their numbers included members of the Yamasee people. Juricek, *Colonial Georgia and the Creeks*, 39.
23. Ivers, *British Drums on the Southern Frontier*, 13.
24. Sweet, *Negotiating for Georgia*, 20–3.
25. See Juricek, *Colonial Georgia and the Creeks*, 39–40, for a more in-depth discussion of Tomochichi's background and the ties between the Creeks and the Yamacraws. It seems clear now that Tomochichi was a Lower Creek chief from the town of Apalachicola.
26. Oglethorpe, 'Curious Account of the Indians', February 1733, *Collections of the Georgia Historical Society*, vol. 2 (Boston: Freeman and Bolles, 1842), 62. Oglethorpe recounted this speech in a short description of the Yamacraws. As

it does not appear in any other sources, its precise content is difficult to verify. However, as Tomochichi made several other similar speeches and gift presentations throughout the 1730s, it seems clear that, at a minimum, Tomochichi presented Oglethorpe with a buffalo skin and a friendly speech upon the arrival of the English in the Southeast. Benjamin Ingham, 'Mr. Ingham's Journal of His Voyage to Georgia, May 1, 1736, Savannah', in Trevor R. Reese (ed.), *Our First Visit in America: Early Reports from the Colony of Georgia, 1732–1740* (Savannah: Beehive Press, 1974), 175. Francis Moore, 'A Voyage to Georgia; Begun the 15th of October, 1735', *Our First Visit in America*, 106.

27. Jacobs, *Diplomacy and Indian Gifts*, 13.
28. Peter Gordon, 'Journal of Peter Gordon', in Trevor R. Reese (ed.), *Our First Visit in America: Early Reports from the Colony of Georgia, 1732-1740* (Savannah: The Beehive Press, 1974), 20.
29. 'The First Conference with the Lower Creeks', 18–21 May 1733, *Georgia Treaties*, 14. In an early 1733 letter sent to his wife by Georgia bailiff Thomas Causton, the author described the preferred dress of the Yamacraws: 'The King and Chiefs wear Coats and Drawers and a piece of Cloth tied about their Legs like Boots. The Queen and her Daughters wear Common printed Calicoe, Jacket and Petticoat without any Head Cloaths.' While it is not clear how widespread the use of European cloth for clothing was among the lower-ranking Indians, the goods were evidently of great value to the Indian headmen.
30. See Braund, *Deerskins & Duffels*, 68–71, 88–9 for a detailed discussion of the deerskin traded by the Creeks, including descriptions of tanning processes and other methods of dressing the skins.
31. It was cheaper for the British government to buy the items in England and ship them than to buy the goods from other British merchants in North America. Harman Verelst to William Stephens, Westminster, 24 March 1742, in CRG 29, 241.
32. Three extensive lists from 1742, 1749 and 1755 give a reasonable sampling of the kinds of items shipped during the mid-1700s. Harman Verelst to William Stephens, Westminster, 24 March 1742. Georgia Historical Society Bevan Papers, box 1, folder 5, 'Presents Delivered by William Stephens', 10 August 1749, 'Presents Delivered to Two Headmen of the Cussetaws', 22 August 1749. 'Memorial of Benjamin Martyn to the Board of Trade', 28 January 1755, in CRG 27, 29–31.
33. See Christopher R. Miller and George R. Hamell, 'A New Perspective on Indian-White Contact: Cultural Symbols and Colonial Trade', *Journal of American History* 73 (1986): 311–28. Braund, *Deerskins & Duffels*, 122–3.
34. The British and the Yamacraws had had earlier 'treaty' conferences in which cessions of land were made and discussed, but these cessions had to be ratified by the Creek people. These Creek ratifications occurred in the summer of 1733.
35. This cession is not mentioned explicitly in the treaty. However, the Creek leader Malatchi later indicated that the Creeks had made an oral confirmation of the Yamacraws cession during the treaty conference in May 1733.
36. 'The First Conference with the Lower Creeks', 18–21 May 1733, *Georgia Treaties*, 13.
37. Sweet, *Negotiating for Georgia*, 39.

38. 'The First Conference with the Lower Creeks', 18–21 May 1733, *Georgia Treaties*, 14.
39. The English did not technically consider the Creeks or the Yamacraws to be a 'sovereign' nation. They believed that the British Crown had ultimate title over all the lands in the Southeast. This was not to deny Indian ownership of the land they inhabited, according to John Juricek. It meant that the British Crown had ultimate sovereignty over the land. As a result, to obtain territory from the Indians in a way that did not contradict British law, the English could not buy the land from the Indians. The transfer of land could not be a legal conveyance of property. They could receive it as a gift. Juricek, *Colonial Georgia and the Creeks*, 91–3.
40. Juricek, *Colonial Georgia and the Creeks*, 91–3.
41. Francis Moore, 'A Voyage to Georgia: Begun the 15th of October 1735', in *Our First Visit in America,* 106.
42. Benjamin Ingham, 'Mr. Ingham's Journal of His Voyage to Georgia, May 1, 1736, Savannah', *Our First Visit in America*, () 176. For a more in-depth discussion of this gift offering as well as Senauki's larger role in Georgia-Creek relations, see Julie Anne Sweet, 'Senauki: A Forgotten Character in Early Georgia History', *Native South* 3 (2010): 65–88.
43. The conversion of the Indians was undertaken by a number of British missionaries in the Southeast. However, in the end, the push to Christianise the Indians in the region resulted in few converts. Overall, religion failed to become an effective means to bind the Indians of the Southeast to the British. Sweet, *Negotiating for Georgia*, 78–96.
44. Patricia Galloway, '"So Many Little Republics": British Negotiations with the Choctaw Confederacy', *Ethnohistory* 41, no. 4 (Fall, 1994): 513–37; Galloway, '"The Chief Who Is Your Father"', *Powhatan's Mantle* (), 345–70; Gilles Havard, *The Great Peace of Montreal of 1701*, 129.
45. Galloway, '"So Many Little Republics"'; Galloway, '"The Chief Who Is Your Father"'.
46. From the evidence available, it does not seem possible to determine exactly what the Yamacraws meant when they called the British king their 'father'. However, since Yamacraws society was matrilineal, it seems reasonable to conclude that the Yamacraws used the term 'father' to classify their British allies as friendly relatives rather than authoritarian patriarchs. Galloway, '"So Many Little Republics"'; Galloway, '"The Chief Who Is Your Father"'. See also Snyder, *Slavery in Indian Country*, 55–6, 111–26, for a further discussion of kinship as a crucial element of Native diplomacy.
47. 'The First Conference with the Lower Creeks', 2 June 1733, *Georgia Treaties,* 13.
48. 'Patrick Mackay to Thomas Causton', 27 March 1735, Coweta, in CRG 20, 290.
49. 'Thomas Causton to Patrick Mackay', 10 April 1735, Savannah, in CRG 20, 317.
50. Richard White, *The Roots of Dependency: Subsistence, Environment, and Social Change among the Choctaws, Pawnees, and Navajos* (Lincoln: University of Nebraska Press, 1983), 36.
51. 'Patrick Mackay to Thomas Causton', 27 March 1735, Coweta, in CRG 20, 290.

52. Though it is impossible to determine Tomochichi's precise motivations, especially in view of the fact that there are no Indian sources, his success at assuming a central role with regard to British–Indian relations in the Southeast suggests his considerable diplomatic skills.
53. For an in-depth discussion of Oglethorpe and Tomochichi's trip to London, see Sweet, *Negotiating for Georgia*, 40–60.
54. 2 June 1734, *Journal of the Earl of Egmont*, 57.
55. 'First Meeting of Tomochichi's Party with the Trustees', *Georgia Treaties*, 20.
56. 'First Meeting of Tomochichi's Party with the Trustees', *Georgia Treaties*, 20–1.
57. *Journal of the Earl of Egmont*, 60–2.
58. 'Alured Clarke's Account of the Royal Audiences', 3 August 1734, *Georgia Treaties*, 22.
59. 'Alured Clarke's Account of the Royal Audiences', 3 August 1734, *Georgia Treaties*, 22. Wilbur Jacobs has argued that despite the popularity among Indians of clothes as gifts, the Indians only wore European clothing when they were among the English. Jacobs, *Diplomacy and Indian Gifts*, 50–1.
60. Sweet, *Negotiating for Georgia*, 40–1.
61. 11 September 1734, *Journal of the Earl of Egmont*, 63.
62. 28 August 1734, *Journal of the Earl of Egmont*, 62.
63. 11 September 1734, *Journal of the Earl of Egmont*, 64.
64. 11 September 1734, *Journal of the Earl of Egmont*, 63.
65. 11 September 1734, *Journal of the Earl of Egmont*, 63.
66. They had done so in their 1735 Act for Maintaining the Peace with the Indians in the Province of Georgia, in 'By-Laws and Laws', in CRG 1, 31–47.
67. 'Tomochichi's Audience with King George II and Queen Caroline', *Georgia Treaties*, 21.
68. William Bartram, *Bartram on the Southeastern Indians*, Gregory A. Waselkov and Kathryn E. Holland Braund (eds) (Lincoln: University of Nebraska Press, 1995), p. 146.
69. In the writings of William Bartram, it seems clear that the primacy of the village was true for all the Indian nations he visited, which included the Choctaws, the Cherokees, and the Chickasaws.
70. 'Oglethorpe to the Duke of Newcastle', 17 April 1736, *Georgia Treaties*, 62.
71. 'Oglethorpe to the Duke of Newcastle', 17 April 1736, *Georgia Treaties*, 62.
72. The Creek Indians did agree to cede this territory, but they did so years later. Juricek, *Colonial Georgia and the Creeks*, 110–1.
73. John Juricek has determined that, when it came to negotiations over land, the Creeks and the English differed over what they thought they were negotiating about. Creek chiefs thought their differences with the English were over land ownership. The British thought the overriding issue was territorial sovereignty. The Indians, it seems, were unaware of the distinction. The British did not enlighten them because ambiguity served their purposes. In the end, the British were duplicitous toward the Indians about sovereignty, not land ownership. Juricek, *Colonial Georgia and the Creeks*, 60–3, 133–8.
74. This is not to downplay the violence that dominated European and Indian relations in the Southeast throughout the seventeenth and eighteenth centuries. For a more in-depth discussion, see Matthew Jennings, *New Worlds of*

Violence: Cultures and Conquests in the Early American Southeast (Knoxville: University of Tennessee Press, 2011).

75. See Juricek, *Colonial Georgia and the Creeks*, for a further discussion of Anglo-Creek understandings of and clashes over land. He argues that much of the scholarly confusion over the exact details of the land agreements made between Oglethorpe and the Creeks stems from the fact that most of them during this early period were oral agreements, so there is no official written record. The exceptions are the 1733 and 1736 treaties. See particularly 42–6.
76. Another critical struggle for land centred around a gift of land given by the Creeks to their kinswoman, the half Creek, half British trader and interpreter Mary Musgrove. Musgrove wanted the land grant to be recognised by the British so she could sell parts of it. Acknowledging her right to the land as a British subject would have violated English law, and the Georgia officials refused. This refusal infuriated the Creeks, who saw it as an affront to their authority to bestow land on their kinswoman. Over the course of the 1740s and 1750s, the land grant erupted into a bitter struggle over sovereignty between the British and the Creeks. It was eventually quelled with compromise in 1757. For more in-depth discussions, see Michele Gillespie, 'The Sexual Politics of Race and Gender: Mary Musgrove and the Georgia Trustees', in Catherine Clinton and Michele Gillespie (eds), *The Devil's Lane: Sex and Race in the Early South* (New York: Oxford University Press, 1997); Michael D. Green, 'Mary Musgrove: Creating a New World', in Theda Perdue (ed.), *Sifters: Native American Women's Lives* (Oxford: Oxford University Press, 2001) and Juricek, *Colonial Georgia and the Creeks*.
77. Braund, *Deerskins & Duffels*, 136–7, 147–53.

8

Retrenchment, Reform and the Practice of Military-Fiscalism in the Early East India Company State

James Lees

In 1765 the British East India Company was granted the *diwani*, or right to collect revenue, in the provinces of Bengal, Bihar, and Orissa by the Mughal emperor Shah Alam II. This grant, which was made in return for the Company's military support and an annual tribute of some two million rupees,[1] marked the beginning of a process which, within 50 years, would transform the Company from a commercial body into the Indian subcontinent's dominant territorial power.

At this time Bengal and its adjacent provinces were home to an estimated population of between 20 and 30 million people,[2] and its public revenue was calculated at approximately one-quarter of that of the entire British Isles.[3] The newfound wealth gained from the taxation of Bengal's largely agrarian population would be used to fund existing commercial ventures and also to subsidise the weaker economies of the Company's other territorial possessions in Bombay and Madras. However, in order to exploit fully this potentially lucrative source of income, the Company needed to be able to impose its governmental authority on these newly acquired subjects. The political economy of the early Company state was to be based on the creation of an environment of civil stability – through the application of the government's armed forces – which would be conducive to economic growth.

The realisation of this aim was not to be a simple task. Jon Wilson has shown that the Company failed to recognise how Indian rural society operated in the eighteenth century and attempted instead to govern by its own rigidly defined notions of the landlord-tenant relationship. In precolonial Bengal it was fairly common for *raiyats* (peasant cultivators) to negotiate tenancy terms with their landlord, or *zamindar*, through the withholding of rent.[4] However, the early Company administrators interpreted such attempts at negotiation as resistance to their governmental authority and refused to be drawn into a dialogue with the cultivators. This incomprehension helped fuel the civil unrest which was endemic to rural life in India during the final quarter of the eighteenth century.

The character of north Indian society in this period was strongly informed by the proliferation of weapons and martial skills throughout the rural population. Dirk Kolff has demonstrated that there existed in Hindustan a considerable military labour market made up of agriculturalists who used *naukari* (military service) as a supplementary source of income.[5] Particularly during the opening decades of Company rule, *zamindars* regularly engaged large bands of armed retainers, and there was considerable employment to be found with merchants and other travellers as caravan guards, as constables under the local *faujdar* (the district chief of police under the Mughal system), or even, in many cases, as *dakaits* (bandits). Although much of this mercenary employment came in the form of short-term contracts (the bulk of the cultivator's time being consumed with agrarian concerns), in north India most 'soldiers' had an agrarian income, and most peasants had some familiarity with arms, even if they did not earn a full-time living from that skill.[6] Therefore, there existed throughout north Indian society the will and the capacity, at a local level, to oppose the authority of the Company's government, and thereby to threaten the territorial revenue stream which sustained it.

The political economy of the Company state may be defined by the term 'military-fiscalist', a form of government which was not new to the subcontinent, having previously been practiced by various indigenous polities, and, in parallel with the Company, by the Mysorean state under Hyder Ali and his son Tipu. Contemporary Anglo-Indian assumptions regarding the military-fiscal cycle – the conquering of territory in order to extract revenue from the population, which in turn is required to defray military costs – have been most fully examined by D. M. Peers. Focusing on the 1820s, Peers argues that the enormous expense of maintaining an army to enforce the Company's political hegemony was one of the main driving forces behind British territorial expansion in India.[7] Military conquest was the main means of increasing the Company's control over revenue-bearing territory, and the civil stability provided by the presence of the army helped to ensure a reasonably consistent flow of revenue into the government's treasury. However, the army itself was a considerable financial burden: while it enabled the state to collect revenue, it simultaneously consumed the lion's share of these funds. In broad terms, the Company's profit consisted of whatever portion of the collections survived the ravages of its own military expenditure.

Likewise, from the 1760s onward, the government at Fort William realised that, in the militant environment of rural Bengal, the degree of social stability necessary to guarantee the steady accumulation of territorial revenue could only be achieved through the use of armed force, a method with serious financial implications arising from the cost of training, supplying, and paying the troops needed to police its territories. Although these provincial duties were undertaken, on occasion, by the regular army's sepoys (indigenously recruited infantrymen), in an attempt to reduce its crippling operational overheads the Company frequently sought to replace them on this service with small bodies of relatively cheap, but poorly trained, Indian paramilitaries, often referred to as 'revenue troops' on account of their role in securing the collections. Several varieties of paramilitary were employed in this way, ranging from armed peons and *barqandazes* (mercenaries who were largely untrained and often without firearms) to militia companies composed of invalided sepoys, and units of locally raised *sibandi* revenue police. The common characteristic shared by all these district forces was that, in addition to being few in number, they were, in comparison with the regular native infantry battalions, ill disciplined and equipped, and lacking an adequate executive infrastructure.[8] Qualitatively inferior, cheaply maintained troops were deemed by Calcutta to be sufficient for what was considered a 'subordinate service'.[9] From the grant of the *diwani* in 1765 to the gradual assertion of the Company's subcontinental dominance during the 1810s, an examination of the colonial government's efforts to glean a greater margin of profit from the military-fiscal cycle through experimentation with various incarnations of revenue paramilitary reveals much about the dynamics of Anglo-Indian political economy. This chapter seeks to draw out some of the implications of that retrenchment for the long-term development of the Company state.

After 1765, Bengal's police nominally remained the responsibility of the Mughal Nizamat (the governmental body charged with implementing criminal justice), and the precolonial Mughal police framework remained in place.[10] Under this system, the police *faujdars*, maintaining contingents of between 500 and 1,500 men[11] depending on the extent of their jurisdictions, were intended to operate in conjunction with local *zamindars* to keep the peace.[12] At the village level, a network of hereditary watchmen, or *dusadhs*, and the semi-military *paiks*, paid for by land grants or a share of local produce, continued to operate.[13] The maintenance of the government's authority at a district level should, then, have been under the charge of these *faujdari-zamindari* forces, but the ineffectiveness of the province's police network,[14] at least until Cornwallis's reforms of the 1790s[15] began to take effect, meant that in practice the Company had to take direct responsibility for suppressing any eruptions of disorder within its territories. Necessary though it undoubtedly was, objections to service of this nature were severe. The use of the army as a district police force was profoundly unpopular in government circles, as is reflected in the governor-general Sir John Shore's minute of June 1795:

> The employment of regular troops in ... Provincial Duties is pregnant with Evils of a most serious nature. ... The native troops acquire from it unmilitary habits and sentiments ... even the health of the native troops is injured by it. ... Whilst the practice continues the Company have not a regular army.[16]

Such service exposed the men employed in it to the endless pursuit of groups responsible for low-level resistance, in an unhealthy climate and often through rugged terrain on the fringes of the Company's territory.[17] The operational environment of these provincial duties necessitated the practice, much disliked by the authorities in Calcutta, of dispersing troops in small detachments at far-flung outposts. This piecemeal distribution removed the troops from the controlling influence of the higher command structure and was found to be extremely detrimental to the maintenance of discipline, breeding, in the words of the governor-general Warren Hastings, 'a Universal Spirit of Rapine and Licentiousness'[18] among the isolated groups of sepoys and, not infrequently, their officers too, who were likewise cut off from the supervision of their superiors.

Understandably, the Company's military high command viewed revenue service as hard and thankless work. Disciplined regular regiments, it was argued, whose training and maintenance represented a significant investment of time and money, would be depleted, either by violence or disease, in warding off the gnat bites of low-level resistance, rather than carrying out their intended function of enabling warfare against other Indian powers. The favoured alternative was, as has been indicated, to restrict the use of the army in this policing role as far as possible and, instead, to provide each district collector with a small number of cheaper irregular troops to act as an immediate armed force, the presence of which would 'obviate the ostensible and apparent necessity for the frequent employment of Military Detachments on provincial service'.[19] These paramilitaries would, in theory, enable the collector to impose the Company's governmental authority locally and to safeguard the production and collection of territorial revenue within the district, while at the same time protecting the regular regiments from exposure to these attritional duties.

The paramilitaries which routinely operated in lieu of the army acted 'as Guards for Cutcherries, Treasuries and Factories', and as escorts for 'Goods and Treasure',[20] but perhaps their most important role was 'enforcing the respect due to the authority of Government' and, more specifically, 'apprehending such as violate the Peace of the Country, or oppose the authority of Government'.[21] They were expected to be 'conducive to the Establishment of good order and Police throughout the country',[22] but during the period up to the 1810s, the corps was often very thinly spread, sometimes fewer than two companies being allotted even to major districts; less fortunate collectors might have to make do with only a handful of locally raised armed peons, the expenditure on which was closely monitored by Calcutta.[23]

This underresourcing of the district administrations, in terms of the quantity and quality of the armed forces detailed to support local government, would ultimately prove self-defeating, since it undermined the two mutually supporting pillars of the Company's military-fiscal state, those of military prestige and the collection of territorial revenue.

The forces which Calcutta allocated as an expedient to spare the army and to bolster Bengal's ailing police structure were reconfigured several times between 1766 and 1810, and the management of these revenue troops was marked by a shifting compromise between minimum possible expense and minimum acceptable efficiency. Initially, revenue service was performed by bodies of armed peons. The evident inadequacy of these motley bands led to the creation in 1766 of a corps of regular-style infantry units, dedicated solely to the revenue service. These were the *pargana* battalions, established by Lord Clive, the first governor of Bengal under the *diwani*. Taking their name from the basic unit of territorial revenue administration, a corps of 11 battalions was formed, with the standard Bengal native infantry complement of European officers, NCOs, and sepoys, and comprising approximately 9,000 men.[24] It was at this juncture that the corrosive effect on discipline of provincial duties began to be fully realised. Finding themselves independent of any large military formation, the detachments of *pargana* battalion sepoys deployed across the districts took to racketeering and extortion on their own account. Nor was such behaviour confined to the private soldiers; their European officers were also corrupted by the 'opportunities of their remote situation and the temptation of unresisted power'.[25] They frequently ignored the local magistrates, chiefs and district supervisors, to whom they were theoretically subordinate, and often became moneylenders in their own right, torturing *zamindars* who defaulted in the repayment of personal loans. The example of this widespread abuse of power on the part of the *pargana* battalions' officers led to Calcutta's strict instructions to their successors on revenue service that they were not permitted to 'punish or confine' individuals arbitrarily, to 'lend or borrow money...or to have any Dealing of any kind whatever with any Dewan, Zamindar, Farmer, Ryot or other Dependent officer of the Revenue'.[26]

Considerable sums of money could be accumulated in this way, and consequently, in spite of the unmilitary nature of the service, postings to these lucrative battalions became a source of jealousy and intense competition amongst officers throughout the army as, in the words of Warren Hastings, 'the Tribute which Vassalage is ever willing to pay to Despotism grew into Right of Perquisite'.[27] In 1783 a minute from the governor-general detailing the history of the revenue service observed that

> the Contagion spread...for the same officers belonged to each Establishment, some returning with disgust from a field of Emoluments to the moderate pay and scanty Perquisites of the Army, and others envious and eager to succeed them.[28]

This illustrates a central problem with the way in which the Company chose to manage its revenue troops. Revenue service was seen as an undesirable duty and one which damaged the discipline of the officers and men engaged in it. Yet, feeling unable to tackle the 'contagion' at its source by attempting to exert greater control over the activities of its soldiers through better training and allowances, the Company's plan was merely to place its revenue troops in a state of quarantine and hope for the best. In 1773, the *pargana* battalions were disbanded, and, after a brief period in which the regular army assisted in provincial duties,[29] a corps of militia, composed principally of invalided European officers and sepoys, was raised in their place. No soldier, commissioned or otherwise, who had served in the militia would ever be permitted to serve again in the regular army, and thus any indiscipline was confined entirely to those units. It is also noteworthy that the basic militia unit attached to a district was company sized and commanded by a subaltern. The new system was therefore much more economical than its predecessor, not requiring highly paid senior officers to command it or a battalion staff to see to its administration. Furthermore, the militia, as a corps, was nearly a third smaller than the *pargana* battalions which it replaced.[30] Unfortunately, a significant saving and isolation from the regular army were not enough to satisfy Calcutta. By 1783, further economies were being called for, and the formation of a cheaper *sibandi* corps, which eventually operated in lieu of the militia in Bengal during 1784–1785, was demanded.[31]

One of the many objections raised to the continuance of the militia as a district police force was that its sepoys were too highly paid and also received *batta* (an additional sum, originally intended as compensation for foreign service): it was argued that 'the emoluments of the Corps now under consideration [the *sibandi* units] ought to be levelled to the standard of the subordinate service to which they are devoted'.[32] Rather than maintaining well-trained and equipped revenue battalions and keeping them as a distinct body from the army, the Company persisted in the view that, as revenue duties were subordinate and degenerate, economy was a more valuable quality than efficiency with regard to the revenue troops.

Finding the *sibandi* corps raised under the 1783 initiative to be wholly inadequate for the role,[33] in 1785 Hastings was forced to disband them, pursuing the unpopular measure of deploying four regular Bengal native infantry regiments, stationed at Rangpur, Bhagalpur, Dhaka and Midnapur, 'to secure the Collection of the Revenues and maintain the Peace of the Country'.[34] For the sake of their internal discipline, these regiments were to be kept constantly on the march and never, on any pretext, divided into anything smaller than a European officer's command.[35] The small number of regular troops assigned to this task across the province (approximately 2,800) was to be offset by their operating in conjunction with bodies of armed peons and *barqandazes* based at each district headquarters.[36]

In 1795, the forces available to the district collector were reconfigured once more, when pressure to release regular troops from these police duties led to the reintroduction of a *sibandi* corps to replace the Bengal infantry regiments which had been circulating in the districts for several years. Like the *pargana* battalions and the militia, the *sibandi* units were supposed to be armed and equipped in the regular manner,[37] but this aside they were very much inferior. One key problem, cited by their many detractors, was that as they were a curious civil–military hybrid, the *sibandi* sepoys were not subject to martial law.[38] Also, whereas the number of officers on active service with a regular native infantry battalion would comfortably be in double figures, the commander of a *sibandi* battalion, usually a captain or lieutenant seconded from the regular army, was the sole commissioned officer in charge of a roughly equivalent number of sepoys, who were trained only 'to a certain Degree of discipline'.[39]

The reasoning behind the establishment of such a substandard force may once more be traced back to a determination on the part of the Company to spend less money on what was perceived to be an inferior service. The *sibandi* were to be paid 'without...any extra allowance whatever'.[40] Also, by only allowing one officer per battalion, and that a junior one, the Company saved a considerable sum in executive pay and allowances. This thriftiness inevitably attracted the sort of recruits who might be expected to join a poorly paid and degraded service, and then allowed their commander insufficient means to create and maintain discipline, either in terms of regulations or reliable subordinates with which to impose them. If well-disciplined regular troops were barely able to operate on revenue duty unscathed, then it seems obvious that these quasi-military replacements would fare rather worse. In the period following 1795 there were repeated complaints about the 'defective'[41] nature of these *sibandi* units, followed by their inevitable disbandment for misconduct.[42] They were raised specially for revenue duties, but they were not 'specialists' in any meaningful sense.

Finally, in 1803 the governor-general Richard Wellesley, exasperated by the 'inefficient state'[43] of the *sibandi* corps, whom he considered to be 'altogether unfit for service',[44] decided to replace them with a system of 'provincial battalions'. Seven of these battalions were to be raised, based in Benares, Burdwan, Chittagong, Dhaka, Murshidabad, Patna, and Purnea, replacing the existing *sibandi* corps as they became operational. By March 1804, the Benares and Patna battalions were nearly ready to enter service, while there had been considerable progress in recruiting for the Burdwan unit,[45] and the *East India Register and Directory* for 1810 shows that the last of the battalions entered service at Dhaka in that year.[46] Each battalion was commanded by a regular European subaltern, who was to be assisted by a further European officer acting as adjutant 'when officers can be spared from the regular corps for that purpose'.[47] In the interests of promoting good order, the battalions were made wholly subject to martial law,[48] and the recruits were to be 'properly disciplined'[49] before joining their units. Also, commanding officers of the nearest bodies of regular troops were enjoined to inspect their local provincial battalions at least once every six months and to report on their state to the governor-general.[50] In terms of overall size, the combined battalions formed a body of approximately 5,000 men, rather fewer even than the militia had been;[51] possibly this is a reflection of the relative tranquillity of Bengal 20 years on, although the indications would seem to be that *dakaiti* (banditry) in this period was as rife as it had ever been under British rule.[52]

This plan marked a departure, if not a radical one, from the previous parsimony which had characterised the government's attitude toward the revenue service: at over 31,000 rupees per month, the payroll costs of the new provincial battalion system were 2,000 rupees more than the previous *sibandi* establishment, even if the new corps was rather smaller than its predecessor.[53] It was not without its flaws, however: the enlisted men of the provincial battalions were denied *batta*, nor were they entitled to the invalid *thannah*, the Company's pension settlement for its retired native soldiers. Moreover, it was decided that 'such of the present Sebundies as are willing and able to serve in the reformed Battalions are to be received and enrolled in those Corps'.[54] Therefore, the old *sibandi* sepoys, whose indiscipline had been censured so strongly, would remain a presence in the new system, perhaps tainting fresh recruits with the lax attitude bred by their previous service. For this reason, some contemporaries saw the provincial battalions as 'nurseries of vice', and Peers, writing on these irregular formations after 1813, has remarked that 'low rates of pay, minimal supervision and poor training meant that these units could not always be depended on'.[55] Yet for all this, the corps was certainly an improvement on its immediate predecessor, and it seemed to signal the government's realisation, finally, that its district officials urgently needed to be supported by a more reliable system of armed force if they were to perform their duties to Calcutta's satisfaction.

For the 50 years after 1765, the main principle guiding Calcutta's approach to the provision of armed forces for the use of district officials appears to have been that of reducing overheads. In the later eighteenth century, Bengal was divided into some thirty districts,[56] yet in 1777 there were only 35 companies of militia for the revenue service[57] based at Buxar and Burdwan (two companies each), Dhaka (six companies), Dinajpur (one company), Fort William (nine companies), Murshidabad (eight companies), and Patna (seven companies).[58] Again, in 1785 there were a mere nine *sibandi* revenue units, nominally based at Bhogalpur, Burdwan, Calcutta, Dhaka, Dinajpur, Murshidabad, Patna, Rangpur, and Tippera. Less than half of these units were the equivalent of a single battalion (Calcutta, Dhaka, Murshidabad, and Patna), while one, Dinajpur, was only about two-thirds of a battalion's strength. The remaining four units contained under 240 *sibandi* sepoys, with Rangpur's allowance being just 160, and rather fewer for Tippera.[59] These troops were intended to be a source of immediate armed force which a collector or other civil officer could utilise in suppressing resistance in the area under his jurisdiction, whether this took the form of unrest among the *raiyats*, the misbehaviour of *zamindars*, or the depredations of various kinds of bandit. Yet in 1785, when the Bengal army was some 40,000 strong, the body detailed for service in the districts was made up of a mere 4,228 paramilitary troops, meaning that, at best, the Company's military presence in much of its territory, particularly in northern and eastern Bengal, was marginal, not to say insignificant, with appreciable consequences for the collection of territorial revenue and its remittance to Calcutta.

Furthermore, if this corps was overstretched at the provincial level, then the same applies to the deployment of its troops within individual districts. From the inception of the Company state, the conditions of revenue service necessitated the use of a host of small, isolated parties to counter the myriad threats, both internal and external, to the security of their districts, and to guard numerous points of strategic and commercial value. A report on the disposition of the militia sepoys in Murshidabad district during 1783 shows that the majority, acting as 'Field and Cantonment Guards', were deployed in bodies of between 20 and 50 sepoys among the local commercial factories.[60] At the provincial level, 20 years later, the forces undertaking these duties were still being divided into small detachments: of the 40 posts listed in the returns of 1803, 21 were manned by fewer than 100, and 12 by fewer than 50 sepoys.[61] Throughout the entire period, but particularly before the 1790s, it was by no means uncommon for single-figure parties of sepoys to be dispatched to coerce individuals or to guard *aurungs* (warehouses) or customs posts, against the repeated instructions of Calcutta to avoid this dilution of force wherever possible.[62]

Retrenchment was certainly the dominant theme in the official correspondence emanating from Calcutta, which railed against the 'Useless, Heavy and Unnecessary Expense'[63] of maintaining any but the smallest body of the cheapest troops for revenue service. However, the saving of a few thousand rupees on military pay and perquisites was not the sole consideration in restricting the quantity and quality of the armed forces available to district officials.

Commenting on the state of the militia in 1783, John Stables, a former Bengal army officer and member of the Supreme Council, declared with some vehemence that, 'in my opinion the Corps of

Militia Sepoys... in their present constitution are highly prejudicial to the army in general... ought to be greatly reduced, and [are] dangerous in case of an invasion to be trusted with English arms'.[64] Countering this, Warren Hastings argued that Stables's opinion arose 'from a mistaken conception of the use and design of the Establishment'.[65] The militia units were intended for policing duties, and the idea that they would be entrusted with protecting British India against invasion was 'never once entertained or suggested'.[66] Plausible though it appears at first sight, Hastings's response may also be interpreted as a wilful distortion of the issue. Firstly, it presupposes that by 'dangerous' Stables meant 'incompetent'. An equally valid reading of his objection is that the presence of an under-officered, semi-military body dispersed throughout the *mofussil* (rural hinterland) could potentially form a dangerous 'fifth column' in the event of an invasion by a hostile power, disrupting the Company's fragile system of political economy and providing an armed core around which discontented elements in local society could rally. This fear continued to haunt a much more firmly established British colonial state over a century later, as evinced by the controversy surrounding the proposed formation of an Indian army reserve after 1857.[67] Secondly, even if we accept Hastings's apparent reading of Stables's objections, the governor-general rather disingenuously implied that in the event of a military emergency, restrictions would be placed on the use of revenue troops, when in fact all military resources, however substandard, were likely to be called upon should the situation deteriorate sufficiently. If they were the only troops available for immediate use (and regular troops were not usually stationed in significant numbers on the northern and eastern frontiers), then the revenue troops would surely be mobilised. Thirdly, even if, somehow, it could be guaranteed that the militia or *sibandi* would not be used in regular warfare, this did not remove the potentially damaging consequences arising simply from their existence: great harm lay in such troops *looking* like the Company's regular soldiers and representing the Company's government in Indian society.

Writing in the early 1820s, but drawing on an experience of service in India which stretched back some 40 years, the hawkish soldier and administrator Sir John Malcolm observed that the existence of the Company state was, and always had been, enabled 'solely by opinion',[68] that is, by the opinion of indigenous society that the Company's government was capable of overcoming armed resistance to its authority. Indian public opinion, Malcolm believed, could be influenced in this way only by a concerted effort on the part of Company officials to act as a single body, ensuring that their daily conduct projected a uniform image of their rule as backed by irresistible military strength applied with justice. This combination threatened annihilation for individuals who dared to resist the Company's authority, while, simultaneously, it sought to remove any perception of unjust government which might serve as a trigger for resistance.

The 'whole fabric' of the Company's government, Malcolm maintained, rested on the 'wise and politic exercise of... military power',[69] and accordingly, Britain's Indian empire had to be considered as 'always in a state of danger'.[70] Such was the strength of Malcolm's conviction that his nation's positive 'reputation and character' enabled the subjugation of a huge indigenous population that he went so far as to write, 'We can contemplate no danger so great as the smallest diminution of the reputation upon which the British Empire in the East is founded.'[71] As one Company officer put it, shortly after the publication of Malcolm's *Political History*, 'our strength is in the high opinion the natives entertain of the European character; weaken that opinion and you undermine the foundation of our power'.[72]

The Company's servants were, then, acutely convinced of the importance of 'reputation', not least in terms of its impact on the Company's capacity to govern, with relatively limited resources, a vast and, at best, ambivalent population. Much attention was paid to the Indian public's perception of the Company's military establishment. Indeed, there was a widespread belief, remarked upon by the future Duke of Wellington in 1804, that the Company's power depended as 'much upon its reputation as distinguished from its real force'.[73] In this context, Stables's comment that the employment of a substandard, quasi-military body was 'highly prejudicial to the army in general' can be interpreted as meaning that it was prejudicial to the daunting reputation which the Company's regular army enjoyed in Indian society.

Arguing against the replacement of the militia sepoys with a cheaper establishment of *sibandis*, Hastings sought to emphasise that the militia was already an inexpensive, irregular force, writing that 'they are cloathed with the Military Garb, and armed with firelocks of which they know but the practice common to the rest of the people, because these Engines of their occupation are found to command respect'.[74] In other words, they looked like regular sepoys, and this facade was intended to disguise the fact that they were not selected, drilled, and officered to the high standards of the Bengal army. Here is a clear example of the Company trading on the prestige of its regular regiments to augment the reputation of cheaper, substandard imitations, and thereby, in saving a few rupees, devaluing the priceless commodity which sustained its rule.

The 'Engines' of the regular army's occupation, the uniform and accoutrements, commanded respect because they were identified with an army which had met with considerable success on the battlefields of India for several decades. Accordingly, the red-coated sepoy was believed to be highly professional and personally courageous. To clothe the invalid sepoys and paramilitaries of the militia in the same uniform was to allow the civilian population to place the professional and the irregular on an equal footing. While it might be useful to enhance the status of such troops by bathing them in the reflected glory of the regular army, it must be remembered that the deception could cut both ways, and that the negative qualities of the irregulars could in turn tarnish the reputation of the Company's army as a whole. After all, the militia, and later the *sibandi* and provincial units, were composed of troops which, by the nature of their local employment in a policing role, would receive considerable public exposure. It was they, not the army, who were routinely tasked with the suppression of resistance within the districts, and it was on the conduct and appearance of this relatively small corps – of whom Warren Hastings had said 'they are not regular, they are not disciplined, they are not soldiers'[75] – that many Indians would base their opinion of the Company's capacity to enforce its rule.[76] As the century drew to a close, more importance was attached to making a clear distinction between regular and irregular troops in the eyes of the population at large. In 1786, there was outrage at the practice adopted by some wealthy Indians of dressing their retainers in the same uniform as the Company's sepoys. They became 'in this dress the terror of the Common People and often Commit the most Oppressive Acts for which the Company's sepoys bear the Odium'.[77] The *sibandi* corps formed under the plan of 1795 were to wear uniforms 'different from that of the [regular] sepoys',[78] and while the provincial battalions formed in 1804 were originally intended to be clothed in a uniform 'which is to correspond as nearly as possible with the uniforms of the regular native corps',[79] it was finally decided that they would be issued with one identical to that worn by the *sibandi* units.[80] There was now a much reduced chance of the regular native army, the prop of the Company's government, exciting the contempt of the population through a false comparison with the poorly trained and ill-led revenue paramilitaries.

The structure of armed force which supported the Company's government in Bengal during the 50 years after 1765 was, then, not straightforwardly composed of 'the army' and a district police force, extending upward from village *paiks* and *dusadhs* to *kotwals* (town police officers), the district *faujdar* and his subordinates, and, later, the police *darogahs* (constables). Throughout the second half of the eighteenth century, Bengal's police network was in disarray, and the effects of Cornwallis's sweeping police reforms of the 1790s would take years to be fully felt. Further, as has been seen, there was considerable reluctance on the part of Calcutta to spread the Bengal army across the province on policing operations, particularly while major Indian powers continued to threaten the Company's heartland. Kolff has argued that the colonial government could not exert something approaching a monopoly on the use of arms over its Indian subjects until as late the 1810s, after its major subcontinental opponents had been defeated.[81] It is surely no coincidence that, in tandem with the Company's rise to political and military supremacy, the army began to be more widely dispersed in many, relatively small and scattered posts, explained by Peers as the army's redeployment as a police force to monitor local society. With the removal of the last great Indian power which could seriously contend with the Company for subcontinental hegemony, there was no immediate threat that required the routine concentration of the army in readiness for mobilisation, so now the secondary function of policing local society could be attended to.

Until this point in the early nineteenth century, Calcutta's reluctance to dilute the strength of the Bengal army in low-level 'pacification' operations meant that district officials had to make do with a secondary corps, variously composed of militia, *sibandi*, or provincial battalions, supported by whatever armed peons and *barqandazes* could be recruited without incurring the wrath of Calcutta. It was with this force – undermanned and, in the main, badly trained, equipped, and officered – that they were expected to impose the Company's governmental authority, guaranteeing the operation of the civil, and later criminal, courts, and, most importantly, safeguarding the development of the rural economy and shielding the revenue stream from the disruption brought about by various kinds of armed resistance.

As the editors of this volume have reminded us in their foreword, it was characteristic of European imperial political economy in this period that colonial powers were beginning to attach increasing importance to the internal development of conquered territory. In particular this meant the implementation of improved technologies of cultivation and production in combination with the establishment of a government monopoly on the use of violence. In the context of British India, this may be seen in attempts to develop the Company state from the very end of the eighteenth century through the raft of measures mentioned above, which were designed to enhance revenue yields, professionalise the colonial bureaucracy, and, crucially, to create a standing army which could act as a military police force throughout Indian society.

However, in the earlier period covered by this chapter, such notions of colonial governance were still at a formative stage. The political economy of the early Company state was characterised by a brand of military-fiscalism which was largely untempered by concerns over longer-term development; indeed, it was military-fiscalism carried to its logical extreme, with colonial administrators attempting to extract a greater margin of profit from the military-fiscal cycle by substituting relatively inexpensive paramilitaries for regular troops on provincial duties. Rather than increasing the Company's net gain, this emphasis on reducing the overheads of colonial government arguably hindered the development of its revenue-bearing territory, because it resulted in the creation of a service which simply could not sustain the civil stability necessary to promote the best possible economic growth. Furthermore, the example of a degraded branch of the Company's armed forces also had the potential to jeopardise the authority drawn from the prestige of the regular army which underpinned its rule. In both regards, the colonial government's efforts to manipulate the military-fiscal cycle through a policy of retrenchment towards its provincial policing commitments during the 50 years after 1765 can be seen as ultimately self-defeating.

Notes

1. P. J. Marshall, *Bengal: The British Bridgehead; Eastern India 1740–1828* (Cambridge: Cambridge University Press, 1987), 90.
2. Ibid., 151.
3. P. J. Marshall, 'Hastings, Warren (1732–1818)', *Oxford Dictionary of National Biography*, vol. 25 (Oxford: Oxford University Press, 2004), 784.
4. Jon E. Wilson, *The Domination of Strangers* (London: Palgrave Macmillan, 2008).
5. Dirk A. H. Kolff, *Naukar, Rajput and Sepoy: The Ethnohistory of the Military Labour Market in Hindustan, 1450–1850* (Cambridge: Cambridge University Press, 1990).
6. Ibid., 185.
7. Douglas M. Peers, *Between Mars and Mammon: Colonial Armies and the Garrison State in India, 1819–1935* (London: I. B. Tauris, 1995).
8. Ibid., 98.
9. Extract of Bengal revenue consultations, 11 November 1783, British Library (India Office Records) F/4/8/709.

10. This remained the case until 6 April 1781, when the office of the *faujdar* was abolished and the judges of civil courts became magistrates with executive and police duties. Cf. Bankey B. Misra, *Central Administration of the East India Company, 1773–1834* (Manchester: Manchester University Press, 1959), 127.
11. Ibid., 303.
12. However, in eighteenth-century Bengal, 'the number of *Faujdars* being very small, the *Zamindari* was the true local unit of police administration in the countryside'. Basudev Chatterji, 'The Darogah and the Countryside: The Imposition of Police Control in Bengal and Its Impact (1793–1837)', *Indian Economic and Social History Review* 18, no. 1 (1981): 22.
13. Misra, *Central Administration*, 127.
14. There are strong indications that many of the *zamindars* were actually complicit in rural banditry: 'Their country houses were robber strongholds, and the early English administrators of Bengal have left it on record that a gang-robbery never occurred without a landed proprietor being at the bottom of it'. Cf. William Wilson Hunter, *The Annals of Rural Bengal* (London: Smith, Elder and Co., 1868), 69–70. Whether or not this was as widespread as Hunter suggests, Chatterji agrees that the *faujdari-zamindari* police system 'was found unworkable in the course of the second half of the eighteenth century'. Cf. Chatterji, 'The Darogah and the Countryside', 22.
15. Cornwallis's 'Regulation XXII' of 1793 empowered local magistrates to appoint *darogahs* (police constables) and heralded the beginning of a more regular and extensive rural police network. Cf. Chatterji, 'The Darogah and the Countryside', 26.
16. Secret Department, minute and resolution of the governor-general in council, 29 June 1795, BL (IOR) F/4/8/709.
17. Report of Capt. J. Browne (Browne Report), C. O. Rajemahal, to W. Hastings, 15 February 1778, BL Add. Ms. 29210, f.149. Cit. G. J. Bryant, 'Pacification in the Early British Raj', *Journal of Imperial and Commonwealth History*, 14, 1 (October 1985), 3.
18. Governor-general's minute, 2 October 1783, BL (IOR) F/4/8/709.
19. Extract Bengal revenue consultations, 12 August 1783, BL (IOR) F/4/8/709.
20. Ibid.
21. Ibid.
22. Ibid.
23. For example, the admonition addressed to the collector of Rangpur in 1783 for raising extra *barqandazes*. Committee of Revenue to R. Goodlad, 20 January 1783, W. K. Firminger, *Bengal District Records: Rangpur*, vol. 3 (Calcutta: Bengal Secretariat Book Depot, 1968), 7. See also the wrangling over the unauthorised hiring in 1773 of a body of irregular troops by a junior army officer to supplement his company, isolated in the newly annexed Tippera in [No. 146] F. Bentley to C. Bentley, 8 July 1773, Firminger, *Bengal District Records: Chittagong*, vol. 1 (Calcutta: Bengal Secretariat Book Depot, 1928), 103.
24. R. Clive to H. Verelst, 19 April 1766, BL Mss. Eur. E231, f.14. Cit. Bryant, 'Pacification in the Early British Raj', 8.
25. Governor-general's minute, 2 October 1783, BL (IOR) F/4/8/709.
26. Extract of Bengal Revenue Consultations, 12 August 1783, BL (IOR) F/4/8/709.

27. Ibid.
28. Governor-general's minute, 2 October 1783, BL (IOR) F/4/8/709.
29. 'The Purgunnah Corps were abolished and the Militia Corps gradually installed in their stead. For some time indeed the regular Battalions were stationed in various parts of the Province.... They were withdrawn in good time', Governor-general's minute, 2 October 1783, BL (IOR) F/4/8/709.
30. The *pargana* battalions numbered approximately 9,000 men, while in 1783, at the height of calls for its disbandment on financial grounds, the corps of militia sepoys was comprised of 6,327 men. Extract of Bengal Revenue Consultations, 11 November 1783, BL (IOR) F/4/8/709.
31. Bengal military (incomplete) and civil statement, 1784–1785, BL (IOR) L/MIL/8/1, 75–8.
32. Extract of Bengal revenue consultations, 11 November 1783, BL (IOR) F/4/8/709.
33. One of many examples of this inadequacy may be found in the correspondence concerning a party of the Dhaka *sibandi* corps, which, having been entrusted with guarding several renowned *dakaits* after their apprehension by the local *shikdar* (the police officer in charge of a *pargana* under the Mughal system), allowed them to escape. The sepoys whose negligence or complicity had led to this were court-martialled, subjected to corporal punishment, and dismissed from the service. [2.21.] M. Day to W. Hastings, 23 June 1784, S. Islam, *Bangladesh District Records: Dacca District (1784–1787)* (Dhaka: University of Dhaka, 1981), 74.
34. Extract of a letter from the governor-general and council, 31 January 1785, BL (IOR) F/4/8/709.
35. Ibid.
36. Extract of letter from the governor-general, 24 August 1795, BL (IOR) F/4/8/709.
37. Ibid.
38. Extract Bengal Judicial Letter, 10 March 1804, BL (IOR) F/4/173/3076.
39. Extract of a letter from the governor-general, 24 August 1795, BL (IOR) F/4/8/709.
40. Ibid.
41. Extract Bengal judicial letter, 10 March 1804, BL (IOR) F/4/173/3076.
42. Extract military letter from Bengal, 27 November 1800, BL (IOR) F/4/94/1894.
43. Extract military letter from Bengal, 1 February 1804, BL (IOR) F/4/173/3076.
44. Extract Bengal judicial letter, 10 March 1804, BL (IOR) F/4/173/3076.
45. Ibid.
46. *East India Company Register and Directory*, 1810, 2nd edn (London, 1810), 84.
47. Extract Bengal military consultations, 25 August 1803, BL (IOR) F/4/173/3076.
48. Extract Bengal judicial letter, 10 March 1804, BL (IOR) F/4/173/3076.
49. Ibid.
50. Extract military letter from Bengal, 1 February 1804, BL (IOR) F/4/173/3076.
51. Ibid.
52. Ascoli, *Early Revenue History of Bengal*, 245–6, cit. Bryant, 'Pacification in the Early British Raj', 9.
53. Extract Bengal judicial letter, 10 March 1804, BL (IOR) F/4/173/3076.

54. Ibid.
55. Peers, *Between Mars and Mammon*, 98.
56. Cf. Bengal military and civil statement, 1786–1787, BL (IOR) L/MIL/8/2, 30.
57. Bengal military consultations, 22 January to 31 December 1777, proceedings of the governor-general and council, 21 August 1777, BL (IOR) P/18/44, 109.
58. Ibid., 162.
59. *Sibandi* returns for 1785 in Bengal military (incomplete) and civil statement, 1784–1785, BL (IOR) L/MIL/8/1, 75–7.
60. Militia returns, extract Bengal revenue consultations, 12 August 1783, BL (IOR) F/4/8/709.
61. Encl. J. Sherer to T. Philpot, 19 July 1803, BL (IOR) F/4/173/3076, 41–7.
62. A typical example of this practice may be seen in the despatch of four *sibandi* sepoys by the collector of Dhaka to deliver a summons to a recalcitrant *zamindar*, whose forces promptly overpowered the sepoys and placed them in close confinement. [5.74] M. Day to W. Cowper, 1 March 1785, Islam, *Bangladesh District Records: Dacca*, 124.
63. Extract of Bengal revenue consultations, 11 November 1783, BL (IOR), F/4/8/709.
64. Ibid.
65. Governor-general's minute, 2 October 1783, BL (IOR) F/4/8/709.
66. Ibid.
67. Adrian Preston, 'Sir Charles MacGregor and the Defence of India, 1857–1887', *Historical Journal* 12, no. 1 (1969): 58.
68. John F. Malcolm, *Political History of India from 1784 to 1823*, vol. 2 (London: J. Murray, 1826), 146.
69. Ibid., 2: 245.
70. Ibid., 2: 76.
71. Ibid., 1: 144–5.
72. Select committee on the East India Company, PP, 13 (1831–1832), lv, cit. Peers, *Between Mars and Mammon*, 63.
73. D. G. Boyce, 'From Assaye to the "Assaye": Reflections on British Government, Force, and Moral Authority in India', *Journal of Military History* 63, no. 3 (1999): 646.
74. Governor-general's minute, 2 October 1783, BL (IOR), F/4/8/709.
75. Ibid.
76. The negative associations of these paramilitary substitutes, at least for the Anglo-Indian community, may be observed in the change over time in the meaning of the term *sibandi* or, anglicised, 'sebundy'. It was used during the eighteenth century loosely to describe a body of irregular troops employed on revenue service, originating in the Persian *sihbandi* (*sih* meaning 'three'), signifying three monthly or quarterly payments. The far-reaching effects on the public imagination of the Company's cheap quasi-military forces can be seen in the fact that the meaning of the term altered during its passage into colloquial usage. It came to signify 'a sort of militia, or imperfectly disciplined troops' quite distinct from its roots in the language of territorial revenue. As late as 1869 a corps of labourers raised at Darjeeling was denominated 'the Sebundy Corps of Sappers and Miners'. Cf. William Crooke (ed.), *Hobson-Jobson: A Glossary of Colloquial Anglo-Indian Words and Phrases and Kindred*

Terms, Eytmological, Historical, Geographic and Discursive (Delhi: Munshiram Manoharlal, 1968), 805.

77. Extract of a letter from the secretary to the General Department under date 3 April 1786, encl. [5.140] J. Spottiswood to M. Day, 11 April 1786, Islam, *Bangladesh District Records: Dacca*, 186.
78. Extract of a letter from the governor-general, 24 August 1795, BL (IOR) F/4 /8/709.
79. Extract Bengal Military Consultations, 25 August 1803, BL (IOR) F/4 /173/3076.
80. Extract Military Letter from Bengal, 1 February 1804, BL (IOR) F/4 /173/3076.
81. Kolff, *Naukar, Rajput and Sepoy*, 3. Also, the final British victory in the Second Anglo-Maratha War (1803–1805) ended any effective resistance on the part of the Marathas, the third war (1817–18) being essentially a matter of small-scale pacification: 'The defeat of Sindia and the confederation of the Maratha princes of Nagpur and Indore in the [Second] Anglo-Maratha War ... confirmed the British as the inheritors of the old Mughal supremacy'. Cf. John Pemble, 'Resources and Techniques in the Second Maratha War', in D. M. Peers (ed.), *Warfare and Empires: Contact and Conflict between European and Non-European Military and Maritime Forces and Cultures* (Aldershot: Ashgate, 1997), 275.

9

How Feeding Slaves Shaped the French Atlantic: Mercantilism and the Crisis of Food Provisioning in the Franco-Caribbean during the Seventeenth and Eighteenth Centuries

Bertie Mandelblatt

In September 1789 the Deputies for Industry and Trade of the French National Assembly published a short pamphlet whose main concern was the dietary habits of the 400,000 slaves of the French colony of Saint-Domingue.[1] The Deputies were particularly interested in the relationship between bread made from French wheat flour and *vivres du pays* (local foodstuffs), referring to manioc, yams, squash, and the other crops cultivated on the island. A central aspect of this relationship was the differentiation between the diets of white planters and their slaves, who in fact consumed, the Deputies claimed, very little bread made of wheat flour:

> Bread...only appears on the tables of Whites where it is always accompanied by a great quantity of the local foodstuffs that Creoles often prefer to European bread. It appears only rarely at the festive gatherings of the *Nègres*....It is so little required that a plantation of 200 *Nègres* scarcely consumes more than 4 barrels of flour a year.[2]

The Deputies' interest in the food practices of the slaves of Saint-Domingue should not surprise us. Food provision was one of the ongoing crises of colonial development, and the continued production of French wealth from Caribbean sugar plantations depended on constant attentiveness to its management.

The late 1780s, moreover, was an era rocked by crises in France in which wheat grain, flour and bread played a pivotal role, and the National Assembly's concern extended to colonial as well as to domestic consumption.[3] In their pamphlet, the Deputies wanted to demonstrate that wheat flour imported from France was of little consequence in the provisioning of Saint-Domingue, the most populous and productive of the French sugar colonies in the Caribbean at this time, because slave consumption of it was so low. The pamphlet's central argument was structured around two propositions: the first that 'It is not true that the provision of French flour to Saint-Domingue is insufficient, and that it is the cause of death by starvation of ten to twelve thousand *Nègres* each year'; and second that 'The famine that currently reigns in the colony only strikes White planters and *Nègres* cannot be dying of it.'[4] In a curious but telling reversal of priorities, the fact that slaves were not starving (according to the Deputies' calculations) far outweighed in importance any incidental suffering of white planters, a situation described here as unlikely and overblown.

This pamphlet was published to refute aggressively documents submitted earlier that month to the Committee of Trade and Agriculture by the two Deputies to the National Assembly from Saint-Domingue, M. de Cocherel and M. de Raynaud.[5] These original documents had described a state of general famine on Saint-Domingue and the insufficiency of French flour imports, and pleaded for formal permission to allow foreign flour (i.e., from the United States) to be imported onto the island. In their disdainful response to these colonial demands for liberty of trade in regards to food provisioning and in their defence of metropolitan merchants, the Deputies were taking part in a debate over the provisioning of the French sugar colonies that had been going on since the French had formally established colonial settlements in the Caribbean a century and a half earlier. The debate was marked by distinct antipathies between metropolitan merchants and colonial planters, and it was carried on between the merchants via their representatives in local Chambers of Commerce and *parlements*, and colonists via their representatives in the metropole and a variety of high-profile commentators who published tracts on life in the colonies.

The subject of this debate was, above all, what Dale Miquelon has called the 'mercantilist dilemma' of early modern colonial expansion.[6] Since the formal demise of the last chartered company to operate in the French Atlantic in 1674, the trade in provisions to the French sugar islands was nominally controlled by private French traders, which set two opposing forces against each other. On the one hand, colonial settlers (both free and enslaved) lived in anomalous situations where stable and adequate local food production proved impossible to establish, and they thus depended heavily on the importation of food provisions via transatlantic or intra-Atlantic trades, for both survival and colonial development. On the other hand, the metropolitan merchants to whom fell the responsibility and, increasingly, the benefit of organising and maintaining transatlantic food provision networks asserted their right to profit from these endeavours.

Historians of Atlantic trade recognise the structural nature of the food provision crisis and the dynamic ways the value of imported food commodities developed alongside and in relation to the value of the export commodities produced for profit on the islands.[7] Therefore, while metropolitan merchants and colonial planters all claimed that their undertakings were to the ultimate economic benefit of France, the value of the provisioning trades ensured that their descriptions of colonial dietary habits were frequently strategic or rhetorical. That is, while famine and starvation were real problems in French Caribbean colonies throughout this period, they often served to mask the real subject at stake in these commercial debates – colonists' insistence on their right to trade with foreigners and metropolitan merchants' entrenched opposition to this perceived violation of their commercial privileges. The articulation of these tensions and the decisions made in their resolution reveal the role played by food provision to the Antilles, and more broadly speaking, colonial consumption, in the development of French political economy during the *ancien régime*.

Indeed, the duration of this basic conflict covered the entire sweep of French political and economic power in the Caribbean – from the initial colonial ventures that took place under the aegis of chartered commercial companies in the 1620s until the social, political and economic revolutions that began on Saint-Domingue in 1791. Although geographically the conflict served to bolster the transatlantic trade networks connecting the French port cities of Rouen, Nantes, La Rochelle, and Bordeaux to the main Caribbean centres of sugar production on Martinique, Guadeloupe and Saint-Domingue, it also affected the further corners of the prerevolutionary French Atlantic. At various points in this history, Plaisance, France's outpost on Newfoundland; New France (Canada, Acadia, and then Louisbourg on Île Royale, Louisiana); Carénage on Sainte-Lucie and Môle St. Nicolas on Saint-Domingue; and Kourou on the northern coast of la Guyane each played or were imagined to play key roles in the provisioning of the French Caribbean.

Although all French colonial settlements experienced periodic provisioning difficulties, those in the Caribbean were more systemic and provoked more protest for a variety of reasons, not least because these colonies generated progressively higher profits and thus received greater attention from the metropole than did, for instance, Canada or Louisiana. As planters turned towards sugar cultivation in the mid-seventeenth century, less and less land became available on which to grow food for local consumption; the disproportionate dedication of land to the cultivation of export crops created a serious inability to produce a stable local food supply.[8] The demographic factor was equally significant: through the eighteenth century, colonial and specifically slave populations represented substantial and rapidly growing groups of consumers, far larger than any that existed in other French colonial settlements.[9] These populations and the patterns of their consumption became integral aspects of the political economy of the overall French Atlantic. In all these realms, then, the provisioning situation in the Caribbean colonies presented intensified versions of the difficulties of developing stable and adequate systems of subsistence characteristic of most French (and other European) colonial ventures during these decades.

The crisis over food provision reached huge proportions and formed a structural element of French transatlantic trade during these eras because it rose out of the coercive mobilisation of huge populations of displaced and enslaved Africans. Histories of Atlantic trade are too often evacuated of the presence of slaves as consumers because of their focus on colonial merchants, their connections and their concerns.[10] Studying networks of food provision means placing slave consumption where it belongs at the centre of this analysis of French trade policy, and allows a critical reappraisal of its role in French political economy, both imperial and metropolitan.

This chapter will chart the development of the metropolitan regulatory framework of this provisioning crisis during the seventeenth and eighteenth centuries, beginning with Jean-Baptiste Colbert who was responsible for implementing the measures that formed the core mercantilist framework governing France's globalised trade, and that lasted, in some form, until the French Revolution.[11] It will show how Colbertian mercantilism itself shifted in meaning in relation to food provision, and how it was both challenged and, paradoxically, reinforced by growing interest in liberal economic theories and the intellectual influence of the physiocrats and other philosophes. The rise and fall of support for inter-colonial trade between the French Antilles and France's North American colonies, and the constant threat of *l'interlope*–illicit trade with foreigners–provided continuous counterpoints to the changes in legislation that governed the flow of food provisions around the French Atlantic.

Richelieu, Colbert and French Atlantic trade, 1626–1683

Although private French merchants had been present in the Caribbean basin since the beginnings of European occupation in the fifteenth century, the formal beginnings of French colonisation there in the seventeenth century dramatically changed the way trade was envisioned.[12] Since the early seventeenth century, the French had begun to show interest in chartering public companies to undertake colonising endeavours in the Americas and in the Indian Ocean to compete with the Spanish, the Dutch and the English who were dominating Atlantic and Indian Ocean trades.[13] In 1626, the Cardinal de Richelieu chartered the Compagnie de Saint-Christophe under the leadership of Pierre Belain d'Esnambuc and Urbain de Roissey to formally establish the first French settlements on the island of Saint-Christophe (St. Kitts). From this initial base, colonising expeditions to Martinique and Dominica were planned and carried out in 1635 under the auspices of the Compagnie des Îles d'Amérique, a new iteration of the earlier company which also oversaw a colonising expedition to Guadeloupe, launched from Dieppe in the same year.

Richelieu's overriding interest in these years was in expanding France's navigational capacities vis-à-vis Spain and Holland: overseas commerce was envisioned both as a means to this end and a natural extension of it.[14] Commerce, as initially represented in the charters of these companies, including the *Lettres patentes* which declared Richelieu the 'Grand Maître, Chef et Surintendant du commerce de France', constituted not only the benefit derived from the import into France of colonial goods but also the activities associated with the provisioning of the three vessels: the 45,000 *livres* intended to pay for three vessels and to 'provision them with the food, arms, equipment and men necessary for the voyage and for the settlement on the said Islands, together with other merchandise that could be considered suitable and useful there'.[15] From the beginnings of French colonial expansion, then, both export and import aspects of commerce figured largely in its institutional structure.

When Colbert came to power in the 1660s, he brought to existing mercantilist ideas a renewed interest in industry, manufacturing, and above all, external trade, and in the ways that wealth and power could be derived from them.[16] As far as colonial matters went, the French colonies in the Caribbean had been more or less abandoned by the Crown, literally sold off to their governors during the tenure of Mazarin, who had succeeded Richelieu as chief minister in 1643. On the one hand, Colbert saw in the Caribbean colonies a chance to build up France's stock in bullion by developing the trade in tropical commodities (tobacco, sugar, indigo and ginger) that had unmistakable potential for growth. Sugarcane had been introduced mid-century to the islands as a plantation crop and was by now clearly the most lucrative of these.[17] Buying the islands back from their proprietors, Colbert chartered another commercial company in 1664, the Compagnie des Indes occidentales (CIO), to undertake the development of the plantation system in exchange for a monopoly on sugar sales.[18] He saw no reason to deviate from the model of African slaves cultivating sugarcane on plantations that had been in place from the earliest days of Portuguese African exploration and was now proving so profitable.[19]

On the other hand, Colbert understood that reinvesting in the French Caribbean colonies was a way of wresting their commercial control from the Dutch, who in the first two-thirds of the seventeenth century were the strongest merchant-nation in Europe and who maintained a stranglehold on colonial trade to and from the Caribbean, including the French and English islands.[20] Dutch traders were able to extend more credit to French and English planters than traders from their own countries, and thus bound them into exchange networks in which all profits from the export commodities being produced (chiefly tobacco) went directly into Dutch hands.[21] In the French case, the inadequacies of the first two commercial companies that had been given responsibility for the maintenance of the tiny French colonies meant that the French settlements on St. Christophe, Martinique and Guadeloupe were well accustomed to trade with Dutch merchants when Colbert surveyed the scene. These settlements depended entirely on the most important commodities brought by the Dutch: food and slaves.

The Dutch at this time had more than seven times the shipping capacity of the French, and therefore Colbert's first task was to build up the navy.[22] Concurrently, he threw his efforts into encouraging and protecting the CIO, issuing ordinances and *arrêts* throughout the early years of the company, mandating that all trade to the islands be restricted to the CIO, and denying colonists the right to trade with any foreign merchants.[23] In order to permit the CIO to operate with as few overhead costs as possible, Colbert also issued ordinances removing all taxes and duties from the commodities that the company shipped across the Atlantic to the islands, although to little effect.[24]

By the end of the War of Devolution (1667–1668), the CIO was much weakened.[25] War was a tremendous disruption to provisioning networks, and the resulting disorder permitted both private French and foreign traders to replace the company's provisioning vessels with greater ease than before. The first significant opening appeared in 1669 when Colbert personally took over the issuing of passports to private merchants to prevent the possibility of foreign trade, showing a greater interest in the role of private trade within the monopolistic control of colonial expansion than is usually attributed to him.[26] Writing to the governor-general of the islands, Jean-Charles de Baas, who was well aware of the unfeasibility of relying on the CIO for provisions, Colbert stated,

> It is not at all His Majesty's wish that the Company should operate alone in the islands; on the contrary, he wishes to encourage all Frenchmen to trade there and to establish entirely free commerce. Until there is an adequate number, the Company is obliged to bring goods and to then sail to Guinée to acquire the slaves necessary for the islands, in so doing ridding you of your need for the Dutch. This is the only objective you must have.[27]

Indeed Colbert saw nothing against the best mercantile interests of France in the operations of private French traders, regardless of how this business was conducted on the islands. His prevailing concern was to replace Dutch supply networks with robust French ones, and to ensure that these traders were not bringing to the islands non-French goods, among which food provisions such as flour and Irish salt beef figured largely.[28] The attempts to control trade in both exported and imported goods were represented by three laws which were enacted between 1670 and 1671 and which laid down the tenets of *l'Exclusif* as it would exist up until, and indeed after, its eventual formalisation in 1717. The first was a 10 June 1670 ordinance that banned all trade with foreigners; the second a 30 December 1670 *arrêt* that stipulated only French traders in possession of passports issued by the Domaine d'occident had the right to trade in the West Indies; and the third was a 4 November 1671 ordinance that forbade French traders from trading non-French goods on the islands.[29] This last ordinance, which began 'Having been informed that despite the edicts that prohibited trade with foreigners, most French vessels sailing to the French islands to trade, have been found loaded with Beef, Lard, Canvas and other goods from foreign countries,' repeated the penalties that foreign trade entailed (a 500 *livres* fine; confiscation of the vessel and goods; and corporal punishment for recidivism) and provided measures by which captains could demonstrate the provenance of their cargos. Even at this early date, de Baas expressed misgivings about the consequences of these sizable constraints on the supply of foodstuffs, building materials, and other provisions critical to the development and maintenance of plantations.[30]

Private traders grew steadily in importance in the Caribbean as the CIO began to fail. By the end of 1671, largely because private French trade had increased more than tenfold over the previous decade, Colbert urged the director of the CIO to close his accounts in the West Indies, and the company's liquidation was begun the next year. By this time another war had broken out, placing even greater emphasis on private supply lines and thus increasing the dependency of colonists on private traders.[31]

As this trade legislation shows, the relationship of the CIO as a state-funded organism to private capital and to private traders was more complex than commonly appears in the older historiography of French mercantilism, which presents the efforts of the French Crown to centrally enforce mercantilist directives as if they were in opposition to the wishes and interests of private French merchants. From this point of view, these traders reacted negatively to the Crown's efforts, leading to the downfall of chartered companies and the establishment of representative bodies of merchants such as the Conseil de Commerce and municipal Chambers of Commerce. The failure of the CIO was inevitable, the argument goes, as was the failure of all chartered companies, because private traders were more able to flexibly and efficiently respond to the colonial demand.[32] However, more recent historical work argues convincingly that the centralised control and promotion of colonial trade of Colbert and his successors in all its forms was welcomed and even petitioned for by private traders, including the formulation of *l'Exclusif* and, indeed, the creation of commercial chartered companies such as the CIO.[33] Pierre Boulle has contended, for instance, that the chartered company system was systematically undermined as a strictly mercantilist tool to the advantage of private individuals who were often shareholders in the companies whose privileges they were contravening or whose trade they were replacing, a process, Boulle has argued, that was nevertheless necessary for the development of trade.[34] The maximisation of private profits at whatever cost to the state, an emerging feature of modern capitalism, became a defining feature of French Atlantic trade. By the end of the seventeenth century, the profits generated by the trade in foodstuffs for growing colonial and slave populations began to play a distinct role within the broader calculations of these private profits.

As a final note about food provisioning in this early period, Colbert's deliberate promotion of intercolonial trade in the 1670s between New France and the Antilles had the potential to redefine the trade relationship between French colonies and their metropole, as well as to provide the growing colonial populations of the French Antilles with another source of food provisions. The development of colonial settlements in complementary ecological zones logically entailed the possibility of complementary intercolonial trades, particularly in foodstuffs, since the climate and physical geography of the Saint Lawrence Valley resembled northern France much more than that of the Antilles, and with sustained agricultural development had the potential to produce the wheat flour, livestock, salted provisions, peas, and lumber needed by the colonial populations in the Caribbean.[35] Two other benefits that continued to sustain interest in intercolonial trade between the 1670s and 1763 were the shortness of the voyages from the eastern continental seaboard or the Gulf of Mexico to the Caribbean relative to the transatlantic voyage that metropolitan traders were obliged to make, and the promise of keeping trade and the profit generated by that trade within the French sphere.[36]

And indeed intercolonial trade between Québec and the Antilles was a recurring feature in Colbert's correspondence between the 1660s and 1680s with the *intendants* of Canada, Jean Talon and Jacques Duchesneau; with Frontenac, its governor; and with Pélissier, the director of the CIO.[37] The first short-lived attempts to stimulate this trade were made: Talon sent three ships from Quebec to Cayenne and Tortuga laden with 'dried fish, peas, beer, flour and pork' in 1670, two more in 1671 and a last one in 1672, the year he returned to France, and Duchesneau continued at the same pace.[38] These small numbers of vessels had little impact on the overall food provisioning of French colonists in the Caribbean. The problems with this trade far outweighed its theoretical advantages: the Quebec winters meant that the Saint Lawrence Seaway was closed to shipping for six months of the year; the increasing population of Canada in the 1670s made agricultural surpluses rarer; and, overall, private colonial merchants did not have the capital to develop their own networks.[39] Because of a lack of immediate profits, these early attempts to create a self-sustaining trade between Canada and the

Antilles were dependent on metropolitan merchants, who soon gave it up. Although this trade was revived slightly in the mid-1680s, it was not until the War of Spanish Succession (1700–1713), and more specifically the establishment of the fort of Louisbourg, that Canadian salt fish and dried peas would be exported in significant amounts to the French Caribbean islands.

The economic reality of encouraging and sustaining this trade within a mercantilist framework increasingly determined by metropolitan private capital meant that intercolonial trade during the *ancien régime* never received the unequivocal support it needed from the Ministère de la Marine. Colonial settlements of North America did indeed have surplus provisions for a profitable trade with the French Antilles in the eighteenth century, but they were the British colonies of the eastern seaboard, not the French ones of the Saint Lawrence River Valley. By 1700 the British settlements were already much more densely populated than New France, and, critically, they were geographically closer to the Caribbean, permitting smaller, less expensive ventures to be launched.[40] References to British–North American traders selling provisions to the French islands in the Caribbean begin in the 1670s, and their growing presence was both a continuing threat to protectionist trade legislation for the next 120 years and an essential feature of the provisioning of the French islands.[41] In conclusion, the indispensability of importing food provisions for a growing colonial slave population provided the theoretical possibility, never realised, of revising the mercantilistic framework to allow for the strengthening of intercolonial bonds, including the bolstering and diversifying of colonial economies, a shift towards which Colbert and local colonial officials showed themselves receptive. It also provided the means by which New Englanders were able to gain a critical foothold in the French Caribbean, shaping the geographies of trade routes, jeopardising the coherence of the French trading sphere, and influencing the formation of colonial trade policy for generations to come.

Food provisioning 1684–1763: *l'Exclusif* and the attempts to prohibit foreign trade

As I have argued, private French traders held a privileged position, one that emerged during the period of chartered commercial companies and grew in importance. With the foundation in 1700 of the Conseil de commerce, a consultative body of bureaucrats and merchant-deputies established to provide economic advice to Louis XIV, merchants were able to collectively articulate their wishes to the French Crown.[42] As the century progressed, the increasing control of the Antilles trade by private traders entailed increasing restrictions on the practice of trade, which was limited to a select, although expanding, number of French Atlantic port cities, and thus trade became centralised in the hands of powerful groups of merchants resident there.[43] The legislation that they advised the Crown to pass was intended to protect the Antilles' trade from illicit French traders from ports other than their own, but more notably from foreign traders in the Caribbean: Dutch, English, and Spanish merchants, and the aforementioned 'New England trade,' the scourge of eighteenth-century French colonial trade policy.

The main principles of the regulatory system that emerged after Colbert were codified in two sets of documents, the *Lettres patentes* of 1717 and of 1727, which with substantial modification after 1763 governed colonial trade until the Revolution. Prior to 1717, almost constant warfare had prevented the effective application of the initial Colbertian edicts passed to restrict trade to the French islands and forbidding French colonists to buy from foreigners.[44] The desperate situation faced by French colonists in the Caribbean, in particular during the War of the Spanish Succession, and the increase in illicit trade in provisions led to merchant pressure on Louis XIV and Jérôme de Pontchartrain to regulate this trade.[45] Despite a small increase in the levels of trade between the Antilles and Canada during this time, and the strong interest in such a trade expressed by Vaucresson, the *intendant* of the Îles du Vent, the war disrupted shipping routes and made a legitimate intercolonial trade almost impossible.[46]

At the peace signed at Utrecht in 1713, trade and colonial matters occupied a central place in the negotiations.[47] These concerns were further concretised four years later with the 1717 *Lettres patentes*, which opened trade with the French Antilles to thirteen privileged port cities – Calais, Dieppe, le Havre, Rouen, Honfleur, St. Malo, Morlaix, Brest, Nantes, la Rochelle, Bordeaux, Bayonne and Sète – and before 1763 another seven ports would be added to this list (Marseilles, Dunkirk, Vannes, Cherbourg, Libourne, Toulon and Caen).[48] Vessels leaving from these cities were required to return directly to them after having completed their business, thus discouraging intercolonial trade. All goods declared to be destined for the islands were free of duty, which held true for goods imported from abroad in order to be reexported to the Caribbean, such as salt beef from Ireland.[49] In this way, these ports became warehouses for all commodities exported from and imported to the Antilles. Predictably, the effect of this legislation on the cities in question was electrifying, in particular on Nantes, St. Malo, Le Havre and above all, Bordeaux. These cities experienced strong growth in the eighteenth century, doubling (Nantes) or tripling (Bordeaux) their populations, as industries grew to support the transatlantic maritime traffic including the reexport of tropical goods, as port hinterlands developed agricultural resources to meet demand, and as domestic consumption of tropical commodities increased. Food provisioning for the islands and for departing vessels continued to figure among the dominant activities spurring on development in these Atlantic ports and their hinterlands.[50]

The intended effect in the Caribbean of these *Lettres patentes* was to curb the growing illicit trade with foreign merchants, the scale of which, although difficult to calculate with precision, almost certainly overshadowed that of intercolonial trade in the provision of foodstuffs to the French islands during the *ancien régime*.[51] The reaction in 1717 to the arrival of this legislation on the French islands was immediate: it precipitated the most important colonists' revolt to date, a revolt which spread throughout the Isles du Vent, and in which the royal militia itself rose up against royal authority.[52] Varenne and Ricouart, the governor and *intendant*, wrote to the Conseil de la Marine about the beginnings of rebellion on Guadeloupe:

> Seditious souls have been gathering with arms in Saint-Anne's parish, declaring their misery and insolently claiming that they are perishing with hunger since trade with the English has been forbidden to them and because the little beef sent by French traders is at an exorbitant price.... We are obliged to advise the Council that if 5 or 6000 barrels of beef are not immediately forthcoming from France (in the expectation of more) then it is feared that all of Guadeloupe will rise up, and that the rebellion will spread to Martinique.... It is imperative to quickly send beef and flour or even greater disorder is to be feared.[53]

In this report, the two officials confirmed that the food provisioning of the islands and its regulation were directly connected to the security of colonial rule and to the continued development and profitability of colonial settlements; more broadly, the transatlantic politics of food provisioning influenced colonists' understandings of their dependency on the metropole, and, by consequence, their degree of loyalty or rebelliousness.

Another clause of the 1717 *Lettres patentes* stipulated that commodities such as salt fish produced in Terre-Neuve were to be free of duty when entering the Antilles, thus equalizing the islands' privileges with those of France and permitting, or even encouraging, the resumption of an intercolonial trade based in the Americas that had, as yet, played a minor role in the provisioning of the French Caribbean islands. Consequently, the 1720s saw the return of this trade based on the still attractive principle that the colonies could provision each other while maintaining all profits within the French sphere. A direct trade between New France and the Antilles had picked up as a result of the construction of Louisbourg on Île Royale (Cape Breton Island), which became an extremely lucrative entrepôt for goods coming from all over the region (including New England and New France) as well as from France and from the West Indies.[54] Louisbourg, given its more favourable position on the Atlantic, was more successful as a French Atlantic trading hub than Quebec or Plaisance had ever been, and the years of its existence (1714–1758) marked the pinnacle in French intercolonial trade. For instance, while 39 vessels sailed between New France and the Caribbean between the 1670s and 1729, this number grew to 478 between 1730 and 1746, and then fell slightly to 376 between 1748 and 1757. The number of vessels sailing in the opposite direction was smaller, although it followed the same general movement of growth: from 35, it grew in the same years as above to 362 and then fell to 248.[55]

In October of 1727, soon after Louis XV began his personal rule, a new version of the *Lettres patentes* was enacted to regulate all commerce that took place among the French colonies, and specifically to create a completely closed commercial system operating between France and the Antilles.[56] The prohibition on trading with foreigners that was noted in a single clause of the 1717 *Lettres patentes* became the entire focus of these new regulations. The only exception to the general rule that provisions (other than slaves) had to be of French origin was salt beef from Ireland, which, although Irish, was still to be transported by French ships after being warehoused in French Atlantic ports.[57] Remarkably, it was a commodity of such vital import to the islands that these regulations were amended two months later to allow French vessels to cross the Atlantic to the Antilles directly from Irish ports laden with the beef, thus bypassing French Atlantic ports entirely for one year, an annual decree that was reissued until 1741.[58]

The legislation closed the waters for one league around all French possessions and included new, harsher penalties imposed on those convicted of trading with foreigners.[59] Although perhaps 'regressive and ineffective' in the long term,[60] these regulations had the medium-term effect of stimulating the trade in foodstuffs between Canada and the Antilles, as Canada became one of the few legitimate sources of provisions for the islands. During the late 1720s and into the 1730s this trade stabilised for a twenty-year period, although the Canada–Antilles trade never played a crucial role in provisioning the islands compared to other sources of provisions. In the year 1736, for instance, an average one in these twenty years, Irish salt beef imports to the islands carried by French traders through French Atlantic ports equalled 60,000 barrels, whereas that of Canadian fish equalled about 6,500 barrels.[61]

The difficulty at the heart of the efforts to encourage this legitimate intercolonial trade in foodstuffs was the distinctly uneven balance of trade between the two French colonial centres of New France and the Antilles, which highlighted the vast differences in economic production, consumption patterns and demographics between them, and which was never resolved.[62] Simply put, the value of Canadian exports to the Antilles far outweighed the value of French Caribbean exports to Canada. The dried cod, wheat flour, lumber, peas, tar, pitch and fuel oil which left Canada for the Antilles were essential provisions on the islands, whose collective populations (of whom more than three-quarters were slaves by 1730) more than quadrupled those of New France.[63] The cargoes of vessels sailing from the Antilles to either Canada or Louisbourg, on the other hand, were made up almost exclusively of sugar by-products: specifically *sirops*, sugar syrups of differing grades, and *guildive* (or *tafia*), the rough sugarcane brandy distilled from the syrups (i.e., rum).[64] Due to the strictures of *l'Exclusif*, planters were forbidden from selling or shipping their semi-refined sugars to Canada or Louisbourg, and there was a negligible market for *tafia* in France, where imports had been banned in 1713 to protect the interests of producers of French grape brandy.[65] Moreover, unfortunately for the desperate planters of the Antilles, there was both a glut of *sirops* and *tafia* at Louisbourg because of their double availability via English sugar planters and a lack of extensive North American markets for these relatively dispensable goods. Indeed the very accumulation of Antillean *sirops* and *tafia* lead to their unique position in the exchanges between the islands and New England and New France, in which they played central roles in both the application of *l'Exclusif* and in New England's industrial development.[66]

Between 1749 and 1750, the provisions trade between Canada and the Antilles suddenly doubled in volume, and it maintained this rate until the outbreak of the Seven Years' War in 1756. Although it is possible that this increase was due to an overall growth in the mercantilist 'empire' that was developing (certainly the sugar trade between the Antilles and Europe was experiencing exponential growth), it is also likely that trade goods from Canada were at this point becoming a mask for contraband trade from New England.[67] In fact, the New England trade assumed more and more material and symbolic importance during the Seven Years' War, even after the loss of Louisbourg in 1758. The renewal of Franco-British hostilities resulted in the British occupation of every French island in the Caribbean except Saint-Domingue, which created legitimate trading channels with the British colonies of the eastern seaboard, critically weakening French transatlantic and intercolonial trading networks and indeed French power in the region overall.

Food provision 1763–1789: the aftermath of the seven years' war

The years following the defeat of France and prior to the onset of the French and Haitian revolutions saw a swift succession of changes to colonial trade policies, and to provisioning policies in particular. According to the Treaty of Paris which concluded the Seven Years' War, France lost all of its North American possessions (save its fishing rights off the 'French Shore' of Newfoundland and the tiny islands of St. Pierre and Miquelon in the Gulf of the Saint Lawrence) – all claims made to territories in the Ohio and Mississippi valleys were renounced, New France went to the British, and Louisiana west of the Mississippi went to the Spanish, and finally, three of its Caribbean possessions (Saint Vincent, Dominica and Grenada) and its possessions in Senegal and India went to the British. However, despite the British occupation during the war, all other Caribbean possessions were retained, and Sainte Lucie, contested up until now, was gained. Any hopes for provisioning France's Caribbean colonies through legitimate intercolonial trade with the northern colonies were henceforth dashed.

Despite this, the Duc de Choiseul who negotiated the treaty on behalf of France, and many others, considered the treaty a success for France – the profits being made from the sugar islands far outweighed the profits derived from the collapsed fur trade, from fishing, or from any other of the commodity trades that had developed in the northern colonies.[68] According to a revivified mercantilism that found new voice in the writings of Montesquieu and Voltaire, the success and value of colonies still depended on the degree to which they could be manipulated to produce and export an array of profitable commodities as unlike those available in France as possible, with the understanding that colonies would consume metropolitan goods, including food provisions.[69] Profits from production dictated the success of colonies and assured the colonial utility of the French Antilles, certainly in comparison to the *quelques arpents de neige* [several acres of snow] to the north which had produced such disappointing returns.[70]

Choiseul's reorganisation of France's overseas colonies after 1763 also reflected the growing influence of the physiocrats, whose writings emerged mid-century, and who had distinctly different views on colonial development and on slave-based colonial regimes in particular.[71] The exaltation of agriculture by writers such as Quesnay, Mirabeau, and Du Pont de Nemours, of the role it played in the functioning of state economies, and of the agrarian ideal more generally, resulted in their pressure within France to remove all tariffs and duties on the grain trade. In relation to France's colonies and in a reversal of mercantilist thinking, colonial utility was to be found in the capacity of colonies to produce commodities in accordance with the metropolitan agricultural model: to extend this model, not to provide a contrast to it.[72] Overseas as well as in France, agricultural productivity was an end in itself, and this focus led to dramatic shifts in the way the provisioning for France's thriving sugar colonies was envisioned.[73]

The clearest example of this shift is Choiseul's disastrous 1763 expedition to Kourou in la Guyane which was expressly intended to establish a replacement for the loss of Canada and Louisiana.[74] While the central initiative was one of settlement and the creation of a new Atlantic base from which France could launch its future offensives against Britain, a secondary goal was to provide an ongoing and legitimate source of provisions for the Îles du Vent, now even more dependent on metropolitan merchants and foreign trade than before the war. In language that mirrored closely that of Jean Talon and Colbert almost a century earlier, a memo addressed by Louis XV to Étienne François Turgot and Thibaut de Chanvalon who headed the Kourou expedition, read,

> His Majesty wishes to encourage by all means the types of cultivation and livestock-raising that will build up food supplies so to assure the subsistence of colonists. His Majesty commands them to actively concentrate on the goal of having agriculture and livestock in such abundance that it will be possible to furnish the *Îles du Vent* and to form a habitual trade with them.[75]

However short-lived the Kourou settlement project eventually was, this proposal reintroduced the idea of an intercolonial trade in provisions with markedly different ideas about colonial political economy, most notably because of the opposition of most physiocrats to slavery, in theory if not in practice.[76]

Caribbean colonists and planters who had pushed for freer trade and the right to buy their essential commodities – including provisions and slaves – from non-French merchants, continued their efforts after 1763 with a vociferousness borne of the privations of the war. In this period they made real gains, some of which can be seen as further signs of physiocratic influence. The increasingly strident post–Seven Years' Wars commercial debates underline the fundamental opposition of the self-interest of metropolitan merchants and colonial merchants and planters, parties which both sought to extend and maximise their commercial profits through the manipulation of royal trade policy.[77] Food provisions had a substantial role to play in the articulation of these debates. For instance, the clearest and most formal expression of an advancement of colonial demands for liberty of trade was Jean-Baptiste Dubuc's 1765 *Mémoire sur l'étendue et les bornes des Lois prohibitives*, which formed the basis of the *Exclusif mitigé* that held sway, in one form or another, for the remainder of the period under examination.[78] Dubuc was a high-profile Creole from Martinique who had been named by Choiseul to be the *premier commis des colonies* in 1764, the first time a *colon* had risen to head the administration of the French colonies. The underlying argument of his *Mémoire* was that colonial survival depended on a strictly defined and limited set of exceptions to the already established regime of trade restrictions with non-French merchants. These exceptions were three crucial groups of commodities which Dubuc contended colonists should be permitted to exchange with foreigners: slaves; *sirops* and *tafia*, the classic return cargos; and cod, a critical element for slaves' diets, in particular.[79] Indeed, as Dubuc articulated it, the

> imperious necessity of circumstances [dictate that] our Colonies cannot provide their own subsistence in any measure whatsoever. In particular the inhabitants of the Isles du Vent, much more precarious in this regard than Saint Domingue, have only foreign trade to supply food for their slaves; cod is absolutely indispensable for this purpose.[80]

In this way, slaves and their foodstuffs were named as the commodities at the root of the most important formal challenge to the French regulatory trade policy in the *ancien régime*. To some extent, the centrality of foodstuffs in this demand for freedom of trade was pure rhetoric and served to mask colonists' bald attempts to extend all of their trade with New Englanders for simple commercial gain: slave diets varied by plantation and by island, but they were notoriously lacking in the protein that fish and beef would have provided and depended heavily on the manioc, plantains, and bananas that slaves themselves grew.[81] These calls for the freedom to trade with New Englanders should not be read as if slaves' dietary needs for salt fish, however real, were the prime factor that motivated colonists, nor as if colonists ever satisfied these needs to the best of their ability.

Moreover, in establishing these specific exceptions related to foodstuffs, the *Mémoire* exhibited a strategic political conservatism: the arguments were set firmly within the familiar limits of mercantilist concepts of the commercial primacy of colonies. Dubuc reiterated a definition of colonies based wholly around their consumption of metropolitan products and around a structural relationship with the metropole that favoured the flow of profit in one direction only. It was within this framework, however, that he argued that what brought wealth to the colonies would result in greater wealth for France. On this basis, while defending the need for the preexisting trade restrictions, Dubuc opened the possibility of exceptions to them, always with the proviso that this flexibility would keep smuggling at bay.[82] Regardless of his *Mémoire*'s equivocation and apparent endorsement of the current state of trade restrictions, metropolitan merchants rightly sensed a serious threat to their authority, and the *Mémoire* was vigorously refuted in the Chambers of Commerce in Atlantic port cities.

Of the series of further measures taken in these twenty-five years that continued to undermine the regime of *l'Exclusif*, including the suspension of the one-league clause of the 1727 *Lettres patentes*, two stand out. The first was the creation in 1767 of two free ports in the French Antilles: one at Carénage on Sainte-Lucie for the Îles du Vent, and the other at Môle Saint-Nicolas, on the northern coast of Saint-Domingue.[83] These ports provided bases where French planters could exchange their *sirops* and *tafia* (as well as other goods imported from France) for a strictly limited number of provisions subject to a duty of 1 per cent.[84] The list of provisions, however, did not include foodstuffs, and the omission of salt cod and salt beef caused immense dissatisfaction, provoking petitions from Saint-Domingue that trade in these two foodstuffs be authorised.[85]

In Guadeloupe, the opposition to the exclusion of foodstuffs from the permitted items was so fierce that in April of the following year an *arrêt* extended the commodities permitted to be traded at Carénage to include rice, maize, salt cod, and vegetables, as well as sugar and coffee.[86] Although Carénage and Môle Saint-Nicolas were created in response to the creation of similar free ports by the British on Dominica and

Jamaica, both were ultimately unsuccessful in controlling the volume of illegal trading. Located directly south of Martinique, and far south of both Guadeloupe and the British free port at Dominica, Carénage was too remote and thus too expensive to reach, and was incapable of providing a trading base for all the French Windward Islands.[87] Môle Saint-Nicolas was more successful overall as a free port because Saint-Domingue had a more developed economy and more well-established (illicit) trade links in food provisions with New England due partly to its proximity to the mainland of North America.[88] Nevertheless the cumulative effect of these free ports was, in fact, the reverse of what had been intended. Their presence served to stimulate the growing trade between New England and the French islands.

In some senses, this French-American trading alliance, concretised through the 1778 Treaty of Amity and Commerce, saw some curious reversals by the end of the American War of Independence, as metropolitan France provisioned the thirteen ex-colonies throughout the war on credit, leading to the accumulation by the new republic of a staggering debt towards France.[89] In the year following the treaty of Versailles in 1783, Castries, *secrétaire d'état de la marine*, formulated the second critical measure that undercut the regulatory regime of *l'Exclusif*. After months of preparation and in view of the provisions trade that the American War of Independence had necessitated, Castries issued the *Arrêt du Conseil du 30 août 1784 Concernant le Commerce étranger dans les Isles Françoises de l'Amérique*.[90] This *arrêt* entailed the formal opening of a total of seven free ports (one on each of the lesser Antilles and one per region of Saint-Domingue) open to the goods authorised in 1767 and 1768, but also for the first time to Irish salt beef and coal.[91]

The only essential commodity that was left off the list was flour; it was the subject of fierce debate, but Castries finally decided that it was too early to curtail the exclusivity that metropolitan merchants still maintained in their flour trade with the colonies. There were factors within metropolitan France that equally influenced the availability of flour for transatlantic export: periodic flour shortages raised grain prices, although the development of flour refineries in Normandy and around Nantes broke the quasi-monopoly that Bordeaux had previously had on the colonial market and potentially increased the number of merchants who could take part in the trade and the amount of available flour.[92] Nevertheless, for the following seven years before the Haitian Revolution utterly transformed the organisation of subsistence within what had been Saint-Domingue (as well as the transatlantic trading networks between Hispaniola and France), the provision of wheat flour continued to be in crisis. It was this crisis that was addressed by the 1789 Committee of Trade and Agriculture pamphlet cited in this chapter's opening.

Conclusion

Although the 1784 *arrêt* seemed conclusively to signal the beginning of an era of true liberty of trade, in matter of fact it simply reiterated the central tenets of the original *Exclusif mitigé* propounded by Dubuc's *Mémoire* of 1765. Nevertheless, there was a tremendous outcry in the Atlantic regions of France. The year after, the *Parlement* of Rouen published a *remontrance* in reaction to it that encapsulates the principal features of the eighteenth-century mercantilist trade regulations surrounding the provision of food to the French Antilles with which this chapter has been concerned. The *remontrance* took the form of a letter to Louis XVI and was concerned with the threat to the prosperity of Normandy posed by the authorisation of trade with non-French merchants in the seven free Caribbean ports specified in the *arrêt*.[93] Beginning with Montesquieu's definition of a colony in which the central principle was the 'extension of trade, not the founding of new cities or of a new empire,' the letter narrated a history of France's colonies in the Caribbean defined by trade: the actions of Colbert the progenitor, followed by the promulgation of the *Lettres patentes* of 1717 and 1727, the development of *l'Exclusif*, and then the challenge of an '*Habitant des Isles du Vent*... who undertook to impose a new system, but without the merit of perfect disinterestedness,'[94] a reference to Jean-Baptiste Dubuc. This history traces the lines of the debate between a liberty of trade continuously called for by self-interested colonists and the claims of metropolitan traders capable of provisioning the colonies via a trade which was their right. Unapologetic in its bias, the letter described in detail the grievous impact within France of the relinquishment to foreigners of this trade in colonial provisions – unemployment, depopulation, migration, and the loss of manufacturing skills.

What this letter clarified and made explicit was the pivotal role played by colonial consumption within the metropolitan political economy of the Atlantic regions of France at the end of the *ancien régime*, and the determination of merchant groups to lay claim to and to protect the sources of their profits. Economic growth in France during this period was highly regional, and merchants from Nantes, Bordeaux, Marseilles and Rouen whose economic activities constituted one of the most dynamic sectors of the French economy were well aware of the critical importance of overseas trade, including export food trades destined for colonial consumption.[95] Indeed, economic power put weight behind this type of articulation of collective self-interest which sought to manipulate royal trade policy for the benefit of these merchants. In the language of the Rouen merchants' text, colonial consumption drove the expansion of metropolitan French commerce and allowed France to engage in global trades in tropical export commodities. 'This Kingdom, the most fertile in Europe, cannot consume all it produces; it is with its excess production that it procures goods from the Islands; it is with its wines, its flour, its hemp and its linen that it converts to canvas that it buys colonial commodities', the letter argued; 'Bordeaux alone sends 200,000 barrels of flour.'[96] While the debate over free trade rarely touched on the identity of the ultimate consumers of this flour (the 1789 pamphlet published by the Deputies for Industry and Trade notwithstanding), the probable loss of colonial consumers that would be the consequence of legalising colonial trades in foodstuffs with non-French merchants was keenly felt. In a striking turn of phrase, the Norman petition observed that

> the secret of Commerce is procuring consumers; when they are found they must not be relinquished; when we have an assured source of them, they must not be abandoned in the uncertain hope of finding others. Our Colonists are consumers who belong to us; surrendering them to Foreigners would be renouncing our trade balance advantage.[97]

Over a century and a half the debates over the regulation of the provisions trade show the growing stakes of this trade. The crisis of food provision was structured into the plantation societies that developed on the Caribbean islands first and foremost because the enslaved workforce that rapidly expanded in the second half of the eighteenth century was not permitted to fully control its own subsistence needs. Intercolonial and transatlantic trades developed and strove both to meet provisioning shortfalls and to derive economic benefit from them. By traditional mercantilist injunctions, this economic benefit was restricted to Frenchmen, although challenges to this legal framework in the form of smuggling between New England and the French Antilles was endemic, and indeed the roots of the complex and shifting relationship between the two early republics of France and the United States in the late eighteenth century are to be found in this provisions trade that dates to the mid-seventeenth century. But even when successfully restricted to the French sphere, the problem of which Frenchmen to benefit (planters? traders?) defined the debate over the trades' regulation, touching on the most elemental questions connected to the value of colonies. The result was the increasingly conscious transformation of colonial populations, including slaves, into paradoxically valuable consumers of metropolitan goods, although the real link between slave consumption and provisions such as wheat flour remains to be proven.[98] While slaves' purported choices between manioc and wheat bread on Saint-Domingue perhaps seem marginal to the dramas of revolution in France in 1789, they were, in fact, central to the economic crises that had preceded them.

Notes

The author wishes to thank Pernille Røge, Sophus A. Reinert and an anonymous reviewer for their valued comments; this chapter has benefitted immensely from their feedback.

1. 400,000 is the estimated slave population that appears in the pamphlet; more contemporary estimates of the slave population of Saint-Domingue in 1789 range from 452,000 (Antoine Gisler, *L'Esclavage Des Antilles Françaises XVIIe–XIXe Siècle, Contribution Au Problème de L'esclavage* [Paris: Editions universitaires fribourg suisse, 1965], 34) to 465,429 (Charles Frostin, *Les Révoltes Blanches À Saint-Domingue Aux XVIIe Et XVIIIe Siècles* [Paris: L'École, 1975], 28).
2. *Approvisionnemens de St. Domingue: Réponse des Députés des Manufactures et du Commerce de France* (Versailles: Imprimerie de Pierres, (s. d.)), 8.
3. Cynthia Bouton, 'Les Mouvements de Subsistance Et Le Problème de L'économie Morale Sous l'Ancien Régime Et La Révolution Française', *Annales Historique de La Révolution Française* 319 (2000): 71–100; Judith Miller, *Mastering the Market : The State and the Grain Trade in Northern France, 1700–1860* (Cambridge: Cambridge University Press, 1999), 115–33 and Owen Hufton, 'Social Conflict and the Grain Supply in Eighteenth Century France', *Journal of Interdisciplinary History* 14, no. 2 (1983): 303–31. For the background to the strife of the 1780s, see Miller, *Mastering the Market*, 27–113, and Steven Kaplan, *Bread, Politics and Political Economy in the Reign of Louis XV* (The Hague: Martinus Nijhoff, 1976).
4. *Approvisionnemens de St. Domingue*, 32–51.
5. These debates had been taking place for six months at this point. On 1 April 1789, the Marquis du Chilleau and François de Barbé Marbois, the governor and intendant of Saint-Domingue, had passed the first ordinance permitting the entry of American flour, followed up on 9 May with an ordinance permitting the export of colonial goods in exchange. See Manuel Covo's forthcoming PhD thesis, *1783–1806* (École des Hautes Études en Sciences Sociales, Paris), for a detailed discussion of the role of Saint-Domingue/United States trade in French revolutionary political economy.

6. Dale Miquelon, 'Canada's Place in the French Imperial Economy: An Eighteenth-Century Overview', *French Historical Studies* 15, no. 3 (Spring 1988): 434.
7. Louis-Philippe May, *Histoire Économique de la Martinique (1635–1763)* (Paris : Marcel Rivière, 1972), 75–84; Clarence Gould, 'Trade between the Windward Islands and the Continental Colonies of the French Empire, 1683–1763', *Mississippi Valley Historical Review* 25, no. 4 (March 1939): 473; Richard Pares, 'Merchants and Planters', *Economic History Review*, supplement 4 (Cambridge: Cambridge University Press, 1960); Richard Sheridan, *Sugar and Slavery: An Economic History of the British West Indies* (Kingston, Jamaica: Canoe Press, 2000, 1974), 259–60 and Sheridan, 'The Crisis of Slave Subsistence in the British West Indies during and after the American Revolution', *William and Mary Quarterly* 33, no. 4 (October 1976): 615–41.
8. Locally cultivated provisions (manioc, yams, sweet potatoes, peas, etc.) continued to play a central role in the diet of slaves in particular. For the historical development of slave gardens in the French Caribbean, see Vincent Huyghues-Belrose, *Le Jardin Créole À La Martinique: Une Parcelle Du Jardin Planétaire* (Fort-de-France: Parc naturel régional de la Martinique, 2010).
9. In 1713, the population of New France was 16,500 (15,000 Canadians and 1,500 Acadians) while that of the French Antilles was 75,000 (15,000 white colonists and 60,000 slaves). By 1763, the population of French Canada was 85,000, while that of the Antilles was 351,000 (35,000 white colonists and 316,000 slaves). Paul Butel, *L'Économie française au XVIIIe siècle* (Paris: SEDES, 1993), 114–5. For population statistics, see also James Pritchard, *In Search of Empire: The French in the Americas, 1670–1730* (Cambridge: Cambridge University Press, 2004), appendices I–II, 423–31.
10. For the French Atlantic, see inter alia Paul Butel, *Les Négociants Bordelais, l'Europe Et Les Îles Au XVIIIe Siècle* (Paris: Aubier, 1974) and Olivier Pétré-Grenouilleau, *Les Négoces Maritimes Français, XVI–XXe Siècle* (Paris: Belin, 1997).
11. See also Paul Cheney, *Revolutionary Commerce: Globalization and the French Monarchy* (Cambridge, MA: Harvard University Press, 2010).
12. For the early generations of French settlement in the Caribbean, see Philip Boucher, *France and the American Tropics to 1700: Tropics of Discontent?* (Baltimore, MD: Johns Hopkins University Press, 2008).
13. Pierre H. Boulle, 'French Mercantilism, Commercial Companies and Colonial Profitability', in Leonard Blussé and Femme Gaastra (eds), *Companies and Trade: Essays on Overseas Trading Companies during the Ancien Regime* (The Hague: Leiden University Press, 1981), 97–117.
14. Boucher, *France and the American Tropics to 1700*, 63–9.
15. Louis-Élie Moreau de Saint-Méry, *Loix Et Constitutions Des Colonies Françoises de l'Amérique Sous Le Vent* (Paris, 1784–1785), tome 1, 18–9.
16. Jacob Soll's recent claim that Colbert showed little interest in colonial matters because of the lack of paperwork they generated in his archive (Jacob Sollis, *The Information Master: Jean-Baptiste Colbert's Secret State Intelligence System* [Ann Arbor: University of Michigan Press, 2009], 113–9) is an unconvincing account of the role of overseas trade in Colbert's overall economic and commercial activity. See inter alia L. Cordier, *Les Compagnies À Charte Et La Politique Coloniale Sous Le Ministère de Colbert* (Paris: A. Rousseau,

1906); E. Benoit du Rey, *Recherches Sur La Politique Coloniale de Colbert* (Paris: A. Pedone, 1902) and Stewart Mims, *Colbert's West India Policy* (New Haven, CT: Yale University Press, 1912). See also Pierre Clément (ed.), *Lettres, Instructions, Mémoires de Colbert* (Paris: Imprimerie Impériale, 1861), tome 3, 2e partie, 387–649, for a selection of Colbert's letters and instructions on colonial affairs written between 1662 and 1682.

17. Robert Batie, 'Why Sugar? Economic Cycles and the Changing of Staples on the English and French Antilles, 1624–54', *Journal of Caribbean History* 8, no. 9 (1976): 1–41; Christian Schnakenbourg, 'Note Sur Les Origines de L'industrie Sucrière En Guadeloupe Au XVIIe Siècle (1640–1670)', *Revue Française D'histoire d'Outre-Mer* 55, no. 200 (1968): 267–311 and May, *Histoire Économique de la Martinique*, 87–90.
18. Pierre Bonnassieux, *Les Grande compagnies de commerce: étude pour servir à l'histoire de la colonisation* (Paris: Plon, 1892), 369–77.
19. Philip Curtin, *The Rise and Fall of the Plantation Complex*, 2nd edn (Cambridge: Cambridge University Press, 1998), 17–20; António de Almeida Mendes, 'Les Réseaux de La Traite Ibérique Dans l'Atlantiques Nord (1440–1640)', *Annales. Histoire, Sciences Sociales* 4 (2008) (63e année): 739–68 and Mims, *Colbert's West India Policy*, 287–309.
20. Immanuel Wallerstein, *The Modern World System II: Mercantilism and the Consolidation of the European World Economy 1600–1750* (New York: Academic Press, 1980), 37–40; Pritchard, *In Search of Empire*, 190; Johannes Postma and Victor Enthoven (eds), *Riches from Atlantic Commerce: Dutch Transatlantic Trade and Shipping, 1585–1817* (Leiden: Brill, 2003); Paul Butel, 'France, the Antilles and Europe, 1700–1900', in James D. Tracy (ed.), *The Rise of Merchant Empires: Long-Distance Trade in the Early Modern World, 1350–1750* (Cambridge: Cambridge University Press, 1990), 153–73
21. Pares, 'Merchants and Planters', 27; Paul Butel, 'France, the Antilles and Europe', 154; May, *Histoire Économique de La Martinique*, 105.
22. May, *Histoire économique de la Martinique*, 108–9.
23. There were a few exceptions to these restrictions: until 1669, trade could be carried out by private French to whom the CIO had allocated permissions (Bonnassieux, *Les Grande compagnies de commerce*, 373).
24. See for example *l'Arret du Conseil d'Etat, pour la décharge de tous les droits de Ville sur les Bestiaux, Vins, Eaux-de-Vie* (12 février, 1665), reprinted in Moreau de Saint-Méry, *Loix Et Constitutions*, tome 1, 134.
25. May, *Histoire Économique de la Martinique*, 109–10.
26. Charles Cole, *Colbert and a Century of French Mercantilism*, vol. II (New York: Columbia University Press, 1939), 27–36 for a closer description of Colbert's efforts at excluding foreign traders; Pritchard, 194; Mims, 225–6; Bonnassieux, 373.
27. Colbert to de Baas, 3 July 1670, in Clément, *Lettres, Instructions*, tome 3, 2e partie, 188.
28. Cole, vol II., 16–7; Bonnassieux, 375 and Boulle, 106–9.
29. *Ordonnance du Roi, qui défend le Commerce Étranger aux Isles* (4 juin 1670), reprinted in Moreau de Saint-Méry, *Loix Et Constitutions*, tome 1, 195–6; *Arrêt Du Conseil D'État Touchant Les Passeports Pour Négocier Aux Indes Occidentales* (30 décembre 1670), reprinted in Moreau de Saint-Méry, *Loix Et Constitutions*, tome 1, 206–7; *Ordonnance Du Roi qui défend le transport des Bœufs, Lards, Toiles et autres Marchandises... dans les Isles* (4 novembre 1671), reprinted

in Moreau de Saint-Méry, *Loix Et Constitutions*, tome 1, 253–4. See also Schnakenbourg, 301–2; G. Saint-Yves, 'Les Antilles françaises et la correspondance de L'intendant Patoulet', *Journal de la Société des Américanistes* 4, no. 1 (1902): 59.

30. CAOM, C8[A] 1, folio 29 (15 janvier, 1670), de Baas à Colbert.
31. May, 110–1; Pritchard, 295–300.
32. The standard accounts of French mercantilism that espouse this view are the volumes by Charles Cole already cited; Eli Fr. Heckscher, *Mercantilism*, rev. edn by E. F. Soderlund, 2 vols. (London: Allen and Unwin, 1955) and Lionel Rothkrug, *Opposition to Louis XIV: The Political and Social Origins of the French Enlightenment* (Princeton, NJ: Princeton University Press, 1965). For a brief discussion of this historiography, see Thomas J. Schaeper, 'Colonial Trade Policies Late in the Reign of Louis XIV', *Revue française d'histoire d'outre-mer* 67 (1980): 203.
33. Jonathan Howes Webster, 'The Concerns of Bordeaux's Merchants and the Formation of Royal Commercial Policy for the West Indies', *Proceedings of the Western Society for French History* 2 (1974): 12–20; Jonathan Howes Webster, 'The Merchants of Bordeaux in Trade to the French West Indies, 1664–1717' (PhD diss., University of Minnesota, 1972), esp 376–436; Boulle, 105–9, 115–7.
34. Boulle, 109.
35. Allana G. Reid, 'Intercolonial Trade during the French Regime', *Canadian Historical Review* 32, no. 3 (September 1951): 242 and Gould, 473–5.
36. The principal works on this trade are Jacques Mathieu, *Le Commerce entre New France et les Antilles au XVIIIe siècle* (Montréal: Fides, 1981) and 'La Balance Commerciale Nouvelle-France–Antilles Au XVIIIe Siècle', *Revue D'Histoire De L'Amérique Française* 25, no. 4 (March 1972): 465–97; Gould, 473–90; Dorothy Burne Goebel, 'The "New England Trade" and the French West Indies, 1763–1774: A Study in Trade Policies', *William and Mary Quarterly*, 3rd series, 20, no. 3 (July 1963): 331–72 and Reid, 236–51. On intercolonial trade between 1670 and 1730, see Pritchard, 197–201. On the trade in wheat flour between New France and the Antilles, see Louise Dechêne, *Le Partage des subsistances au Canada sous le régime français* (Montréal: Boréal, 1994).
37. For example, Jean Talon assured Colbert that 'within fifteen years, we will be producing enough surpluses to supply the Antilles' (CAOM, Col C[11a] 2 f. 1453–153v, 4 October, 1665); Colbert observed to Talon that 'colonists' lives will improve as commerce picks up, especially that with the islands' (CAOM Col C[11a] 3 f. 11–18, 20 February, 1668) and in a 1670 memo, Pélissier listed the goods that Canada could export to the islands – 'dried fish, flour, *froment*, oats, green peas, fish oil' (CAOM Col C[11a] 3 f. 146–149, 15 December 1670).
38. Reid, 243; Mims, 315–8.
39. As obstacles to this trade, Pritchard adds the disruption of shipping caused by the Dutch War (1672–1678) and the discrepancy between sizes of vessels desired by Colbert and available to colonists, 198; see also Reid, 243; Gould, 475.
40. The total population of the thirteen British colonies in 1700 was 251,000, as compared to New France's total population of 16,856 (James James McCusker, *The Rum Trade and the Balance of Payments of the Thirteen Continental Colonies, 1650–1775* [PhD diss., University of Pittsburgh, 1970], table B-26, 584; Pritchard, appendix 1, 423).

41. CAOM C^{8A} 1 f. 316–22, le sieur Duclerc (20 January 1670).
42. Thomas Schaeper, *The French Council of Commerce 1700–1715: A Study of Mercantilism after Colbert* (Columbus: Ohio State University Press, 1983), esp 61–2, 125, 241–2; David Kammerling Smith, 'Structuring Politics in Early Eighteenth-Century France: The Political Innovation of the French Council of Commerce', *Journal of Modern History* 74 (September 2002): 490–537.
43. See Webster, especially his dissertation, for an examination of the Bordeaux merchants' effect on the formation of colonial trade policy.
44. The War of Devolution (1667–1668); the Dutch War (1672–1678); the Nine Years' War (1688–1697) and the War of the Spanish Succession (1701–1713).
45. Jacques Petitjean-Roget, *Le Gaoulé: la révolte de la Martinique en 1717* [Société d'histoire de la Martinique, 1966], 167–93, treats in detail the trade and provisioning crisis of this war.
46. Pritchard, 199–220; Gould, 477–9; Reid, 245. For Vaucresson's interest in stimulating this trade during the War of the Spanish Succession, see CAOM C^{8A}16 f. 333 (2 May 1708) and CAOM C^{8B}2 item 92 (1 June 1708).
47. Dale Miquelon, 'Envisioning the French Empire: Utrecht, 1711–1713', *French Historical Studies* 24, no. 4 (Fall 2001): 653–77.
48. *Lettres Patentes du rois portant Règlement pour pe Commerce des Colonies Françoises*, Avril 1717. Reprinted in René-Josué Valin, *Nouveau commentaire sur L'Ordonnance de la marine du mois d'août 1681* (La Rochelle, 1766), I, 417–21.
49. Jean Tarrade, *Le commerce colonial de la France À La fin de L'Ancien Régime: L'Évolution du régime de l'Exclusif de 1763 à 1789* (Paris: Presses universitaires de France 1972), I: 88–9.
50. Jean-Pierre Poussou, 'L'Âge atlantique de l'Économie française (vers 1680–1780)', *Information Historique* 59, no. 1 (1997): 28. A detailed calculation of the value of colonial food trades to the metropolitan economy remains to be done. See Guillaume Daudin for the broad role played by all external trade within the domestic economy (*Commerce et prosperité: la France au XVIIIe siècle* [Paris: Presses de l'Université de Paris-Sorbonne, 2005], 351–431, esp 390–1); on hinterland development, Richard Drayton, 'The Globalisation of France: Provincial Cities and French Expansion, 1500–1800', *History of European Ideas* 34, no. 4 (December 2008): 424–30. For Bordeaux, see Francisque-Michel, *Histoire du commerce et de la navigation À Bordeaux* (Bordeaux: Feret and Fils, 1870), tome 2, 285–90 and for Bordeaux's colonial wine trade, see Christian Huetz de Lemps, *Geographie du commerce de Bordeaux À La fin du règne de Louis XIV* (Paris: La Haye, 1975), 121–3.
51. Pritchard, 203–8; Tarrade, I: 95–101. For a wider discussion of smuggling, see Wim Klooster, 'Inter-imperial Smuggling in the Americas, 1600–1800', in Bernard Bailyn and Patricia Denault (eds), *Soundings in Atlantic History: Latent Structures and Intellectual Currents* (Cambridge, MA: Harvard University Press, 2009), 141–80.
52. The classic work on this revolt is Petitjean-Roget's *Le Gaoulé.*
53. CAOM C^{8A}22 f. 133 (1 May 1717).
54. Christopher Moore, 'The Other Louisbourg: Trade and Merchant Enterprise in Ile Royale, 1713–1758', in Eric Krause, Carol Corbin and William O'Shea (eds) *Aspects of Louisbourg: Essays on the History of an Eighteenth-Century French Community in North America* (Sydney, Nova Scotia: Louisbourg Institute, 1995), 228–49 and John McNeill, *Louisbourg and Havana: Atlantic Empires of*

France and Spain, 1700–1763 (Chapel Hill: University of North Carolina Press, 1985), esp 180–202.

55. Mathieu, 153.
56. An exception was made to these restrictions in terms of trade with Spanish colonies in the Caribbean and on the mainland of the Americas Tarrade, I: 94–5; Pritchard, 201–2).
57. Moreau de Saint-Méry, *Loix et constitutions*, III: 234.
58. Bertie Mandelblatt, 'A Transatlantic Commodity: Irish Salt Beef in the French Atlantic', *History Workshop Journal* 63 (Spring 2007): 18–47.
59. Goebel, 332.
60. Pritchard, 192.
61. Gould, 485–6.
62. Gould, 485–7; Dechêne, 20–1 for Canadian food provisions shipped from Louisbourg to the French Antilles between 1721 and 1741; see Mathieu's conclusion, 210–6, for the effects of the uneven balance of trade.
63. Pritchard, appendix 1, 423–4
64. Another term for *tafia* is *guildive*. Its cheapness and ubiquity often rendered it a substitute for the provisions that planters were ostensibly obliged to provide their slaves.
65. Bertie Mandelblatt, 'L'Alambic dans l'Atlantique: production, commercialisation, et concurrence d'eau-de-vie de vin et de rhum dans l'Atlantique français jusqu'à 1713', *Histoire, Économie et Société*, no. 2 (2011): 63–78.
66. Tarrade, vol. I, 173–4, 329–31. For the uses of French and other foreign West Indian molasses in the eighteenth-century New England rum industry, see McCusker, 396–431.
67. Gould, 488–9 and Donald Chard, 'The Price and Profits of Accommodation: Massachusetts-Louisbourg Trade, 1713–1744', in Eric Krause et al. (ed.), *Aspects of Louisbourg*, 209–27.
68. For a recent examination of the French negotiations of the Treaty of Paris, see Helen Dewar, 'Canada or Guadeloupe? French and British Perceptions of Empire, 1760–1763', *Canadian Historical Review* 91, no. 4 (December 2010): 637–60.
69. On Tarrade, I: 14–6 and E. Daubigny, *Choiseul et la France d'outre-mer après le traité de Paris: Étude sur la politique coloniale au XVIIIe siècle* (Paris: Librairie Hachette, 1892), 19–27. See also Charles de Secondat, baron de Montesquieu, *The Spirit of the Laws*, Anne M. Cohler, Basia Carolyn Miller and Harold Samuel Stone (trans.) (ed.) (Cambridge: Cambridge University Press, 1989 [1748]), bk 21, chap. 21, 390–3, for his statements on the functions of colonies.
70. Voltaire, *Candide: ou l'optimisme* (Paris: Éditions A.-G. Nizet, [1759], 1979), chap 23, 191.
71. See Pernille Røge's contribution to this volume for a more detailed discussion of postwar physiocractic influence on colonial policy. See also Cheney, *Revolutionary Commerce*, 141–67.
72. André Labrouquère, *Les idées coloniales des Physiocrates: documents inédits* (Paris: Presses universitaires de la France, 1927).
73. In this regard, see chiefly Victor de Riquetti, marquis de Mirabeau, *Philosophie rurale: ou Économie générale et politique de l'agriculture* (Amsterdam: les Libraires associés, 1763).

74. A site of repeated French colonial expeditions before this period, la Guyane experienced several more after the Seven Years' War: David Lowenthal, 'Colonial Experiments in French Guiana, 1760–1700', *Hispanic American Historical Review* 32 (1952): 22–43; see also Marion F. Godfroy-Tayart de Borms, 'La guerre de Sept ans et ses conséquences atlantiques: Kourou ou L'Apparition D'un nouveau système colonial', *French Historical Studies* 32, no. 2 (Spring 2009): 167–91.
75. Jacques François Artur, *Histoire des colonies françoises de la Guianne: transcription Établie, présentée et annotée par Marie Polderman* (IBIS Rouge Éditions, 2002), 716.
76. Marcel Dorigny, 'The Question of Slavery in the Physiocratic Texts: A Rereading of an Old Debate', in Manuela Albertone and Antonino De Francesco (eds), *Rethinking the Atlantic World: Europe and America in the Age of Democratic Revolutions* (London: Palgrave Macmillan, 2009), 147–62.
77. See Røge in this volume for an examination of the provisioning activities of Le Mercier de la Rivière, Martinique's physiocratic *intendant* during the Seven Years' War. See also Goebel, 337; Labrouquère, 147–56; Tarrade, vol. I, 179–80.
78. Tarrade, vol. I, 185–280. Dubuc's *Mémoire* appeared, amongst other places, in the *Journal de L'Agriculture, du commerce et des finances,* tome 3, partie 3 (décembre 1765): 87–122.
79. Jean-François Brière, *La pêche française en Amérique du Nord au XVIIIe siècle* (Montréal: Fides, 1990), 4, 59–60, 257 and for a summary of the deep-rooted structural problem with provisioning slaves in the French Caribbean with French dried cod from Newfoundland, Brière, 257–8.
80. Jean-Baptiste Dubuc, 'Mémoire sur L'Étendue et les bornes des Lois prohibitives', *Journal de L'Agriculture,* tome 3, partie 3 (décembre 1765): 117–8.
81. Malnourishment, including protein deficiency, was a central cause of the high mortality rates of slaves, and was recognised as such during the eighteenth century: see Jean-Barthélemy Dazille, *Observations sur les maladies des nègres: leurs causes, leurs traitements et les moyens de les Prévenir* (Paris: Didot le jeune, 1776), 262–6; for a discussion of the diets of French Caribbean slaves, see Gabriel Debien, 'La nourriture des esclaves sur les plantations des Antilles françaises aux XVIIe et XVIIIe siècles', *Caribbean Studies* 4, no. 2 (1964): 3–27.
82. Tarrade, vol. I, 241–3.
83. Reprinted in Moreau de Saint-Méry, 5: 121–6; Tarrade, vol. I, 287–327; Goebel, 362–4.
84. The list included lumber in various forms, all livestock, hides, leather, pelts, pitch and tar. Tarrade, vol. I, 317–8.
85. These petitions, in the form of *représentations*, are signalled at the end of the entry in Moreau de Saint-Méry (5: 121–6) and appear in CAOM C^{9A}134 f. 14, f. 81 (1768).
86. Martin Durand-Molard, *Code de la Martinique, nouvelle Édition* (Saint-Pierre, Martinique: 1807–1814), II: 565–7; C. A. Banbuck, *Histoire politique, Économique et sociale de la Martinique sous L'Ancien Régime, 1635–1789* (Paris, 1935), 273.
87. Goebel, 364–9. Dominica instead became a trading hub for French planters seeking flour, salt cod and slaves.
88. Goebel, 369–72.

89. Tarrade, vol. II, 527–30; for French-American trade during the War of Independence, see Paul Cheney, 'A False Dawn for Enlightenment Cosmopolitanism? Franco-American Trade during the American War of Independence', *William and Mary Quarterly*, 3rd series, 63 (July 2006): 459–84; on the question of debt see Allan Potofsky, 'The Political Economy of the French-American Debt Debate: The Ideological Uses of Atlantic Commerce, 1787 to 1800', *William and Mary Quarterly*, 3rd series, 63, no. 3 (July 2006): 489–516.
90. Reprinted in Moreau de Saint-Méry, 6: 561–6.
91. Tarrade, vol. II, 539–41, 545.
92. Tarrade, 542.
93. *Lettre du Parlement de Rouen au Roi, au Sujet de l'Arrêt du Conseil du 30 août 1784* (Paris, 1785), 3.
94. *Lettre du Parlement de Rouen*, 9.
95. The debates over the role of overseas trade in the economic growth of Europe are vast and reach back notably to Eric Williams. See, inter alia, Guillaume Daudin, 'Do Frontiers Give or Do Frontiers Take? The Case of Intercontinental Trade in France at the End of the Eighteenth Century', in P. C. Emmer, O. Pétré-Grenouilleau and J. V. Roitman (eds), *A Deux Ex Machina Revisted: Atlantic Colonial Trade and European Economic Development* (Leiden, the Netherlands: Brill, 2006), 200–24.
96. *Lettre du Parlement de Rouen*, 37.
97. *Lettre du Parlement de Rouen*, 29–30.
98. Evidence, in fact, points to whites (including those attached to French naval garrisons) and free people of colour as being the foremost consumers of wheat flour throughout the French Antilles: by 1763 in Martinique, for example, bakers had to be licensed by the island's Sovereign Counsel, and all ship captains, merchants and other 'sellers of flour' were required to report to the Counsel the names of those to whom they sold flour. ('Ordonnance...Concernant les boulangers et la vente des farines de 1 septembre, 1763', *Code de la Martinique*, Saint Pierrre [Martinique]; imprimerie P. Richard, 1767, 491–2.)

Select Bibliography

Acres, Marston, 'Huguenot directors of the Bank of England', *Proceedings of the Huguenot Society* 15, no. 2 (1933–1937), 238–48.

Alden, Dauril, *Royal Government in Colonial Brazil: With Special Reference to the Administration of the Marquis of Lavradio, Viceroy, 1769–1779* (Berkeley, CA, 1968).

Allen, Robert C., 'Britain's Economic Ascendancy in a European Context', in Leandro Prados de Escosura (ed.), *Exceptionalism and Industrialisation: Britain and Its European Rivals, 1688–1815* (Cambridge, 2004), 15–34.

——, *The British Industrial Revolution in Global Perspective* (Cambridge, 2009).

Anthony, David W., *The Horse, the Wheel, and Language: How Bronze-Age Riders from the Eurasian Steppes Shaped the Modern World* (Princeton, 2007).

Ardanaz, Daisy Ripodas, *Refracción de Ideas en Hispanoamérica Colonial* (Buenos Aires, 1983).

Armitage, D., *The Ideological Origins of the British Empire* (Cambridge, 2000).

Backhaus, Jürgen G., 'The German Economic Tradition: From Cameralism to the Verein für Socialpolitik', in Manuela Albertone and Alberto Masoero (eds), *Political Economy and National Realities* (Turin, 1994), 320–56.

Barbieri, Katherine, *The Liberal Illusion: Does Trade Promote Peace* (Ann Arbor, 2002).

Batie, Robert, 'Why Sugar? Economic Cycles and the Changing of Staples on the English and French Antilles, 1624–54', *Journal of Caribbean History* 8/9 (1976): 1–41.

Bell, D., *The Idea of Greater Britain: Empire and the Future of World Order, 1860–1900* (Princeton, 2007).

Benians, E. A., 'Adam Smith's Project of an Empire', *Cambridge Historical Journal* 1 (1925): 249–83.

Bennett, Colin, 'What Is Policy Convergence and What Causes It?' *British Journal of Political Science* 21, no. 2 (1991): 215–22.

Benoit du Rey, E., *Recherches Sur La Politique Coloniale De Colbert* (Paris, 1902).

Benôt, Yves, 'L'*Encyclopédie* et le droit de coloniser', in R. Desné and M. Dorigny (eds), *Les lumières, l'esclavage, la colonisation* (Paris, 2005), 164–72.

Bonnassieux, Pierre, *Les Grande Compagnies De Commerce: Étude Pour Servir À L'histoire De La Colonisation* (Paris, 1892).

Boucher, Philip, *France and the American Tropics to 1700: Tropics of Discontent?* (Baltimore, 2008).

Boulle, Pierre H., 'French Mercantilism, Commercial Companies and Colonial Profitability', in Leonard Blussé and Femme Gaastra (eds), *Companies and Trade: Essays on Overseas Trading Companies during the Ancien Regime* (The Hague, 1981), 97–117.

Bouton, Cynthia, 'Les Mouvements De Subsistance Et Le Problème De L'Économie Morale Sous L'Ancien Régime Et La Révolution Française', *Annales Historique De La Révolution Française* 319 (2000): 71–100.

Boyce, D. G., 'From Assaye to the "Assaye": Reflections on British Government, Force, and Moral Authority in India', *Journal of Military History* 63 (1999): 643–68.

Brading, D. A., 'Bourbon Spain and Its American Empire', in Leslie Bethell (ed.), *Cambridge History of Latin America*, vol. 1 (Cambridge, 1984), 389–439.

Brewer, John, *The Sinews of Power: War and the English State, 1688–1783* (London, 1989).

Brière, Jean-François, *La Pêche Française En Amérique Du Nord Au XVIIIe Siècle* (Montréal, 1990).

Bruhns, Svend, *Bibliografiens Historie I Danmark, 1700- og 1800- Tallet* (Aalborg, 2004).

Burke, Peter, 'Tacitism, Scepticism, and Reason of State', in J. H. Burns and Mark Goldie (eds), *The Cambridge History of Political Thought, 1450–1700* (Cambridge, 1991), 479–98.

——, *Languages and Communities in Early Modern Europe* (Cambridge, 2004).

Butel, Paul, *Les Négociants Bordelais, L'Europe Et Les Îles Au XVIIIe Siècle* (Paris, 1974).

——, 'France, the Antilles and Europe, 1700–1900', in James D. Tracy (ed.), *The Rise of Merchant Empires: Long-Distance Trade in the Early Modern World, 1350–1750* (Cambridge, 1990), 153–73.

——, *L'Économie Française Au XVIIIe Siècle* (Paris, 1993).

Calazans Falcon, Francisco José, *A Época Pombalina (Política, Econômia e Monarquia Ilustrada)* (São Paulo, 1982).

Cárcel, Ricardo García, *La Leyenda Negra: Historia y Opinión* (Madrid, 1992).

Cardoso, José Luís, 'Nas Malhas do Império: A Economia Política e a Política Colonial de D. Rodrigo de Souza Coutinho', in Cardoso (ed.), *A Economia Política e os Dilemas do Império Luso-Brasileiro 1790–1822* (Lisbon, 2001), 63–109.

Carlos, Ann M., Jennifer Key and Jill L. Dupree, 'Learning and the Creation of Stock Market Institutions: Evidence from the Royal African and Hudson's Bay Companies, 1670–1700', *Journal of Economic History* 58, no. 2 (1998): 318–44.

Carpenter, Kenneth E., *Dialogue in Political Economy: Translations from and into German in the 18th Century* (Boston, 1977).

Carrato, José Ferreira, 'The Enlightenment in Portugal and the Educational Reforms of the Marquis of Pombal', *Studies in Voltaire and the Eighteenth Century* 168 (1977): 359–93.

Carreira, Antonio, *As Companhias Pombalinas de Grão Pará e Maranhão e Pernambuco e Paraíba* (Lisbon, 1983).

Carruthers, Bruce G., *City of Capital: Politics and Markets in the English Financial Revolution* (Princeton, 1996).

Carter, A. C., 'The Huguenot Contribution to the Early Years of the Funded Debt, 1694–1714', *Proceedings of the Huguenot Society* 19, no. 3 (1955): 21–41.

Cashin, Edward J., *Lachlan McGillivray, Indian Trader: The Shaping of the Southern Colonial Frontier* (Athens, 1992).

Castro, Concepción de, *Campomanes: Estado y Reformismo Ilustrado* (Madrid, 1996).

Chanier, Paul, 'Le Dilemme de Mirabeau: Cantillon ou Quesnay?', in Michel Vovelle (ed.), *Les Mirabeau Et Leur Temps: Actes Du Colloque D'Aix-En-Provence, 17 Et 18 Décembre 1766* (Paris, 1968), 23–35.

Charbit, Yves and Arundhati Virmani, 'The Political Failure of an Economic Theory: Physiocracy', *Population* 57, no. 6 (2002): 855–83.

Charles, Loic, 'The Tableau Economique as Rational Recreation', *History of Political Economy* 36 (2004): 445–74.

Chartier, Roger, *The Order of Books* (Stanford, 1994).

Chatterji, Basudev, 'The Darogah and the Countryside: The Imposition of Police Control in Bengal and Its Impact (1793–1837)', *Indian Economic and Social History Review* 18, no. 1 (1981): 19–42.

Chaussinand-Nogaret, Guy, *Choiseul – Naissance De La Gauche* (Paris, 1998).

Cheney, Paul, 'A False Dawn for Enlightenment Cosmopolitanism? Franco-American Trade during the American War of Independence', *William and Mary Quarterly* 63 (2006): 459–84.

——, *Revolutionary Commerce: Globalization and the French Monarchy* (Cambridge, MA, 2010).

Clark, Henry C., *Compass of Society. Commerce and Absolutism in Old-Regime France* (Lanham, 2007).

Clément, Alain, '"Du Bon Et Du Mauvais Usage Des Colonies": Politique Coloniale Et Pensée Économique Française Au XVIIIe Siècle', *Cahiers D'Économie Politique* 56 (2009): 101–27.

Cordier, L., *Les Compagnies À Charte Et La Politique Coloniale Sous Le Ministère de Colbert* (Paris, 1906).

Curtin, Philip, *The Rise and Fall of the Plantation Complex*, 2nd edn (Cambridge, 1998).

Daudin, Guillaume, *Commerce et prosperité: la France au XVIIIe siècle* (Paris, 2005).

——, 'Do Frontiers Give or Do Frontiers Take? The Case of Intercontinental Trade in France at the End of the Eighteenth Century', in P. C. Emmer, O. Pétré-Grenouilleau and J. V. Roitman (eds), *A Deux Ex Machina Revisited: Atlantic Colonial Trade and European Economic Development* (Leiden, 2006), 200–24.

Davids, Karel, 'From De la Court to Vreede. Regulation and Self-Regulation in Dutch Economic Discourse from c. 1660 to the Napoleonic Era', *Journal of European Economic History* 30, no. 2 (2001): 245–89.

Davies, K. G., 'Joint-Stock Investment in the Later Seventeenth Century', *Economic History Review* 4, no. 3 (1952): 283–301.

Davis, Harold E., *The Fledgling Province: Social and Cultural Life in Colonial Georgia, 1733–1776* (Chapel Hill, 1976).

Davis, Natalie Zemon, *The Gift in Sixteenth-Century France* (Madison, 2000).

Daubigny, E., *Choiseul Et La France D'outre-Mer Après Le Traité de Paris: Étude Sur La Politique Coloniale Au XVIIIe Siècle* (Paris, 1892).

Debien, Gabriel, 'La Nourriture Des Esclaves Sur Les Plantations Des Antilles Françaises Aux XVIIe Et XVIIIe Siècles', *Caribbean Studies* 4, no. 2 (1964): 3–27.

Dechêne, Louise, *Le Partage Des Subsistances Au Canada Sous Le Régime Français* (Montréal, 1994).

Dewar, Helen, 'Canada or Guadeloupe? French and British Perceptions of Empire, 1760–1763', *Canadian Historical Review* 91, no. 4 (2010): 637–60.

Díaz, Laura Rodríguez, *Reforma E Ilustración En La España Del Siglo XVIII* (Madrid, 1975).

Dickson, P. G. M., *The Financial Revolution in England: A Study in the Development of Public Credit, 1688–1756* (London, 1967).

Dorigny, Marcel, 'The Question of Slavery in the Physiocratic Texts: A Rereading of an Old Debate', in Manuela Albertone and Antonino De Francesco (eds), *Rethinking the Atlantic World: Europe and America in the Age of Democratic Revolutions* (London, 2009), 147–62.

Drayton, Richard, *Nature's Government: Science, Imperial Britain, and the 'Improvement' of the World* (New Haven, 2000).

——, 'The Globalisation of France: Provincial Cities and French Expansion, 1500–1800', *History of European Ideas* 34, no. 4 (2008): 424–30.

Eco, Umberto, *La Ricerca Della Lingua Perfetta Nella Cultura Europea* (Bari, 1993).

Elliott, J. H., *The Old World and the New 1492–1650* (Cambridge, 1970).

——, 'A Europe of Composite Monarchies', *Past and Present* 137 (1992): 48–71.

——, *Empires of the Atlantic World: Britain and Spain in America 1492–1830* (New Haven and London, 2006).

Ethridge, Robbie, 'Creating the Shatter Zone: Indian Slave Traders and the Collapse of the Southeastern Chiefdoms', in Thomas J. Pluckhahn and Robbie Ethridge (eds), *Light on the Path: The Anthropology and History of the Southeastern Indians* (Tuscaloosa, 2006), 207–18.

Fabian, Bernhard, *The English Book in Eighteenth-Century Germany* (London, 1992).

Fitzmaurice, Andrew, 'The Commercial Ideology of Colonization in Jacobean England: Robert Johnson, Giovanni Botero, and the Pursuit of Greatness', *William and Mary Quarterly* 64 (2007): 791–820.

Fox-Genovese, Elizabeth, *The Origins of Physiocracy – Economic Revolution and Social Order in Eighteenth-Century France* (London, 1976).

Fraginals, Manuel Moreno, *El Ingenio: Complejo Económico-Social Cubano del Azúcar* (Havana, 1978).

Frostin, Charles, *Les Révoltes Blanches À Saint-Domingue Aux XVIIe Et XVIIIe Siècles* (Paris, 1975).

Gallay, Alan, *The Indian Slave Trade: The Rise of the English Empire in the American South, 1670–1717* (New Haven, 2002).

Galloway, Patricia, '"So Many Little Republics": British Negotiations with the Choctaw Confederacy', *Ethnohistory* 41, no. 4 (1994): 513–37.

Gauthier, Florence, 'À L'origine de La Théorie Physiocratique Du Capitalisme, La Plantation Esclavagiste. L'expérience de Le Mercier de La Rivière, Intendant de La Martinique', *Actuel Marx* 32 (2002): 51–72.

Gerace, Michael P., *Military Power, Conflict and Trade* (London, 2004).

Gillespie, Michele, 'The Sexual Politics of Race and Gender: Mary Musgrove and the Georgia Trustees', in Catherine Clinton and Michele Gillespie (eds), *The Devil's Lane: Sex and Race in the Early South* (New York, 1997), 187–201.

Gisler, Antoine, *L'Esclavage Des Antilles Françaises XVIIe–XIXe Siècle, Contribution Au Problème de L'esclavage* (Paris, 1965).

Godfroy-Tayart de Borms, Marion F., 'La Guerre de Sept Ans Et Ses Conséquences Atlantiques: Kourou Ou L'apparition D'un Nouveau Système Colonial', *French Historical Studies* 32, no. 2 (2009): 167–91.

Goebel, Dorothy Burne, 'The "New England Trade" and the French West Indies, 1763–1774: A Study in Trade Policies', *William and Mary Quarterly* 20 (1763): 331–72.

Gould, Clarence, 'Trade between the Windward Islands and the Continental Colonies of the French Empire, 1683–1763', *Mississippi Valley Historical Review* 25, no. 4 (1939): 473–90.

Gould, Eliga, 'Entangled Histories, Entangled Worlds: The English-Speaking Atlantic as a Spanish Periphery', *American Historical Review* 112, no. 3 (2007): 764–86.

Grafton, Anthony, 'A Sketch Map of a Lost Continent: The Republic of Letters', *Worlds Made by Words: Scholarship and Community in the Modern West* (Cambridge, MA, 2009), 9–34.

Green, Michael D., 'Mary Musgrove: Creating a New World', in Theda Perdue (ed.), *Sifters: Native American Women's Lives* (Oxford, 2001).

Gregory, C. A., *Gifts and Commodities* (London, 1982).

Grieder, Josephine, *Anglomania in France 1740–1789: Fact, Fiction, and Political Discourse* (Geneva-Paris, 1985).

Guasti, Niccoló, 'Forbonnais e Uztariz: Le Ragioni di una Traduzione', *Cuadernos Aragoneses de Economia*, 2° epoca, 8, no. 1 (1998): 125–41.

Gujarati, Damodar, *Essentials of Econometrics* (New York, 1992).

Guyatt, N., *Providence and the Invention of the United States, 1607–1876* (Cambridge, 2007).

Haakonssen, Knud, *Natural Law and Moral Philosophy: From Grotius to the Scottish Enlightenment* (Cambridge, 1996).

Hahn, Steven C., *The Invention of the Creek Nation: 1670–1763* (Lincoln, 2004).

Hall, Joseph M., *Zamumo's Gifts: Indian-European Exchange in the Colonial Southeast* (Philadelphia, 2009).

Harris, Bob, *Politics and the Nation: Britain in the Mid-Eighteenth Century* (Oxford, 2002).

Harris, J. R., *Industrial Espionage and Technology Transfer: Britain and France in the Eighteenth Century* (Aldershot, 1998).

Havard, Gilles, *The Great Peace of Montreal of 1701: French-Native Diplomacy in the Seventeenth Century* (Montreal, 2001).

Heal, Felicity, *Hospitality in Early Modern England* (Oxford, 1990).

Herr, Richard, *The Eighteenth Century Revolution in Spain* (Princeton, 1958).

Hirschman, Albert O., *The Passions and the Interests: Political Arguments for Capitalism before Its Triumph* (Princeton, 1977).

Hochstrasser, T. J., 'Physiocracy and the Politics of Laissez-Faire', in Mark Goldie and Robert Wokler (eds), *The Cambridge History of Eighteenth-Century Political Thought* (Cambridge, 2006), 419–42.

Holland Braund, Kathryn E., *Deerskins and Duffels: The Creek Trade with Anglo-America* (Lincoln, 1993).

Hont, Istvan, 'The Language of Sociability and Commerce: Samuel Pufendorf and the Theoretical Foundations of the "Four-Stages" Theory', in A. Pagden (ed.), *Languages of Political Theory in Early Modern Europe* (Cambridge, 1986), 253–76.

——, *Jealousy of Trade: International Competition and the Nation-State in Historical Perspective* (Cambridge, 2005).

——, 'Adam Smith's History of Law and Government as Political Theory', in R. Bourke and R. Geuss (eds), *Political Judgement: Essays for John Dunn* (Cambridge, 2009), 131–71.

Hoppe, Fritz, *A África Oriental Portuguesa no Tempo do Marquês do Pombal* (Lisbon, 1970).

Horsefield, J. K., 'The Stop of the Exchequer Revisited', *Economic History Review* 35, no. 4 (1982): 511–28.

Huber, Thomas, *Studien zur Theorie des Übersetzens im Zeitalter der Deutschen Aufklärung 1730–1770* (Meisenheim am Glan, 1968).

Huetz de Lemps, Christian, *Geographie Du Commerce de Bordeaux À La Fin Du Règne de Louis XIV* (Paris, 1975).

Hufton, Owen, 'Social Conflict and the Grain Supply in Eighteenth Century France', *Journal of Interdisciplinary History* 14, no. 2 (1983): 303–31.

Humpert, Magdalene, *Bibliographie Der Kameralwissenschaften* (Cologne, 1937).

Hutchinson, M. Grice, *The School of Salamanca and Early Economic Thought in Spain, 1177–1740* (London, 1978).

Huyghues-Belrose, Vincent, *Le Jardin Créole À La Martinique: Une Parcelle Du Jardin Planétaire* (Fort-de-France, 2010).

Inikori, Joseph E., *Africans and the Industrial Revolution in England: A Study in International Trade and Economic Development* (Cambridge, 2002).

Israel, Jonathan, 'The Intellectual Origins of Modern Democratic Republicanism (1660–1720)', *European Journal of Political Theory* 3 (2004): 7–36.

Ivers, Larry E., *British Drums on the Southern Frontier: The Military Colonization of Georgia, 1733–1749* (Chapel Hill, 1974).

Jacobs, Wilbur R., *Diplomacy and Indian Gifts: Anglo-French Rivalry Along the Ohio and Northwest Frontiers, 1748–1763* (Lincoln, 1950).

Jaenen, Cornelius J., 'The Role of Presents in French-Amerindian Trade', in Duncan Cameron (ed.), *Explorations in Canadian Economic History: Essays in Honour of Irene M. Spry*, (Ottawa, 1985), 231–50.

Jennings, Matthew, *New Worlds of Violence: Cultures and Conquests in the Early American Southeast* (Knoxville, 2011).

Jones, D. W., *War and Economy in the Age of William III and Marlborough* (Oxford, 1988).

Joucla, Henri, *Le Conseil Supérieur Des Colonies Et Ses Antécédents* (Paris, 1928).

Juricek, John T., *Colonial Georgia and the Creeks: Anglo-Indian Diplomacy on the Southern Frontier, 1733–1763* (Gainesville, 2010).

Kagan, Richard L., *Clio and the Crown: The Politics of History in Medieval and Early Modern Spain* (Baltimore, 2009).

Kaplan, Steven, *Bread, Politics and Political Economy in the Reign of Louis XV* (The Hague, 1976).

Klein, P. W., 'A New Look at an Old Subject. Dutch Trade Policies in the Age of Mercantilism', in S. Groenveld and M. Wintle (eds), *State and Trade: Government and the Economy in Britain and the Netherlands since the Middle Ages* (Zutphen, 1992), 39–49.

Klooster, Wim, 'Inter-imperial Smuggling in the Americas, 1600–1800', in Bernard Bailyn and Patricia Denault (eds), *Soundings in Atlantic History: Latent Structures and Intellectual Currents* (Cambridge, 2009), 141–80.

Koebner, R., *Empire* (Cambridge, 1961).

Kolff, Dirk A. H., *Naukar, Rajput and Sepoy: The Ethnohistory of the Military Labour Market in Hindustan, 1450–1850* (Cambridge, 1990).

Labrouquère, André, *Les Idées Coloniales Des Physiocrates* (Paris, 1927).

Letayf, Marcelo Bitar, *Economistas Españoles Del Siglo XVIII: Sus Ideas Sobre La Libertad Del Comercio Con Indias* (Madrid, 1968).

Llombart, Vicent, *Campomanes, Economista Y Político de Carlos III* (Madrid, 1992).

Loménie, Louis de, *Les Mirabeau, Nouvelles Études Sur La Société Française Au XVIIIe Siècle*, 5 vols. (Paris, 1879–1891).

Lowenthal, David, 'Colonial Experiments in French Guiana, 1760–1700', *Hispanic American Historical Review* 32 (1952): 22–43.

Lucassen, Leo and Boudien de Vries, 'Leiden Als Middelpunt Van Een Westeuropees Textiel-Migratie-Systeem, 1586–1650', *Tijdschrift Voor Sociale Geschiedenis* 22 (1996): 138–67.

Luiten van Zanden, Jan and Maarten Prak, 'Towards an Economic Interpretation of Citizenship: The Dutch Republic between Medieval Communes and Modern Nation-States', *European Review of Economic History* 10 (2006): 111–45.

Lyra, Maria de Lourdes Viana, *A Utopia Do Poderoso Império: Portugal E Brasil, Bastidores Da Política 1798–1822* (Rio de Janeiro, 1994).

MacLeod, Christine, 'The 1690s Patents Boom: Invention or Stock-Jobbing?' *Economic History Review* 39, no. 4 (1986): 549–71.

——, *Inventing the Industrial Revolution: The English Patent System, 1660–1800* (Cambridge, 1988).

Maddison, Angus, *The World Economy* (Paris, 2006).

Magnusson, Lars, *Mercantilism: The Shaping of an Economic Language* (London and New York, 1994).

Mallios, Seth, *The Deadly Politics of Giving: Exchange and Violence at Ajacan, Roanoke, and Jamestown* (Tuscaloosa, 2006).

Mandelblatt, Bertie, 'A Transatlantic Commodity: Irish Salt Beef in the French Atlantic', *History Workshop Journal* 63 (2007): 18–47.

——, 'L'Alambic Dans l'Atlantique : Production, Commercialisation, Et Concurrence D'eau-de-Vie de Vin Et de Rhum Dans l'Atlantique Français Jusqu'à 1713', *Histoire, Économie Et Société* 2 (2011): 63–78.

Marshall, P. J., *Bengal: The British Bridgehead. Eastern India 1740–1828* (Cambridge, 1987).

Martin, Joel W., *Sacred Revolt: The Muskogees' Struggle for a New World* (Boston, 1991).

——, 'Southeastern Indians and the English Trade in Skins and Slave', in Charles Hudson and Carmen Chaves Tesser (eds), *The Forgotten Centuries: Indians and Europeans in the American South* (Athens, 1994), 304–24.

Mathieu, Jacques, 'La Balance Commerciale Nouvelle-France – Antilles Au XVIIIe Siècle', *Revue D'histoire de l'Amérique Française* 25, no. 4 (March 1972): 465–97.

——, *Le Commerce Entre New France Et Les Antilles Au XVIIIe Siècle* (Montréal, 1981).

Mauss, Marcel, *The Gift: The Form and Reason for Exchange in Archaic Societies*, W. D. Halls (trans.) foreword by Mary Douglas (New York, 1990).

Maxwell, Kenneth, *Conflicts and Conspiracies: Brazil and Portugal, 1750–1808* (Cambridge, 1973).

——, *Pombal: Paradox of the Enlightenment* (Cambridge, 1995).

May, Louis-Philippe, *Histoire Économique de La Martinique (1635–1763)* (Paris, 1972).

——, *Le Mercier de La Rivière (1719–1801) Aux Origines de La Science Économique* (Paris, 1975).

McClellan, James E. and Francois Regourd, 'The Colonial Machine: French Science and Colonisation in the Ancien Regime', *Osiris* 15 (2000): 31–50.

McCusker, John J. and Cora Gravesteijn, *The Beginnings of Commercial and Financial Journalism: The Commodity Price Currents, Exchange Rate Currents, and Money Currents of Early Modern Europe* (Amsterdam, 1991).

McNeill, John, *Louisbourg and Havana: Atlantic Empires of France and Spain, 1700–1763* (Chapel Hill, 1985).

Meek, Ronald L., *Social Science and the Ignoble Savage* (Cambridge, 1976).
Melton, James van Horn, *The Rise of the Public in Enlightenment Europe* (Cambridge, 2001).
Mendes, António de Almeida, 'Les Réseaux de La Traite Ibérique Dans l'Atlantiques Nord (1440–1640)', *Annales. Histoire, Sciences Sociales* 4 (2008): 739–68.
Mendonça, Marcos Carneiro do, *O Marquês de Pombal E O Brasil* (São Paulo, 1960).
Merle, Marcel, 'L'anticolonialisme', in Marc Ferro (ed.), *Le Livre Noir Du Colonialisme XVIe–XXIIe Siècle: De L'extermination À La Repentance* (Paris, 2003), 815–62.
Meysonnier, Simone, *La Balance Et L'horloge. La Genèse de La Pensée Libérale En France Au XVIIIe Siècle* (Paris, 1989).
Miller, Christopher R. and George R. Hamell, 'A New Perspective on Indian-White Contact: Cultural Symbols and Colonial Trade', *Journal of American History* 73 (1986): 311–28.
Miller, Judith, *Mastering the Market: The State and the Grain Trade in Northern France, 1700*–1860 (Cambridge, 1999).
Miller, Peter N., *Defining the Common Good: Empire, Religion and Philosophy in Eighteenth-Century Britain* (Cambridge, 1994).
Milo, Daniel, 'La Bourse Mondiale de La Traduction: Un Baromètre Culturel?', *Annales*: *Économies, Sociétés, Civilizations* 29 (1984): 93–115.
Mims, Stewart, *Colbert's West India Policy* (New Haven, 1912).
Minard, Philippe, *La Fortune Du Colbertisme. État Et Industrie Dans La France Des Lumières* (Paris, 1998).
Miquelon, Dale, 'Canada's Place in the French Imperial Economy: An Eighteenth-Century Overview', *French Historical Studies* 15, no. 3 (Spring 1988): 432–43.
——, 'Envisioning the French Empire: Utrecht, 1711–1713', *French Historical Studies* 24, no. 4 (2001): 653–77.
Misra, Bankey B., *Central Administration of the East India Company, 1773–1834* (Manchester, 1959).
Moore, Christopher, 'The Other Louisbourg: Trade and Merchant Enterprise in Ile Royale, 1713–1758', in Eric Krause et al. (eds), *Aspects of Louisbourg: Essays on the History of an Eighteenth-Century French Community in North America* (Sydney, 1995), 228–49.
Morgan, William Thomas, 'A Crisis in the History of the Hudson's Bay Company, 1694–1697', *North Dakota Historical Quarterly* 5, no. 4 (1931): 197–218.
Mulier, Haitsma, E. O. G., *The Myth of Venice and Dutch Republican Thought in the Seventeenth Century* (Assen, 1980).
Murphy, Anne L., 'Lotteries in the 1690s: Investment or Gamble?' *Financial History Review* 12, no. 2 (2005): 227–46.
——, 'Dealing with Uncertainty: Managing Personal Investment in the Early English National Debt', *History* 91, no. 302 (2006): 200–17.
Murphy, Orville T., 'Dupont de Nemours and the Anglo-French Commercial Treaty of 1786', *Economic History Review* 19 (1966): 569–80.
Murray, David, *Indian Giving: Economies of Power in Indian-White Exchanges* (Amherst, 2000).
Neal, Larry, 'The Rise of a Financial Press: London and Amsterdam, 1681–1810', *Business History* 30, no. 2 (1980): 163–78.
Neff, Stephen C., *Friends but No Allies: Economic Liberalism and the Law of Nations* (New York, 1990).

Nijenhuis, Ida, 'De Ontwikkeling Van Het Politiek-Economische Vrijheidsbegrip in de Republiek', in E. O. G. Haitsma Mulier and W. R. E. Velema (eds), *Vrijheid: Een Geschiedenis Van de Vijftiende Tot de Twintigste Eeuw* (Amsterdam, 1999), 233–52.

North, Douglass C. and Barry R. Weingast, 'Constitutions and Commitment: The Evolution of Institutions Governing Public Choice in Seventeenth-Century England', *Journal of Economic History* 49, no. 4 (1989): 803–32.

Nye, J. V. C., *War, Wine, and Taxes: The Political Economy of Anglo-French Trade, 1689–1900* (Princeton, 2007).

O'Brien, Patrick, 'Inseparable Connections: Trade, Economy, Fiscal State, and the Expansion of Empire, 1688–1815', in P. J. Marshall (ed.), *The Oxford History of the British Empire*, vol. 2, *The Eighteenth Century* (Oxford, 1998), 53–77.

O'Rourke, H., *Power and Plenty: Trade, War, and the World Economy in the Second Millennium* (Princeton, 2007).

Oz-Salzberger, Fania, *Translating the Enlightenment: Scottish Civic Discourse in Eighteenth Century Germany* (Oxford, 1995).

Pagden, A., *Lords of the All the World: Ideologies of Empire in Spain, Britain, and France c. 1500–1800* (New Haven, 1995).

Pajares, 'Traducción Inglés-Español en el Siglo XVIII', *El Mundo Hispánico en el Siglo de las Luces* (Madrid, 1996).

Paquette, Gabriel, *Enlightenment, Governance, and Reform in Spain and Its Empire, 1759–1808* (Basingstoke, 2009).

Pares, Richard, 'Merchants and Planters', *Economic History Review Supplement 4* (Cambridge, 1960).

Pedreira, Jorge, 'From Growth to Collapse: Portugal, Brazil and the Breakdown of the Old Colonial System (1760–1830)', *Hispanic American Historical Review* 80, no. 4 (2000): 839–64.

Peers, Douglas M., *Between Mars and Mammon: Colonial Armies and the Garrison State in India, 1819–1935* (London, 1995).

Perrotta, Cosimo, 'Early Spanish Mercantilism: A First Analysis of Underdevelopment', in Lars Magnusson (ed.), *Mercantilist Economics* (Boston, 1993), 17–58.

Pétré-Grenouilleau, Olivier, *Les Négoces Maritimes Français, XVI–XXe Siècle* (Paris, 1997).

Phillipson, N., *Adam Smith: An Enlightened Life* (London, 2010).

Phillipson, Robert, *Linguistic Imperialism* (Oxford, 1992).

Pigman, G. W., 'Versions of Imitation in the Renaissance', *Renaissance Quarterly* 33, no. 1 (1980): 1–32.

Piker, Joshua, '"White & Clean" & Contested: Creek Towns and Trading Paths in the Aftermath of the Seven Years' War', *Ethnohistory* 50, no. 2 (Spring 2003): 320–21.

——, *Okfuskee: A Creek Indian Town in Colonial America* (Cambridge, 2004).

Pincus, S., *1688: The First Modern Revolution* (New Haven, 2009).

Pitts, J., *A Turn to Empire: The Rise of Imperial Liberalism in Britain and France* (Princeton, 2005).

Pocock, J. G. A., 'Josiah Tucker on Burke, Locke, and Price: A Study in the Varieties of Eighteenth-Century Conservatism', *Virtue, Commerce and History: Essays on Political Thought and History, Chiefly in the Eighteenth Century* (Cambridge, 1985), 158–92.

——, *The Machiavellian Moment. Florentine Political Thought and the Atlantic Republican Tradition*, 2nd edn (Princeton, 2003).

——, *Barbarism and Religion*, 4 vols. (Cambridge, 1999–2005).

Potofsky, Allan, 'The Political Economy of the French-American Debt Debate: The Ideological Uses of Atlantic Commerce, 1787 to 1800', *William and Mary Quarterly* 63, no. 3 (July 2006): 489–516.

Prak, Maarten et al. (eds), *Craft Guilds in the Early Modern Low Countries. Work, Power, and Representation* (Aldershot, 2006).

Preston, Adrian, 'Sir Charles MacGregor and the Defence of India, 1857–1887', *Historical Journal* 12, no. 1 (1969): 58–77.

Price, J. M., 'A Note on the Circulation of the London Press, 1704–1714', *Bulletin of the Institute of Historical Research* 21 (1958): 215–24.

Pritchard, James, *In Search of Empire: The French in the Americas, 1670–1730* (Cambridge, 2004).

Quintana, Enrique Fuentes (ed.), *Economía y Economistas Españoles*, vol. 3, *La Ilustración* (Barcelona, 2000).

Ramsey, William L., '"Something Cloudy in Their Looks": The Origins of the Yamasee War Reconsidered', *Journal of American History* 90, no. 1 (2003): 44–75.

——, *The Yamasee War: A Study of Culture, Economy, and Conflict in the Colonial South* (Lincoln, 2008).

Reeder, John, 'Bibliografía de Traducciones, Al Castellano Y Catalán, Durante El Siglo XVIII, de Obras de Pensamiento Económico', *Moneda Y Crédito* 126 (1973): 57–78.

Regourd, François, 'La Société Royale D'agriculture de Paris Face À L'espace Colonial (1761–1793)', *Bulletin Du Centre D'histoire Des Espaces Atlantiques* 8 (1997/1998): 155–94.

Reid, Allana G., 'Intercolonial Trade during the French Regime', *Canadian Historical Review* 32, no. 3 (1951): 236–51.

Reinert, E. S., 'Emulating Success: Contemporary Views of the Dutch Economy before 1800', in Oscar Gelderblom (ed.), *The Political Economy of the Dutch Republic* (Farnham, 2009), 19–39.

Reinert, Sophus A., 'The Italian Tradition of Political Economy: Theories and Policies of Development in the Semi-Periphery of the Enlightenment', in Jomo K. Sundaram and Erik S. Reinert (eds), *The Origins of Development Economics: How Schools of Economic Thought Have Addressed Development* (London, 2005), 24–47.

——, 'Blaming the Medici: Footnotes, Falsification, and the Fate of the "English Model" in Eighteenth-Century Italy', *History of European Ideas* 32, no. 4 (2006): 430–55.

——, 'Lessons on the Rise and Fall of Great Powers: Conquest, Commerce, and Decline in Enlightenment Italy', *American Historical Review* 115 (2010): 1395–425.

——, *Translating Empire Emulation and the Origins of Political Economy* (Cambridge, 2011).

——, 'Another Grand Tour: Cameralism and Antiphysiocracy in Baden, Tuscany, and Denmark-Norway', in Jürgen G. Backhaus (ed.), *Physiocracy, Antiphysiocracy and Pfeiffer* (New York, 2011), 39–69.

Rich, E. E., 'The Hudson's Bay Company and the Treaty of Utrecht', *Cambridge Historical Journal* 11, no. 2 (1954): 183–203.

Robertson, John, *The Case for the Enlightenment: Scotland and Naples 1680–1760* (Cambridge, 2005).
Roche, Geneviève, *Les Traductions-Relais En Allemagne Au XVIIIe Siècle: Des Lettres Aux Sciences* (Paris, 2001).
Rodríguez, Manuel Bustos, *El Pensamiento Socio-Economico De Campomanes* (Oviedo, 1982).
Røge, Pernille, '"Legal Despotism" and Enlightened Reform in the Îles Du Vent: The Colonial Governments of Chevalier de Mirabeau and Mercier de La Rivière, 1754–1764', in Gabriel Paquette (ed.), *Enlightened Reform in Southern Europe and its Atlantic Colonies, c. 1750–1830* (2009), 167–82.
——, 'The Question of Slavery in Physiocratic Political Economy', in Manuela Albertone (ed.), *Governare Il Mondo. L'economia Come Linguaggio Delle Politica Nell'Europa Del Settecento* (Feltrinelli, 2009), 149–69.
Rogers, Ruth R., 'The Kress Library of Business and Economics', *Business History Review* 60, no. 2 (1986): 281–88.
Rommelse, Gijs, 'The Role of Mercantilism in Anglo-Dutch Political Relations, 1650–74', *Economic History Review* 63, no. 3 (2010): 591–611.
Ross, I. S., *The Life of Adam Smith* (Oxford, 1995).
Rossi, Paolo, *Clavis Universalis: Arti Della Memoria E Logica Combinatoriale Da Lullo a Leibniz* (Bologna, 2000).
Rothkrug, Lionel, *Opposition to Louis XIV: The Political and Social Origins of the French Enlightenment* (Princeton, 1965).
Rothschild, Emma, 'The English *Kopf*', in Donald Winch and Patrick K. O'Brien (eds), *The Political Economy of British Historical Experience* (Oxford, 2002), 31–60.
——, 'Global Commerce and the Question of Sovereignty in the Eighteenth-Century Provinces', *Modern Intellectual History* 1, no. 1 (2004): 3–25.
——, *The Inner Life of Empires: An Eighteenth-Century History* (Princeton, 2011).
Rowen, Herbert H., *John de Witt, Grand Pensionary of Holland, 1625–1672* (Princeton, 1978).
Ruiperez, Mariano García, 'El Pensamiento Económico Ilustrado Y Las Compañías de Comercio', *Revista de Historia Económic* 4, no. 3 (1986): 521–48.
Sahlins, Marshall, *Stone Age Economics* (London, 1974).
Sánchez-Blanco, Francisco, *El Absolutismo Y Las Luces En El Reinado de Carlos III* (Madrid, 2003).
Schaeper, Thomas J., 'Colonial Trade Policies Late in the Reign of Louis XIV', *Revue Française D'histoire D'outre-Mer* 67 (1980): 203–15.
——, *The French Council of Commerce 1700–1715: A Study of Mercantilism after Colbert* (Columbus, 1983).
Schelle, Gustave, *Dupont de Nemours et l'école physiocratique* (Paris, 1888).
Schnakenbourg, Christian, 'Note Sur Les Origines de L'industrie Sucrière En Guadeloupe Au XVIIe Siècle (1640–1670)', *Revue Française D'histoire d'Outre-Mer* 55, no. 200 (1968): 267–311.
Schui, Florian, *Early Debates about Industry: Voltaire and His Contemporaries* (Basingstoke, 2005).
Scott, William Robert, *The Constitution and Finance of English, Scottish and Irish Joint-Stock Companies to 1720*, 3 vols. (Cambridge, 1910–1912).
Sée, Henri, 'Les Économistes Et La Question Coloniale Au XVIIIe Siècle', *Revue de L'histoire Des Colonies Françaises* 4 (1929): 381–92.

Shaw, L. M. E., 'The Marquês de Pombal (1699–1782): How He Broke Britain's Commercial Ascendancy in Portugal', *Journal of European Economic History* 27, no. 3 (1998): 537–54.

Sheridan, Richard, 'The Crisis of Slave Subsistence in the British West Indies during and after the American Revolution', *William and Mary Quarterly* 33, no. 4 (October 1976): 615–41.

——, *Sugar and Slavery: An Economic History of the British West Indies* (Kingston, 2000).

Shovlin, John, *The Political Economy of Virtue: Luxury, Patriotism, and the Origins of the French Revolution* (Ithaca, 2006).

Simmons, Beth, Frank Dobbin and Geoffrey Garrett, 'Introduction: The International Diffusion of Liberal Ideas', *International Organisation* 60 (2006): 781–810.

Skinner, A. S., 'Adam Smith and the American Economic Community: An Essay in Applied Economics', *Journal of the History of Ideas* 37 (1976): 59–78.

Skinner, Quentin, *Visions of Politics*, 3 vols. (Cambridge, 2002).

Smith, C. F., 'The Early History of the London Stock Exchange', *American Economic Review* 19, no. 2 (1929): 206–16.

Smith, David Kammerling, 'Structuring Politics in Early Eighteenth-Century France: The Political Innovation of the French Council of Commerce', *Journal of Modern History* 74 (2002): 490–537.

Snyder, Christina, *Slavery in Indian Country: The Changing Face of Captivity in Early America* (Cambridge, 2010).

Snyder, Henry L., 'The Circulation of Newspapers in the Reign of Queen Anne', *The Library* 23, no. 3 (1968): 206–35.

Soll, Jacob, 'Accounting for Government: Holland and the Rise of Political Economy in Seventeenth-Century Europe', *Journal of Interdisciplinary History* 40, no. 2 (2009): 215–38.

——, *The Information Master: Jean-Baptiste Colbert's Secret State Intelligence System* (Ann Arbor, 2009).

Sonenscher, Michael, *Before the Deluge: Public Debt, Inequality, and the Intellectual Origins of the French Revolution* (Princeton, 2007).

Stein, Stanley J. and Barbara H. Stein, *Silver, Trade and War: Spain and America in the Making of Early Modern Europe* (Baltimore and London, 2000).

——, *Apogee of Empire: Spain and New Spain in the Age of Charles III* (Baltimore and London, 2003).

Steiner, George, *After Babel: Aspects of Language & Translation*, 3rd edn (Oxford, 1999).

Steiner, Philippe, 'L'ésclavage Chez Les Économistes Français (1750–1830)', in Marcel Dorigny (ed.), *Les Abolitions de L'esclavage de L. F. Sonthonaz À V. Schœlcher 1793 1794 1848* (Paris, 1995), 165–75.

——, *La "Science Nouvelle" de L'économie Politique* (Paris, 1998).

Stevens, D., 'Adam Smith and the Colonial Disturbances', in A. S. Skinner and T. Wilson (eds), *Essays on Adam Smith* (Oxford, 1975), 202–17.

Stolleis, Michael, *Staat Und Staatsräson in Der Frühen Neuzeit. Studien Zur Geschichte Des Öffentlichen Rechts* (Frankfurt, 1990).

Sweet, Julie Anne, *Negotiating for Georgia: British-Creek Relations in the Trustee Era, 1733–1752* (Athens, 2005).

Tarrade, Jean, 'L'administration Coloniale En France À La Fin de L'ancien Régime: Projets de Réforme', *Revue Historique* 229 (1963): 103–22.

——, *Le Commerce Colonial de La France À La Fin de L'ancien Régime: L'évolution de 'l'Exclusif' de 1763 À 1789*, 2 vols. (Paris, 1972).

Théré, Christine, 'Economic Publishing and Authors', in Gilbert Faccarello (ed.), *Studies in the History of French Political Economy: From Bodin to Walras* (London, 1998), 1–56.

Théré, Christine and Loïc Charles, 'The Writing Workshop of François Quesnay and the Making of Physiocracy', *History of Political Economy* 40 (2008): 1–42.

Thomas, Nicholas, *Entangled Objects: Exchange, Material Culture, and Colonialism in the Pacific* (Cambridge, 1991).

Tijn, Theo van, 'Pieter de La Court, Zijn Leven En Zijn Economische Denkbeelden', *Tijdschrift Voor Geschiedenis* 69 (1956): 304–70.

——, 'Dutch Economic Thought in the Seventeenth Century', in Jan Daal and Arnold Heertje (eds), *Economic Thought in the Netherlands 1650–1950* (Aldershot, 1992), 7–28.

Ulloa, Antonio de, *La Marina: Fuerzas Navales de la Europa y Costas de Berberia* (Cádiz, 1995).

Usner, Daniel H., Jr., *Indians, Settlers, & Slaves in a Frontier Exchange Economy: The Lower Mississippi Valley before 1783* (Chapel Hill, 1992).

Vardi, Liana, *The Physiocrats and the World of the Enlightenment* (Cambridge, 2012).

Velema, Wyger, '"That a Republic Is Better than a Monarchy': Anti-monarchism in Early Modern Dutch Political Thought', in Martin van Gelderen and Quentin Skinner (eds), *Republicanism: A Shared European Heritage*, 2 vols. (Cambridge, 2002), 1: 9–25.

Vilar, P., *A History of Gold and Money, 1450–1920*, J. White (trans.) (New York, 1991).

Viroli, Maurizio, *From Politics to Reason of State: The Acquisition and Transformation of the Language of Politics, 1250–1600* (Cambridge, 1992).

Vries B. De et al. (eds), *De kracht der zwakken. Studies over arbeid en arbeidersbeweging in het verleden* (Amsterdam, 1992).

Vries, Jan de and Ad van der Woude, *The First Modern Economy. Success, Failure, and Perseverance of the Dutch Economy, 1500–1815* (Cambridge, 1997).

Wagener, Hans-Jürgen, 'Free Seas, Free Trade, Free People: Early Dutch Institutionalism', *History of Political Economy* 26, no. 3 (1994): 395–422.

Wallerstein, Immanuel, *The Modern World System II: Mercantilism and the Consolidation of the European World Economy 1600–1750* (New York, 1980).

Webster, Jonathan Howes, 'The Concerns of Bordeaux's Merchants and the Formation of Royal Commercial Policy for the West Indies', *Proceedings of the Western Society for French History* 2 (1974): 12–20.

Wells, John and Douglas Wills, 'Revolution, Restoration and Debt Repudiation: The Jacobite Threat to England's Institutions and Economic Growth', *Journal of Economic History* 60, no. 2 (2000): 418–41.

Weulersse, George, *Le Mouvement Physiocratique En France (De 1756 À 1770)*, 2 vols. (Paris, 1910).

White, Richard, *The Roots of Dependency: Subsistence, Environment, and Social Change among the Choctaws, Pawnees, and Navajos* (Lincoln, 1983).

Wildenberg, Ivo W., *Johan & Pieter de La Court (1622–1660 & 1618–1685). Bibliografie En Receptiegeschiedenis* (Amsterdam, 1986).

Wilson, Jon E., *The Domination of Strangers* (London, 2008).

Winch, D., *Classical Political Economy and Colonies* (London, 1965).

——, *Adam Smith's Politics: An Essay in Historiographic Revision* (Cambridge, 1978).

Wood, Peter H., 'The Changing Population of the Colonial South', in Peter H. Wood, Gregory A. Waselkov and M. Thomas Hatley (eds), *Powhatan's Mantle: Indians in the Colonial Southeast* (Lincoln, 1989), 57–132.

Zanden, Jan Luiten van, *The Long Road to the Industrial Revolution: The European Economy in a Global Perspective, 1000–1800* (Leiden, 2009).

Index

Printed and bound in the United States of America